*The Glorious*

# INDIAN
# SUMMER

## OF 1995

Published by Russell Schneider Enterprises, Inc.
        Post Office Box 347156
        Cleveland, Ohio 44134
Copyright © 1995 by Russell Schneider Enterprises Inc.
All rights reserved
Published November 1995


Printed by Fine Line Litho, Cleveland, Ohio

ISBN 0-9649813-0-0

*The Glorious*

# INDIAN

# SUMMER

## OF 1995

## By Russell Schneider

# About the Author

Russell Schneider was a sportswriter-columnist for The Plain Dealer in Cleveland for 32 years, until leaving the newspaper in June 1993.

He is an even longer fan of the Cleveland Indians, living with them through their (infrequent) best of times, and dying with them through their (frequent) worst of times.

After a two year stint in the U.S. Marine Corps (1946-48), Schneider played minor league baseball in the Indians farm system - he was a good field, light hitting catcher - and was recalled to active duty during the Korean War. He later played and managed semi-pro baseball teams in and around the Cleveland area.

Schneider covered the Indians on a daily basis for fourteen years, from 1964-77. He also covered the Cleveland Browns of the National Football League for six years, from 1978-83, before concentrating on investigative reporting, special assignments and writing a sports column, *Schneider Around,* for the Plain Dealer.

This book, *The Glorious Indian Summer of 1995*, is Schneider's fourth. He recently completed *The Cleveland Indians Encyclopedia,* an all-inclusive history of the franchise from 1901 through 1995, for Temple University Press (publication date: March 1, 1996)

Schneider previously wrote *Frank Robinson, The Making of a Manager*, and also *Covering All The Bases*, the biography of Lou Boudreau. Robinson and Boudreau are former Tribe player-managers, and both are in the Baseball Hall of Fame.

Schneider also published three editions of *Tribe Memories*, a collection of stories about former Indians and events, and *Browns Memories*, a series of profiles of the men who played on that football team that began operations in 1946 as a charter member of the All-America Conference, and joined the NFL in 1950.

Schneider and his wife Catherine have three children, Russell Jr., who played a major role in the writing, editing and production of *The Glorious Indian Summer of 1995*, Bryan, and Eileen, who is married to former Indians pitcher Eric Raich.

# "A Magical Season"
## By Mike Hargrove

Are there words to describe the '95 Indians Baseball season? I don't think so. We've all tried in our own way ... awesome, unbelievable, great, wonderful, incredible, unreal ... but the word that seems to best describe this season to me is ... MAGICAL!

I have been in professional baseball since 1972 and there is nothing that can begin to match this MAGICAL season!

Russ has written this book about this magical season and it is an account of a very special time in any Tribe fan's life.

Although we think we will never forget a detail about this season, rest assured as you read the pages of this book it will stir memories that make goose bumps on all of us.

When I reflect on this '95 season I find that I wish I could just "bottle" it up so that nothing ever happens to the great feelings I have about it. This is what Russ does for all of us ... just bottles up the '95 season.

Although there are moments I know I'll never forget as they are etched so deeply in my mind, I thank Russ for the time and effort he put into putting it all down for all of us.

Please read, highlight special memories, and enjoy this book for many, many years. I just hope it's not another 41 years before another is written about an Indians MAGICAL season!

I salute all Tribe fans.

Mike Hargrove

## Dedication and Acknowledgements

*To my wife, Kay, for her encouragement, patience, and support; and to my son Rusty, for his invaluable help in the writing, editing, and production of this book; and to Joe Simenic, a dear friend, a valued colleague, a remarkable researcher, and one of the best baseball fans anywhere; and to Bob DiBiasio, Bart Swain, Joel Gunderson and Susie Gharrity of the Indians Public Relations Department; and to Burt Graeff of The Plain Dealer, for his splendid idea; and to Indians beat reporters Jim Ingraham of the Lake County News-Herald, Paul Hoynes of The Plain Dealer, and Sheldon Ocker of the Akron Beacon-Journal, for their coverage of the Indians, and their help in putting some of the material together; and to Ed Chukayne for his counsel, artwork and assistance; and to Joe Corrado, Angelo Murracco, and John Krepop, press box attendants at Jacobs Field, for their friendship and help; and to John Hart and Dan O'Dowd, for providing the outstanding personnel that made the 1995 Indians the best team in the American League; and to Mike Hargrove, who was, is and will be my "Manager of the Year" for many years; and to his coaches, Buddy Bell, Luis Isaac, Dave Nelson, Jeff Newman, and Mark Wiley, who worked tirelessly to bring out the best in all of the Indians; and last but certainly not least, to all of the players on the team that brought a championship to Cleveland after 41 years of frustration, and who made possible The Glorious Indian Summer of 1995, When a Season of Dreams Became Reality in Cleveland.*

# The Batting Order

# Prologue

It absolutely, positively was a season of dreams - a season of dreams come true - in Cleveland in 1995 when the Indians redeemed the sins of their predecessors.

They restored baseball to a position of glory in a city that had, for so long, suffered the ignominy of not just having losing teams, but having very bad losing teams.

In 1995, more than 2.8 million fans, a Cleveland record, spun the turnstiles of Jacobs Field, and countless others observed and enjoyed from a distance the deeds and accomplishments of their new heroes.

Even more impressive, the baseball renaissance in Cleveland came to fruition in the wake of the longest, nastiest and most contentious labor dispute in the history of professional sports in America.

It was a 132 day player strike that alienated fans and turned off their interest in many other major league cities, but not in Cleveland.

It did not happen overnight, however, not even in one year or two, 1995 and 1994. Neither was it solely the result of the construction and opening of Jacobs Field, variously described as "a jewel in downtown Cleveland"and, equally appropriate, the city's "field of dreams."

The redemption of the Indians began soon after December of 1986 when Richard E. Jacobs and his late brother, David H., purchased the then terribly mismanaged and under-financed franchise from the estate of F.J. (Steve) O'Neill.

The Jacobses hired Hank Peters to rebuild and operate the organization, and Peters, in turn, brought two of his former front office aides from Baltimore, John Hart and Dan O'Dowd, to work at his side.

Then, but certainly not least, Peters appointed former Tribe first baseman Mike Hargrove manager of the Kinston, North Carolina team in the Class A Carolina League in 1987, promoted him to Williamsport, Pennsylvania of the Class AA Eastern League in 1988, and to Colorado Springs, Colorado of the Class AAA Pacific Coast League in 1989.

Hargrove learned fast and well. Especially well.

A year later, in 1990, Hargrove was named a coach under Indians manager John McNamara, and on July 6, 1991, replaced McNamara.

Then, forced to bite the bullet and take their lumps on the field - the Indians lost a franchise record 105 games in 1991, but doggedly "stayed the course," in Jacobs' words - and devised a plan.

It was a plan that was necessitated by the constantly escalating player salaries and other costs that made operating in Cleveland, then a "small market" city, difficult to compete with wealthier franchises whose resources and revenue streams were much better.

That blueprint for success, called simply, "The Plan," was implemented during that horrendous, humiliating season of 105 defeats. The Indians were the butt of jokes as they staggered to a last place finish, 34 games behind the American League East Division champion Toronto Blue Jays.

The Plan, implemented by Hart and O'Dowd, was to sign to multi-year contracts the young, up-and-coming players the Indians believed had the best chance to succeed, and would give the franchise its best chance for success.

Essentially, it was an arrangement by which the players would be well paid during their early, developmental years, thus ensuring their continued presence when they reached maturity as big leaguers. Most importantly, it also would preclude their taking the club to arbitration, or becoming free agents at the peak of their careers.

When the plan was put into effect, Hart remembers, "We got calls from other clubs asking us, 'What are you doing? Do you realize the gamble you're taking?'" Jacobs, Hart and O'Dowd did.

Hart concedes, "There were a couple of hard years in there. But we had a different agenda. We were the third wheel. There were no stars to be loyal to. We had a revolving door."

And, as he also said, "We did not want to go through 20 arbitration cases."

Not all the players granted multi-year contracts lived up to expectations.

But most of them did - Sandy Alomar, Carlos Baerga, Albert Belle, Kenny Lofton, Charles Nagy, Manny Ramirez, Paul Sorrento and Jim Thome, among others - all of whom have contributed to the Indians' renaissance, and are expected to continue to keep the club as successful as it has come to be.

Now, The Plan is a model for other major league organizations to follow in this era of wild bidding for free agents, and the continuing escalation of player salaries.

And nobody is questioning the Indians' wisdom anymore.

Which is a far cry from the way it used to be, from those bad old days when a .500 record by the Indians was a moral victory.

As Frank Robinson once quipped after he managed the Indians from 1975-77, "Pennant fever in Cleveland is a 24-hour virus."

It often was in the years since the Indians blew the 1954 World Series.

But not anymore. Definitely, not anymore.

# 1

## The Best of Times, the Worst of Times

It was the best of times, but it also was the worst of times ... with apologies to Charles Dickens.

Baseball was back after 132 days of strife that cost the Indians their first appearance in post season play in 40 years.

But baseball also was back with *replacement* players, a.k.a. "scabs," because the strike by the Players Association that began on August 12, 1994, was still going on. Players were still angry at the owners, and the owners were still angry at the players.

It was, however, a new beginning for the Indians - though their names were Biasucci, Campbell, Kuld, Slusarski, Wearing and Yelding instead of Alomar, Baerga, Belle, Lofton, Martinez, Murray, Nagy, and Vizquel.

The beginning of what was to be a season of fulfilled dreams, the renaissance of the Cleveland baseball franchise that had, for so long been a doormat in the American League, took place on the lush, green grass of Chain O' Lakes Stadium in Winter Haven, Florida in late-February. Fifty-two players, most of them young - and all of them eager for the chance to prove themselves - reported to Tribe manager Mike Hargrove who was, admittedly, unsure of his own sentiments.

"I don't know how I feel," Hargrove said publicly. "I just know it's time to play ball, and I'm glad we have some guys who want to do so."

But, privately, Hargrove's opinion of the situation and the players he had inherited was something else, though he discreetly kept it to himself, as did all members of the Indians organization.

One of the replacement players probably said it best on behalf of his non-union teammates. "We're in a no-win situation." said Dan Gray, who had caught and played first base for the Winnipeg Goldeyes of the independent Northern League in 1994. "You want to get your time in, but you don't want to be known as a scab. It's a fine line."

Indeed it was.

Gray, who had undergone surgery on his right shoulder only five months earlier, shrugged and attempted to justify the position in which he'd placed himself by signing an Indians contract.

"My father is in a construction union back home in the Bronx," said Gray, as he tried on his Tribe uniform the day before workouts were to begin. "He told me, 'If I go out on strike the company could hire somebody else and I might never get my job back. It would be like taking food off my table.'

"But in this situation, in baseball, everybody knows that when the strike ends, the replacement players go home. When it's done, it's over - unless we show something and the Indians want to keep us in the organization, either up here with the big club, or in the minors.

"That's why I'm here. I think it's the reason most of us are here. For one more chance," added the 24-year old Gray, who had spent almost four seasons in the minors, originally as a farmhand of the Los Angeles Dodgers.

## "THE RIGHT PLACE, THE RIGHT TIME"

Or, as longtime minor league pitcher David Welch said, "To me, the only reason most of us are not up there before now is that we didn't get a chance. A break is being in the right place at the right time. As far as I'm concerned, this surely is the right place and the right time.

"Maybe if I were in the big league players' shoes, I'd feel like they do. But I'm in David Welch's shoes and I've got to look out for myself."

Few could blame him - or any of the replacement players, although, of course, the regulars certainly did.

"They're nothing but stinkin' scabs," said one who, out of curiosity, attended as a spectator an early workout. He shook hands with one of the replacement players he'd known prior to the strike.

Afterwards he told a reporter, "I wanted to scrub my hand after I shook with him."

That's how bad it was.

Later in spring training, after the Indians had played 14 exhibition games, another striking player, second baseman Carlos Baerga, made a surprise appearance at Winter Haven, strolled through the clubhouse and met with Hargrove and the coaches,.

"It's hard to describe being here. You walk in the clubhouse and there's someone else in your locker. It's strange," Baerga said, without further reference to the non-union players who had replaced him and his regular teammates.

However, while Baerga had nothing else to say, at least publicly, one of the replacement players did.

"Carlos probably was here to make us feel like dirt," he said.

Each replacement player was paid a guaranteed $5,000, plus major league meal money, and would receive an additional $5,000 if they survived the final cut. By opening the season on the major league roster, their salary would be $115,000.

Of the players who started spring training for the Indians that first day, two of them were released even before workouts resumed in the afternoon. It spoke volumes for the caliber of candidates hoping to take advantage of the strike to make it in the major leagues.

A catcher named Al Dumus, whose regular job was making Italian sausage in a Worthington, West Virginia meat processing plant, and a pitcher named Al Jones, who spent the previous four years playing in Taiwan, did not last long.

Dumus was sent packing because he apparently had eaten too much of his own sausage. Though his weight was listed at 189 pounds, the 28-year old Dumus was closer to 240 and was badly out of condition. "I haven't run like that since high school," he said, though his comment should have been that he hadn't *tried* to run the way Indians conditioning coach Fernando Montes ordered.

As for Jones, "He flat-out can't pitch ... how the hell could we have signed him, even as a replacement player?" one of the coaches scornfully asked.

One thing - perhaps the *only* thing - that pleased Mike Hargrove was the attitude of the players. "I saw guys hustling, and I like that," he said.

Otherwise, Hargrove diplomatically stated that he was "reserving judgment" on the players he was inheriting for what would be the start of his fourth full season as Tribe manager.

And throughout the replacement era, Hargrove wisely maintained his unwillingness to publicly evaluate the talent under his direction, though Cincinnati Reds manager Dave Johnson was not so judicious in his comments.

## THE FIRST TRADE

When the first trade in the history of replacement baseball was made between the Indians and Reds on March 2, in which Cleveland sent three players - former major league outfielder Barbaro Garbey, outfielder Mike Palivoda and pitcher Mike Curtis - to Cincinnati for a player (or players) to be named later, Johnson said:

"The Indians got the best of the deal ... they got nobody."

And Curtis quipped, "Now I can be one of the answers in Trivial Pursuit."

Making the situation even more ludicrous, the Indians sent two more players via the waiver route to Cincinnati - outfielder Lee Granger and Gray, the catcher who had talked about wanting a "break" - to make sure the Reds had enough to field a team for the exhibition season.

However, neither Granger nor Gray remained with the Reds for long. Granger was returned to the Tribe because he was unable to play due to a leg injury, and Gray was sent home with a sore shoulder.

Later in spring training Johnson, even more outspoken in his comments, called Replacement Baseball "a travesty."

Reds owner Marge Schott did not appreciate her manager's evaluation, but nobody openly disagreed with Johnson.

In that opener of the Grapefruit League and the first-ever game played by the two teams in the era of Replacement Baseball, the Indians beat the Reds, 3-1, in front of about 1,200 fans at the Plant City, Florida training complex of the Reds.

The best player in the field was Tribe shortstop Ever Magallenes. A longtime minor leaguer, Magallanes received a brief trial with the Indians in 1991, but couldn't make it as a utility infielder, with Felix Fermin the regular shortstop. That was the season the Tribe lost a franchise-record 105 games.

The Indians won with two runs in the fourth inning on singles by Pete Kuld and Shane Turner, and Mike Sarbaugh doubled home an insurance run in the ninth.

The next day, in front of only 1,824 fans who showed up for Cleveland's "home" opener in Winter Haven, the Indians again beat Cincinnati, this time, 8-6, as two veteran minor leaguers hit long home runs, both in the first inning. Mel Wearing, a 6-3, 230 pound first baseman who played for the Thunder Bay Whiskey Jacks in the Northern League, hammered a three-run shot, and Rob Nelson, who played in Mexico and at Tulsa of the American Association in 1994, followed with another homer.

## PROBABLE OPENING DAY LINEUP

The replacement Indians went on to win four of their first seven games, after which Hargrove indicated what "probably" would be the Indians opening day lineup if the strike was not settled by then.

The catcher would be Kuld or Darrin Campbell, Wearing and Nelson would platoon at first base, with Turner or Joe Biasucci at second, Magallenes at shortstop, Adell Davenport or Carlo Columbino at third, Eric Yelding in right field, Shawn Jeter or Dennis Hood in center, and Joe Mikulik in left. and a starting pitching rotation of Dickie Brown, Tim Delgado, Greg Perschke, Tommy Taylor, and Rod Steph, with Darrin Chapin and Mike Soper heading the relief corps.

The Indians' eighth game of the replacement era was televised back to Cleveland and did little to impress fans with the caliber of play. After losing to the Reds, 12-10, Magallenes said, "A game like that gives fans good reason to call us scabs."

There were few dissenters, including Hargrove. "What bothers me most is that we made too many mental mistakes," said the manager.

The game also produced a "first," which also might turn up on a Trivial Pursuit card one of these days.

Yelding was ejected in the seventh inning for arguing a called strike.

Making it particularly noteworthy was that the umpire who gave Yelding the thumb was a fellow named Joe Pitisici who - like all the players on the field - also was a so-called "scab."

Because members of the Major League Baseball Umpires Association had been locked out due to their stalled negotiations with the owners, college and former professional umpires were hired to work in their place.

As *Plain Dealer* reporter Paul Hoynes wrote the next day, "There was an unmistakable symmetry about the ejection."

Through the first 14 games, of which the Indians won eight, including the last five in a row, Biasucci was hitting a robust .529 (18-for-34) with two homers and 15 RBI, which probably contributed to the optimism expressed by Indians owner Richard Jacobs.

When asked for his reaction to Replacement Baseball, Jacobs said, "I'm not discouraged at all by what we've seen in spring training. This is baseball and we've got to protect it. You've got guys playing who have been stockbrokers for 10 years. This is where their dreams are."

But if that's where the replacement players' dreams were, that certainly was not the case with the regular players.

To a man, they were adamant in their resolve to stay out until an agreement was reached.

As Paul Sorrento said from his home in Largo, Florida, "It wouldn't be worth it to cross the line, to go back until the strike is settled. First, if you cross, you'll be blackballed. Second, what are you crossing for? If you're crossing for the money, it's not worth it.

## "IF YOU PLAY, YOU'RE A STRIKEBREAKER"

"There will be some resentment when the big leaguers come back. The union made it perfectly straight to the minor leaguers - if you play, you're a strikebreaker."

Eric Plunk also was outspoken. "I hate to see this happen," he said. "Coming up through the minor leagues, reaching the big leagues was a life-long commitment. You couldn't even go near the big league clubhouse when you were a minor leaguer. It was sacred.

"Now they're giving that opportunity to guys who don't deserve it, who didn't earn it. There was always a thought that it would never happen. But it is about to."

There also were reports that a Cincinnati replacement player left camp because, according to Reds general manager Jim Bowden, "somebody threatened to break his legs."

To which Sorrento responded, "Come on, get serious. Who's going to do something like that?"

Through it all, negotiations between the owners and players union continued sporadically. One day the news was positive and promising, but usually the next day it was negative and depressing.

On one occasion, early in March, Colorado Rockies chairman Jerry McMorris, a member of the owners negotiating committee, said, "Without a miracle, major league players will not be on the field opening day."

Players union head Donald Fehr called it "a pretty clear indication (that) the owners have already decided to blow off the beginning of the season."

Hargrove was among those who were particularly distressed by the lack of progress. Midway through the month of March he said, "It sounds to me like we're going to start the season with replacement players. You hope against hope that it wouldn't come to this, but I'm tired of getting my hopes dashed. Until I hear differently, this is the way we go."

Contributing to the negativism that had been generated was a development that also occurred midway through March involving the National Labor Relations Board.

The regional director of the NLRB in New York issued an unfair labor practices complaint against the owners for removing salary arbitration, competitive bidding for free agents, and anti-collusion provisions in the free agent rules.

It led to the expectation that the five member board would seek a preliminary injunction in federal court in New York requiring the owners to restore the terms of the previous labor contract.

And because the union had said it would end the strike if the injunction were granted, several of the owners hinted they would press for a lockout of the players if the strike ended without a new agreement.

## JACOBS FAVORED A LOCKOUT

Indians owner Richard Jacobs indicated he would favor a lockout "I'd have to know all the ramifications, but I think I'd vote for a lockout," he was quoted as saying. What's more, Jacobs speculated, "I think we'd have enough votes (among the owners to institute a lockout)."

Jacobs also said if the injunction was imposed on the owners, there was a good chance they would appeal.

"The appeal would go right back to the NLRB, the same five people who voted the first time," he said. "That does not sound good unless you have compelling evidence. I think we do."

But, as several others pointed out, the owners would be risking millions of dollars if they proceeded with a lockout.

If such a move were deemed illegal - which very possibly would have been the case - the owners would have been liable for the players' lost wages. In 1987, after a strike by the National Football League Players Association, the NFL Management Council had to pay $30 million in damages for refusing to allow players to return to the field immediately.

In the case of baseball, it also was possible that a lockout would weaken the owners' position in any challenge to their antitrust exemption in Congress or the courts.

And so, the impasse went on, still with no break in sight.

As it turned out, two weeks later the NLRB voted to seek an injunction against the owners. It was issued on March 31 which, in effect, ended the strike because the players agreed to go back to work under the previous agreement.

In the meantime, however, the impasse dragged on, and so did the mixed emotions that many of the players felt, especially those who had previous major league experience.

Yelding was typical of them. "My mother doesn't want me to do it (continue as a replacement player), and neither does one of my best friends, Lance Johnson."

Johnson, the striking center fielder of the Chicago White Sox, constantly called Yelding, urging him not to play.

In 1990, Yelding hit .254 with 69 runs and 64 stolen bases for Houston, but thereafter didn't spend a full season in the big leagues. It's why he eagerly sought another chance with another organization, despite being torn by doubt about doing the right thing.

## YELDING IS TRIBE'S "BEST HITTER"

Hargrove called Yelding - who was batting .348 (23-for-66) with 11 stolen bases.- the Indians' "best hitter," even though Biasucci's average continued to hover around the .500 mark, while leading the team with 18 RBI.

"I'm still praying for guidance to do the right thing, and for the strike to end," said Yelding.

Another former major leaguer who found himself in a similar situation was Junior Ortiz, a back-up catcher for the Indians in 1992 and 1993, who joined the Texas Rangers in 1994.

When he became a free agent in the winter of 1994-95, Ortiz wasted no time signing on as a replacement player with the Chicago White Sox, strike or no strike.

His attitude also was interesting - and so was Hargrove's reaction to seeing Ortiz on the other side of the field when the Indians played and beat the White Sox, 8-5, on March 25.

"I couldn't afford to stay home (in Puerto Rico)," said Ortiz. "I am 35, if I don't play this year, there is no guarantee that the union would get me a job for 1996, or even this year when the strike ended. So why shouldn't I do what I am doing?"

Ortiz classified the talent among the replacement players as being "like a Class A league with a few players who could play at Class AA or Class AAA."

Hargrove, obviously still aware of his position as a member of management, but also a staunch union member as a player, said, "I have no comment," when asked about Ortiz's willingness to break ranks with the union.

Another attitude was articulated by Charles York, a pitcher who arrived in training camp late, but was hopeful of winning a job with the Indians before the team left for Cleveland.

"Sooner or later all this stuff gets to you," he said when the end of spring training was only a week away. "The sign on the wall of the clubhouse says the equipment truck is leaving for Cleveland three days from now, but no one knows if his stuff is going to be on it or not.

"You see guys walking around in the clouds. Some of them are scared. I can see it in their faces. It's not so much the older guys, but the young guys, the guys who aren't sure if they're doing the right thing or not by hanging in here.

"They're saying to themselves, 'If the strike goes on, will I be going to Cleveland, and is it the right thing? And if the strike ends, what happens to me? Either way, am I going to be blackballed?'"

The questions were relevant.

## PERSCHKE OR SLUSARSKI TO PITCH

As the days dwindled down and the date for breaking camp approached - the Indians were to leave Winter Haven on March 30, play exhibition games against Cincinnati in Columbus on March 31, and the New York Mets at Jacobs Field in Cleveland on April 1, and open the season on April 2 in Oakland - Hart, Assistant General Manager Dan O'Dowd, and Hargrove labored over the final replacement roster.

Hargrove said either Perschke or Slusarski would start the opener against the Athletics, unless ... well, you know.

Unless the strike was settled by then.

If not, did Hart believe any of the striking players would cross the line and return to the team? His reply was interesting.

"I've talked to a lot of agents and they told me they don't have any player who wants to be the first one to go back, but they have hundreds who will be the second," said Hart.

The labor situation was still cloudy, though it appeared that a break might be forthcoming three days before the Indians were to leave Winter Haven for their final two exhibition games against the Reds and Mets, and six days prior to the opener in Oakland.

As the Indians were beating Houston, 5-4, to even their Grapefruit League record at 14-14 on March 28, major league club owners and players met in a negotiating session in New York.

"Something's going to happen ... it's going to be real hairy the next few days," predicted Kansas City pitcher David Cone, one of the players who'd been most active in the nearly eight month strike.

A similar indication was given by Fehr, the players union leader. "I think it is fair to say that the series of suggestions that we have received represents some movement by the clubs," he said. But then he cautioned, "I also think it would be incorrect of me to suggest that we thought it was substantial."

And in Columbus, Tribe stars Eddie Murray and Kenny Lofton testified before a standing room only crowd at an Ohio House Commerce and Labor Committee hearing on a bill that would ban replacement games in publicly funded stadiums in the state.

It was sponsored by Rep. Ross A. Boggs Jr., an Ashtabula County Democrat, who said he hoped to have the bill out of committee and voted on by the full House before the end of April.

Murray said he hoped the bill would force the owners to the bargaining table "a little sooner."

But the legislators also fired some tough questions at Murray and Lofton.

As one of them, Rep. Robert L. Corbin, a Dayton Republican, asked, "What ball player is worth $7 million?"

Murray replied, "The person getting it."

Meanwhile, after the Indians' victory over Houston, Wearing again lamented the uncertainty of the situation, and the difficult position all the replacement players were in.

## "WHAT'S GOING TO HAPPEN?"

"It doesn't play on your mind during the game, but it's an after game thought," he said. "You come in, look around the clubhouse and wonder, 'What's going on? What's going to happen?'"

A few nights earlier, Wearing said, he ran into a big leaguer he'd played with in Baltimore's farm system. Wearing wouldn't identify the man, but said they'd been friends. When he tried to say hello, the other player's response was a slight movement of the head and a pursing of the lips.

"The guy gave me the ugly," said Wearing. "He'd seen me hit .326 at Class AAA Rochester in 1992. He'd seen me put up 91 RBI in Double-A and Triple-A that same year, and not get put on the (Orioles') 40 man roster. Did he have any remorse for me? No. So why should I have remorse for him now?

"We're already in deep trouble for just playing in these games. For me, I want it to be showtime. I want to play a couple of games up there. I want people who have never seen me to get a chance to see what Mel Wearing can do."

And then Wearing made a promise to any fans who might not be sure he was good enough to play in the major leagues.

"A lot of guys who just wanted to get in a uniform, to see a big league city, to walk into a big league clubhouse are gone now," he said. "It's gotten down to the guys who know how to play. We're not going to embarrass the city, the tradition, or the uniform."

Two days later - after a 10-6 loss to Detroit and 5-0 victory over the Chicago White Sox that gave them a 15-15 record - the replacement Indians left Winter Haven and headed north.

Negotiations were still going on, but after all the false alarms of the previous five weeks, players and Tribe officials alike were not taking them seriously.

As for the replacement players, they, of course, were hopeful of finally getting a chance in the "Show."

As Mikulik said, "I've got my fingers crossed. It would be a crime for it to end now, like this. A lot of guys here have never stepped on a big league field or lived the big league life. I've played 11 years and never lived it. It would be hard to swallow if it doesn't happen."

Hart didn't have much to say about Mikulik's comment. "I'm not going to think about anything until we get off the plane in Columbus," he said.

## THE 35 MAN REPLACEMENT ROSTER

The 35 man roster included fifteen pitchers - David Welch, Tommy Taylor, Dickie Brown, Darrin Chapin, Joe Slusarski, Bo Magee, Mike Soper, Greg Perschke, Mark Sims, Tim Delgado, Frank Ricci, Greg Williams, Rod Steph, John Hrnsovsky and Steve True; three catchers - Kuld, Darrin Campbell and Steve Soliz; ten infielders - Biasucci, Shane Turner, Carlo Colombino, Mike Sarbaugh, Nelson, Wearing, Adell Davenport, Magallenes, Rouglas Odor and Carmelo Martinez; and seven outfielders - Dennis Hood, Yelding, Mikulik, Shawn Jeter,. Sam Hence, Alex Ramirez and Scott Tedder.

In Columbus on March 31 the Indians lost to Cincinnati, 6-1, in the annual "Ohio Cup" game, in front of a slim turnout of 4,660 fans, and immediately boarded a charter plane for a flight to Cleveland where they'd play a final exhibition against the New York Mets the next day at Jacobs field.

And then it would be on to Oakland for the start of the first season of Replacement Baseball.

By the time they arrived in Cleveland, however, a funny thing had happened in New York.

A U.S. District judge issued an injunction against the owners, ordering them to restore free agent bidding, salary arbitration and the anti-collusion provisions of the expired collective bargaining agreement.

"So what are they going to do ... take this away from us now?" asked Kuld on behalf of his replacement player teammates.

"I know it was never ours to begin with, but it sure felt like ours for a long time."

What the owners did was the only thing that made any sense ... *financial* sense, that is. A lockout could have cost them millions of dollars.

Indians owner Richard Jacobs admitted as much. As he said, "For every day of a lockout it would have cost me $195,000. That got my attention."

Obviously, it got the attention of all the owners, and it was much more prudent to accept the order of the court, welcome back the striking players and negotiate a settlement with the union at the end of the season.

Industry estimates were that the strike cost the 28 owners $700 million in revenues, and the players nearly $300 million in salaries.

Despite the truce that called off the hostilities between labor and management, the Indians played that final exhibition game in Jacobs Field, if only for the satisfaction of the soon-to-be-departed replacement players, and the fans.

## INDIANS REPLACEMENTS WIN, 5-2

In that first and last game between replacement players in Cleveland, the Indians beat the Mets, 5-2.

"It was weird," said Campbell, a former Cleveland high school and sandlot player who caught the game for the Indians. "I was all geeked up, playing in my hometown, in front of my family. I go 1-for-3, throw out a runner and then they drop a bomb on me."

All who played in exhibition games received $5,000, plus an additional $2,000 bonus.

Twenty-three of the 35 players who broke camp with the Indians were kept in the farm system. The other 12 who were not retained were released outright.

Among those released were first basemen Mel Wearing and Mel Nelson, two of the best hitters during the short-lived replacement era.

Sent to Class AAA Buffalo were pitchers Darrin Chapin, Tim Delgado, Greg Perschke and Joe Slusarski, infielder Carmelo Martinez, and outfielders Shawn Jeter and Eric Yelding. Campbell was assigned to Canton-Akron of the Class AA Eastern League.

"When they told us it was over there were some heartaches in that locker room," said Perschke. "It was kind of sad. It looked to me like the owners never really intended to use us. I mean, I have nothing against the Cleveland Indians. They've been super to me. But as a whole, I don't think the owners were ever going to use us in real games."

Said Kuld, who also was among those released, "No, it wasn't worth it. Forty-three days flushed down the toilet because somebody couldn't get off the pot and make up his mind about the money involved in the strike."

And so, the longest, nastiest, and costliest strike in the history of professional sports finally ended.

It was April Fool's Day but, thankfully, this was not a joke.

# Spring Training II
# ....the Sequel

Though he was merely expressing a wish, the words of Jose Mesa would prove to be prophetic when he said on the morning of April 3, "All we can do is work hard and try to win as many games as we can so the fans will come back and see us."

Mesa was speaking as the Indians' chartered plane took off from Cleveland less than 48 hours after a truce was declared, if not a settlement, in what had been a 232 day strike by the Major League Baseball Players Association.

Indians officials and a small contingent of players who'd been in Cleveland waiting out the strike were on their way to Winter Haven, Florida for what General Manager John Hart called "Spring Training II, the Sequel."

The season was re-scheduled to begin for the Indians on April 27 against the Texas Rangers in the new Ballpark in Arlington, and the home opener would be played at Jacobs Field on May 5 against Minnesota.

While all concerned were happy for the return of Major League Baseball - which meant the end of *Replacement* Baseball - Hart was obviously and understandably reserved in his expression of relief that the strike had finally ended.

"Until we get a deal with the union, it won't be the right thing," he said. It was a reference to the fact that the players returned to their teams because of the court ordered reinstatement of baseball's expired collective bargaining agreement that had caused the union to walk off the field on August 12, 1994.

The work stoppage that spoiled the Indians' best season since 1954 and prevented them from reaching postseason play for the first time in 40 years, also cut 18 games from the 1995 schedule, reducing it from 162 to 144 games.

What's more, it wiped out 18 Indians games against western division teams - teams that were among the Tribe's favorite foes in 1994. Then their record was 19-9 versus teams in the American League West (5-0 vs. California, 6-0 vs. Oakland, 3-2 vs. Seattle, and 5-7 vs. Texas).

Little wonder that Hart, along with many of his colleagues on the management side, were less than thrilled with the truce that brought the players back to work without agreeing to agree to a no-strike pledge.

## "THE IMPORTANT THING"

"The important thing," said Hart with resignation, "is that baseball is back. Hopefully, we can solve our problems, iron out our differences down the road. It won't be easy, but we'll be trying."

And once all the players were in camp, Hart met with them in an effort to heal any wounds that might have still festered in the wake of the longest, costliest and nastiest strike in the history of professional sports in America.

"One thing I told the players," said Hart, "was that they will have to show the fans how much they care about the game, how much they love it."

Charles Nagy, the Indians player representative, agreed. "I'm sure we'll feel (the fans') wrath, and deservedly so," he said. "We're going to have to be more conscientious toward the fans than we have been in the past."

Among the happiest Tribesmen to be back in uniform and on the playing field were Paul Sorrento and Jim Thome.

"I never thought I'd be glad to go to spring training, but I am," said Sorrento.

And Thome said of the strike and not playing ball, "I don't think anyone wants to get to that point again. It made me realize how important the game is. It's tough out there in the real world, and this - playing major league baseball - is a fun job."

But while the players were unanimous in their happiness about being back, and that their problems with the owners apparently were behind them, several could not resist voicing their anger at those who wanted to take their jobs.

"Those replacement guys just used the opportunity to open their pockets and take the pay," said Sandy Alomar Jr. "They took the $5,000 bonuses and knew exactly what they were getting into.

"It made me laugh to hear the replacement players say they played the game for the love of it. Love isn't going to pay your bills or help raise your children.

"We love the game, too, but we had to do what was necessary to protect our interests. Anyone in our position would have done the same thing. It wasn't greed. We were just fighting for our rights."

Whatever, Spring Training II, the Sequel, was launched under a blazing Florida sun on April 5. It would continue through April 26, after which the Indians would embark upon what would become their greatest season since 1954.

## TRIBE SIGNS DAVE WINFIELD

One of Hart's first personnel moves was the signing of free agent Dave Winfield to a one year contract.

"He's the right guy for this ball club," said Hart. "Adding David Winfield is adding another potent offensive weapon to one of the best offenses in the American League."

Ironically, the Indians had traded for Winfield on August 31, 1994, even though the strike was then in progress. Because of the work stoppage, Winfield never became an Indian. But Hart didn't lose interest in the 43-year old outfielder, a veteran of 21 seasons in the major leagues.

It also was ironic that Winfield finally wound up with the Indians, the team he rejected 15 years earlier. Then, as a member of the San Diego Padres, Winfield had a no-trade clause in his contract and wouldn't agree to let the Padres send him to Cleveland.

"Things (in Cleveland) were different then," said Winfield. "Now, I'm delighted to be going to the Indians. They - we - have a chance, a good chance to win the pennant and I look forward to being a part of it."

Winfield, who signed for $600,000 plus incentives, was the leader among active players in hits (3,088), home runs (463), and runs batted in (1,829). He was 14th on the all-time hit list.

The presence of Winfield with Eddie Murray gave the Indians two certain future Hall of Famers. Murray would enter the season needing only 70 hits to become only the 19th player in major league history to reach 3,000, which Winfield achieved in 1993 when he played for the Minnesota Twins.

With the addition of Winfield, Hart turned his efforts to finding another starting pitcher, a left-handed reliever and a closer. His primary objectives were Orel Hershiser to bolster the rotation, Paul Assenmacher to balance the bull pen, and former Tribesman Doug Jones, who set a club record of 43 saves in 1990.

As it turned out, Hart was successful in signing Hershiser and Assenmacher, as well as another veteran starter, Bud Black, to free agent contracts. But - fortunately, as it turned out - Hart was unsuccessful in the reacquisition of Jones.

Even before adding a closer, and with spring training less than a week old, Hargrove said, "I've never been associated with a team as complete as this. There's a sense of confidence here that wasn't present this time last year. This team is as close to winning as any I've been around."

## STILL SEARCHING FOR A CLOSER

When Jones rejected the Indians' offer and elected to sign with Baltimore, Hart turned his efforts to Jeff Russell, the reliever who pitched the final two months for Cleveland in 1994. Russell became a free agent when the season was aborted by the strike. So did Mike Jackson, another relief pitcher who had toiled for San Francisco.

However, both Russell and Jackson - again, fortunately for the Indians - wanted more money than Hart was willing to pay, and they went elsewhere. It left the Tribe with a large void to shore up in the bullpen, but one that was filled from an unexpected source.

Mesa, a 28-year old right-hander who'd been acquired by the Indians from Baltimore in a trade for minor league outfielder Kyle Washington on July 14, 1992, became the focal point of Hargrove's first experiment in spring training.

Mesa came to Cleveland with a reputation for having a good arm that could propel a fast ball in the 95-plus miles-per-hour range, though he'd never harnessed it, nor enjoyed much success during parts of four previous major league seasons with the Orioles.

In fact, one of his former teammates called Mesa "the kind of pitcher that gets pitching coaches fired."

In 149 games - 95 as a starter - for the Orioles and Indians prior to 1995, Mesa's won-lost record was an undistinguished 34-45 with a 4.89 earned run average. His totals included six complete games, and two saves, both of them for the Indians in 1994.

"The thing that impressed us about Jose, and led us to think that he might be able to do the job as a closer," Hargrove said, "was his live arm and that great fast ball. We figured that, if he didn't have to pitch more than an inning at a time, and if we didn't overwork him, he wouldn't lose any velocity, or movement on his pitches."

It was a massive understatement, as everyone knows now.

Mesa became the missing link in 1995, as well as the best, most dominant closer in baseball, obliterating not only Tribe relief pitching records but also major league marks.

Five days into Spring Training II, and five days before the Indians' second Grapefruit League exhibition season began, they signed Hershiser to a $1.45 million contract for 1995, with a club option worth $1.5 million in 1996. It completed the starting rotation that already included Dennis Martinez, Charles Nagy, Mark Clark and Bud Black.

## "I WANT TO BE PART OF THAT" - HERSHISER

Hershiser, 36, rejected offers - several of which, he said, were for more money - from other clubs to join the Indians because, "There is an unbelievable opportunity to win here ... a chance to win a world championship.

"The Indians have a quality ballpark, a quality ball club and are located in a quality city. I want to be part of that."

Hershiser pitched for the Los Angeles Dodgers, and was their Most Valuable Player when they beat Oakland in the World Series in 1988. "I want to be part of that again. If I'm not the MVP of the Series, I want to shake the hand of the guy who is the MVP. I want to let the fans and players know that it's worth everything you go through."

Two days later, on April 10, Assenmacher also signed.

Among those applauding the moves the loudest was Alomar, who played his first game for Tribe in 1990 and was a member of the team that lost 105 games in 1991.

"Five years ago," said Alomar, "nobody wanted to come here. If somebody said he did, you thought, 'This guy is out of his mind.' People couldn't wait to leave. Now, this is awesome. This is great."

So was the Indians' Grapefruit League opener on April 13 in Lakeland, Florida, if for no other reason than it marked the resumption of major league baseball - *real* major league baseball - for the first time in more than eight months.

Excluding the exhibitions played by replacement players in March, the game against the Detroit Tigers, a 10-9 Indians victory, was their first since August 10, 1994 when they beat Toronto, 5-3, two days before the season was halted by the strike.

"It seemed like an eternity since we'd been on the field," said Sorrento, who hit the Tribe's first home run in 1995 in the third inning. Rookie outfielder Brian Giles also homered.

Mesa made his first 1995 appearance in the Indians' second game, another poorly-played exhibition that became a 12-8 loss to Houston. Perhaps as a portent of things to come, Mesa struck out the side, after walking the second batter he faced, in the eighth inning.

The highlight of the loosely-played game came in the fifth inning when Winfield pinch-hit for Murray and hammered a two run homer.

The game was umpired by college and former professional arbiters because the regulars were still locked out and without a new contract.

While the 3,145 fans in Joker Marchant Stadium were subdued, perhaps because their "home" team, the Tigers were losing, they showed no hostility - as had been feared by some - toward the players upon their return from the strike.

## HERSHISER'S DEBUT IS IMPRESSIVE

The next day Hershiser's debut also was impressive, though the Indians' record fell to 1-2 in a 7-3 loss to Kansas City. Hershiser pitched the first two innings and gave up one hit and an unearned run.

"The Royals were hitting the top of the ball and pounding it into the dirt, which shows me I was getting good movement on the ball," said the 36-year old veteran who spent the first 12 years of his major league career with the Dodgers.

Alomar saw the same thing. "Hershiser's ball really sinks a lot. He's the type of pitcher who makes my job a lot easier," said the catcher.

A few days later a minor flap surfaced when Players Association head Donald Fehr published a list of players who participated in replacement games. It was compiled, Fehr said, so that major leaguers could identify the "strikebreakers."

"They have a right to know who was trying to take their jobs," said Fehr, though he claimed the union was not suggesting that its members should retaliate in any way. "We don't encourage anybody doing anything ... I'm not concerned about that kind of stuff."

Fehr did say, however, that the union would consider legal ways of making its point to the erstwhile strikebreakers, such as not allowing them into the union should they reach the majors. It was further evidence that the animosity that had been generated was not completely forgotten - nor would it.

Fehr's remarks infuriated two of the Indians' replacement players, Rod Steph and Joe Biasucci, both of whom opened the season at Class AA Canton-Akron.

"What (Fehr) said is terrible, and his comments are stupid," said Steph. "We knew we weren't taking anybody's jobs. We were just filling spots. We just wanted to take advantage of the opportunity for the major league coaches and managers to take a look at us."

Biasucci agreed "Fehr is stupid. I played this spring because I needed a job and had to pay bills. It was a good opportunity for the Indians to see us and have some fun. I made $1,400 a month last year, about as much as some big leaguers make in one at-bat."

On the other hand, Dennis Martinez said there was nothing wrong with Fehr's list.

"It's something the (regular) players asked for," he said. "We want to know what players were involved. There's nothing wrong with that."

But, he added, "No one would try to harm anyone. I understand where (the replacement players) were coming from. I hope they understand that the owners used them. If the owners try to do the same thing again, they'll realize what's going on

"But if some of the same players decided to play again, then you have to think about what kind of individual you're dealing with."

With five days of Spring Training II remaining before their opener against the Rangers in Arlington, Texas, the Indians' exhibition record was 3-2-1 (the tie was a 2-2 extra inning game against Houston that was called when both teams ran out of pitchers).

## ALOMAR IS HURTING

It was then that the first potentially-serious problem surfaced for the Tribe.

Alomar, who underwent surgery on his left knee during the winter, and who was sidelined with injuries on several occasions during his first five seasons with the Indians, limped off the field during pre-game batting practice on April 20.

Four days earlier Alomar had fluid drained from the knee, but it was not considered anything to worry about.

However, Alomar's knee swelled and became progressively more painful, preventing him from getting into a full crouch behind the plate.

"It's nothing to worry about," Alomar insisted, though he subsequently was proved wrong. When the season opened, Alomar was on the disabled list again, with Tony Pena the regular catcher, backed up by Jesse Levis.

Alomar's injuries, since winning the American League "Rookie of the Year" award in 1990, included: in 1991 - an inflamed right rotator cuff, broken index finger and strained right hip flexor - in 1992, torn webbing between two fingers on his right hand and arthroscopic surgery on his left knee; in 1993 - back surgery for a ruptured disk and a strained medial collateral ligament in his left knee; and in 1994 - torn webbing between two fingers on his right hand again.

Of the Indians' 648 games from 1991-94, Alomar played in only 284 of them.

Another injury, this one to rookie reliever Willie Smith, who was competing with Mesa and Paul Shuey for the closer role in the bull pen, suffered a ruptured medial collateral ligament in his right elbow. He required immediate ligament transplant surgery (also known as "Tommy John surgery") and was lost for the season.

"We liked what we saw of Willie," Hargrove said of Smith, who had been signed as a free agent in November 1994. "He was in a battle with Mesa and Shuey, but now it's prettty much up to them (Mesa and Shuey) to win or lose."

It meant that the Indians no longer were considering a deal for an established closer in the trade mart. They had inquired about the availability of Rick Aguillera, Bryan Harvey, Jeff Montgomery, John Hudek, Rod Beck and Randy Myers, but obviously felt their price tags were all too high..

Hudek, who logged 16 saves and a 2.97 earned run average in 42 appearances as a rookie for Houston last year, was appealing to the Indians because of his record and $185,000 salary.

## SWINDELL? THANKS BUT NO THANKS

However, the only way the Astros would trade Hudek was in a package with former Tribe southpaw Greg Swindell who was signed through 1996 in a four-year deal that would pay him about $4 million in each this season and next.

While the Astros said they'd be willing to absorb some of Swindell's salary, negotiations ended when they asked for a package that would include three of the Tribe's best young pitching prospects - Julian Tavarez, Albie Lopez and Chad Ogea.

Through the final day of Spring Training II the umpires were still on strike and replacement umpires worked the exhibition games, much to the consternation of the players, though all kept their concerns discreetly silent.

"Don't ask," said one veteran. "We may be stuck with them (when the season opens) and I don't want anything I might say now to be held against me then."

Another said, "You can't win. If you say something good about them, the real umps will get mad at you. And if you say something bad about the replacement guys, they could get you during the game."

Hargrove was more understanding, probably by design.

"These fellows (replacement umpires) are trying hard, which is to their credit, but they are not as consistent as the regular umpires. That's the biggest difference I've seen. The players have had a difficult time adjusting."

Finally, it was over - "Spring Training II, the Sequel," as Hart called it three-and-a-half weeks earlier in the wake of the strike that, some thought, would kill the game.

On April 25 the Indians left Winter Haven with an 8-3-1 Grapefruit League record, played a final tune-up game in Buffalo against their Class AAA affiliate in the American Association, and headed for Texas with high hopes for a return to glory

Hargrove was not among the prophets of doom as he addressed members of the media after beating the Bisons, 2-1.

"The game will be all right," he said, because, "It's bigger than anything we can do to it. There are legitimate concerns, yes. But baseball will be here long after you and I are gone."

Acting Commissioner Alan "Bud" Selig also expressed optimism, stressed the hope that the old wounds would soon be healed, and encouraged players to do their best to bring the fans back.

"This season is very important, very critical," he said. "We've got to get back to baseball. We've got to be very sensitive to the fans. I'm grateful that we're playing again, but we've got a lot of work to do at the national and club levels."

And with that the Indians embarked upon their mission - to erase four decades of frustration.

## THE FINAL ROSTER FOR 1995

The final roster included 18 players who were with the Indians when the strike ended the 1994 season.

They were: pitchers Mark Clark, Jason Grimsley, Dennis Martinez, Jose Mesa, Charles Nagy and Eric Plunk; catchers Sandy Alomar (on the disabled list) and Tony Pena; infielders Carlos Baerga, Alvaro Espinoza, Eddie Murray, Paul Sorrento, Jim Thome and Omar Vizquel; and outfielders Albert Belle, Wayne Kirby, Kenny Lofton and Manny Ramirez.

Newcomers to the club: pitchers Paul Assenmacher, Bud Black, Dennis Cook, Orel Hershiser, Jim Poole, Paul Shuey and Julian Tavarez; catcher Jesse Levis; infielder David Bell; and outfielders Ruben Amaro and Dave Winfield.

(Black, Cook, Shuey, Tavarez and Levis all previously played for the Tribe, but were not on the Cleveland roster at the end of 1994.)

In uniform, too, was Hargrove's complete coaching staff: Buddy Bell, Luis Isaac, Charlie Manuel, Dave Nelson, Jeff Newman and Mark Wiley.

Still out, however, were the umpires, who were still unable to reach agreement with the owners on a new contract, and it appeared that their replacements would be making the calls when the season began.

# 3

## The First Step
## in a Long Journey

It's been said that every journey, even the longest, begins with a first step.

On April 27, 1995, the Indians took their first step along the road toward redemption - the undoing of 41 years of abject and absolute frustration - in The Ballpark in Arlington, the new home of the Texas Rangers.

Both the result of the game and the fans in attendance were indicative of what was in store for the Indians and Major League Baseball in 1995.

The Indians rocked three Texas pitchers for 13 hits, including home runs by Carlos Baerga, Albert Belle, Eddie Murray, Manny Ramirez and Paul Sorrento, to overwhelm the Rangers, 11-6. It was a particularly impressive debut by Ramirez, who doubled and singled twice to go 4-for-5.

Dennis Martinez yielded two runs (one earned) on four hits in six innings for his first of what would be nine consecutive victories without a loss. The Tribe was coasting, 10-2, when Martinez left, and the Rangers took advantage of Dennis Cook to make the final score appear more respectable.

Attendance was an embarrassment, however, as 32,161 fans paid their way through the gates to see the return of major league baseball, leaving more than 27,000 seats vacant.

Many of the fans expressed their displeasure with the players by booing and jeering during the pre-game introductions, which also was the case elsewhere around the American and National League.

The Toronto Blue Jays drew their smallest crowd ever in the SkyDome where 31,070 fans saw the home team beat Oakland, 7-1, and San Diego and Pittsburgh each drew fewer than 7,500 for their openers.

## "REAPING WHAT WE SOWED"

"We're reaping what we sowed, both the owners and the players," said Orel Hershiser. "We've torn down a product for a failure of will to get an agreement. Any trust we try to build now, fans will probably take with a grain of salt. An educated fan will realize we still don't have a basic agreement."

Nobody could disagree with Hershiser's analysis.

Mike Hargrove was pleased, of course, with the Indians victory, and the way it was achieved. "Every year is different," he said, "but this game was typical of how we played last year," when the Indians would have qualified for the playoffs as the American League's wild card team had there not been a strike. Their 1994 won-lost record was 66-47 (.584) and left them one game behind the Chicago White Sox when the season was suspended.

The Indians' one-sided victory over the Rangers made the prognosticators look like, well, *experts*. Among the reporters at the *Plain Dealer,* Paul Hoynes predicted the Indians would win the AL Central, while columnists Bill Livingston and Bud Shaw both expected them to finish second to Chicago, but to gain a wild card berth in the playoffs.

Beat writers Jim Ingraham of the *Lake County News-Herald* and Sheldon Ocker of the *Akron Beacon Journal*, also picked the Indians to win the AL Central, though only Ingraham said in print that the Tribe would win the pennant.

Hargrove conceded that being picked to win created pressure on the Indians that a Cleveland team had not known in the previous four decades.

"Anytime people expect you to win, the pressure is there," he said. "But if you're asking me if I think this is our last chance to contend, I don't think so. Our front office has been very good at getting the people we need."

The Tribe's impressive victory in the opener also was tempered by the announcement that Sandy Alomar's aching left knee, which had caused him to be placed on the disabled list during spring training, required another operation.

Alomar underwent surgery by Dr. Louis Keppler and would be lost to the Tribe for at least eight weeks, possibly longer.

It meant that Tony Pena, the 37-year old veteran who had been on the roster of the Class AAA Buffalo Bisons when Spring Training II began, would do the catching through the first two months of the season. His backup catcher was Jesse Levis, who had brief stints with the Tribe in each of the previous three seasons.

# THE OPENING VICTORY:
## Indians 11, Rangers 6

| Cleveland | AB | R | H | RBI | Texas | AB | R | H | RBI |
|---|---|---|---|---|---|---|---|---|---|
| Lofton, cf | 3 | 0 | 0 | 1 | Nixon, cf | 5 | 0 | 1 | 2 |
| Vizquel, ss | 5 | 1 | 1 | 0 | Frye, 2b | 5 | 1 | 1 | 0 |
| Baerga, 2b | 5 | 2 | 3 | 1 | W.Clark, 1b | 3 | 1 | 1 | 1 |
| Belle, lf | 5 | 2 | 2 | 3 | Tettleton, dh | 4 | 0 | 0 | 0 |
| Murray, dh | 5 | 1 | 1 | 1 | I. Rodriguez, c | 3 | 1 | 1 | 0 |
| Thome, 3b | 4 | 1 | 0 | 0 | Greer, rf | 4 | 1 | 1 | 2 |
| Ramirez, rf | 5 | 3 | 4 | 3 | Palmer, 3b | 3 | 1 | 1 | 0 |
| Sorrento, 1b | 4 | 1 | 1 | 2 | McLemore, lf | 4 | 1 | 2 | 0 |
| Pena, c | 3 | 0 | 1 | 0 | Gil, ss | 4 | 0 | 0 | 0 |
| **Totals** | **39** | **11** | **13** | **11** | | **35** | **6** | **8** | **5** |

| Cleveland | 036 010 001 - 11 13 2 |
|---|---|
| Texas | 100 100 220 -  6  8 0 |

**E:** Vizquel 2. **LOB:** Cleveland 6, Texas 5. **2B:** Ramirez, Frye, Palmer. **HR:** W.. Clark, Baerga, Belle, Murray, Ramirez, Sorrento. **SB:** McLemore. **SF:** Lofton. **GIDP:** Belle, Tettleton.

| Cleveland | IP | H | R | ER | BB | SO | Texas | IP | H | R | ER | BB | SO |
|---|---|---|---|---|---|---|---|---|---|---|---|---|---|
| De. Martinez (W) | 6 | 4 | 2 | 1 | 0 | 3 | Ke. Gross (L) | 2 | 9 | 9 | 7 | 0 | 2 |
| Cook | 1 2/3 | 4 | 4 | 4 | 1 | 0 | Hereda | 4 | 2 | 1 | 1 | 2 | 1 |
| Plunk | 1 1/3 | 0 | 0 | 0 | 1 | 1 | Alberro | 3 | 2 | 1 | 1 | 2 | 3 |

**HBP:** by Cook (W. Clark). **WP:** Ke. Gross. **PB:** I. Rodriguez. **Umpires:** Mason, Caraco, Bialorucki, Henrichs. **Time:** 3:17. **Attendance:** 32,161.

As impressive as the Indians were in the opener, they stumbled and bumbled the next two days. Some skeptics even accused them of reverting to form as they lost to the Rangers, 10-9 and 6-5.

Mark Clark was hammered for nine runs and knocked out of the box in the second inning on April 28, and the Rangers rallied for a ninth inning run against Paul Shuey to beat the Tribe on April 29.

Clark's performance was, in a word, ugly, although the Indians nullified it by fighting back to forge a 9-9 tie. But then southpaw Jim Poole, a late addition to the relief corps, relinquished a two-out, eighth inning solo homer to Mickey Tettleton. It was Tettleton's second homer of the game, his first, a three-run shot, was struck off Clark in the second inning.

Jeff Russell - the same Jeff Russell who pitched for the Indians in 1994 and was found wanting - blanked his former teammates in the ninth after Kenny Lofton singled with one out and was caught trying to steal. Omar Vizquel followed with another single, but the uprising, inning and game ended as Carlos Baerga popped out.

"That's a play where, if you make it, it's a great one. But if you don't make it, it's not so great," said Hargrove, refusing to second guess Lofton who was running on his own.

## HERSHISER IS SO-SO

Hershiser started the next day and pitched five so-so innings, giving up five runs on six hits, and middle relievers Julian Tavarez, Paul Assenmacher and Eric Plunk held the Rangers scoreless into the eighth.

Shuey, the Indians' No. 1 draft choice (second overall) in 1992, and their big hope to become their closer of the future, took over with one out in the eighth following a 65 minute rain delay.

Shuey maintained the tie the Indians had fashioned with four runs in the seventh, when Sorrento cracked a a two run homer, but lost control in the ninth. He walked two Rangers with one out, and Rusty Greer ended the game with a single to center..

Hargrove was more upset with replacement umpire Jeff Henrichs than he was with Shuey. "Paul threw good pitches to Otis Nixon (who walked with one out and stole second in the eighth) and they were called balls," grumbled Hargrove.,

"And the inning before that (Rangers pitcher) Darren Oliver almost bounced a pitch to Vizquel and Henrichs called it a strike. I don't appreciate that kind of inconsistency."

Obviously, neither did Hargrove appreciate replacement umpires.

The Indians won the next night, beating Texas, 7-6, in 12 innings as Jose Mesa made his first appearance of the season, taking over in the 11th with the game tied, 5-5. After the Indians scored twice in the 12th, Mesa gave up two hits in the bottom of the 12th, one of them Dean Palmer's lead-off homer, but hung on to get credit for the victory.

It boosted the Tribe back to the .500 level, but that wasn't the only reason - perhaps not even the *main* reason - Hargrove was smiling broadly.

The next day, May 1, an open date before the Indians played a three game series in Detroit, the American and National leagues reached agreement with the Major League Baseball Umpires Association, which brought to an end the four month lockout.

"I'm relieved, we all are," said Hargrove. "I'm not faulting the replacement umpires, they tried hard. It's just that they lacked experience and were too inconsistent. Consistency is the key to being a good umpire. The real umps can come in cold and still be better than what we've had."

Then Hargrove quipped, "They might even be smiling for a change."

Another May 1 announcement was that Albert Belle was named the AL's "Player of the Week" after he'd hit .471 (8-for-17) with two homers and six RBI in the Tribe's first four games. It was the third time in his career that Belle was so honored, and would be the first of several more in 1995.

The next day in Detroit for the Tigers' home opener, the Indians were reminded again how angry the fans were at the players for walking off their jobs in 1994.

When the Tigers were introduced, they were booed by the less-than-capacity crowd of 39,398 fans. Then, during the game which the Indians won, 11-1, their second vicotry in three games, unruly fans threw bottles, batteries and other objects onto the field.

## " IT WAS GOING TO BE A WEIRD GAME"

"I knew it was going to be a weird game when even Cecil Fielder was booed," said Vizquel. "He's always been a hero in this town."

At least 20 people ran across the field at various times during the game. They were apprehended by Tiger security personnel, arrested and fined $500 each.

John Hart called the Detroit fans' actions a "disgrace." He asked the American League to ensure that better protective measures be taken to safe-guard the players after Lofton walked off the field in the fifth inning, complaining that he nearly was hit by a thrown object,

"I was all right until they started throwing bottles," said Lofton. "There were whiskey, beer and soda bottles landing within eight to ten feet of me. When I took off to go after a ball, I didn't know when they were going to throw them."

It got so bad that the Indians considered asking the umpires to stop the game and declare it forfeited in their favor, though that probably would not have done any good because the arbiters were replacement umpires working their last game.

Martinez recorded his second victory with a seven inning performance in which he gave up seven hits. He waltzed home after being staked to a four-run uprising in the first inning, highlighted by Jim Thome's three run homer. Later Baerga, Ramirez and Sorrento also homered.

The fans didn't throw anything the next day, but the Indians continued their bombardment of the Tigers, beating them, 14-7. Eddie Murray, Sorrento and Ramirez homered, making a firm believer - and something of a prophet - of veteran Detroit manager Sparky Anderson.

"If the Indians don't win this thing ...," Sparky said, his voice trailing off without finishing the sentence. Finally Anderson shook his head, rubbed a hand across his eyes and added, "Oh, my God!." leaving no doubt about his opinion.

·When Anderson's remark was shared with Hargrove, the Tribe manager smiled and said, "Ask me a month from now and I'll have a better idea.

"We have a good hitting lineup. We've scored a lot of runs. But I don't think anyone expects us to score 10, 11 runs a night."

## 14-19 VS. LEFT-HANDERS IN 1994

Which the Indians didn't the next day, being held to seven hits, one of them Ramirez's fourth homer. They scored only three runs off David Wells, a hard-throwing left-hander against which the Indians were only 14-19 in 1994.

The loss was Hershiser's first American League decision, and though he pitched seven decent innings, two of the six hits he allowed were homers by his former Los Angeles Dodgers teammate Kirk Gibson, and by rookie Bobby Higginson.

It left the Indians with a 4-3 record, tied with Kansas City, 1 1/2 games behind the Milwaukee Brewers, and brought them back to Cleveland for their May 5 home opener against Minnesota.

That also was the day the Indians made their first roster change - and which very well could be considered the turning point in Jose Mesa's career.

It came about circumstantially, even accidentally, as Shuey had suffered a severely pulled right hamstring muscle while pitching the ninth inning in the Indians' victory over the Tigers on May 3.

That night Shuey left the clubhouse on crutches and the next day was placed on the disabled list. It left Mesa as the sole survivor in the competition for the job of closer that Hargrove had set up in spring training.

Mesa made the most of the opportunity, and so did Chad Ogea, who was recalled from Class AAA Buffalo to replace Shuey on the roster.

The Indians home opener at Jacobs Field was totally different from the ugly reception fans gave the Tigers in Detroit three days earlier, and which virtually all the other teams also received throughout the major leagues, with the possible exception of Baltimore and Denver.

"I don't know if I was surprised, but it was really great," Hargrove said of the warm greeting by the capacity crowd of 41,434 fans at Jacobs Field. "I think it says a whole lot about this community."

"I knew it would be different here," said Baerga. "The people in Cleveland are great. They are excited about baseball."

The Indians also were great in beating the Twins, 5-1, reeling off five double plays as Charles Nagy yielded just four hits and a run in seven innings. Rookie Julian Tavarez blanked Minnesota in the eighth and, when he ran into trouble in the ninth, Mesa took his first step in establishing himself as the best closer in the major leagues.

The Twins' first two batters in the ninth reached as Tavarez hit Chuck Knoblauch with a pitch, and Alex Cole singled.

Mesa stalked to the mound, threw a couple of 95-mph fast balls past Kirby Puckett, striking him out, then induced Matt Merullo to bounce into a double play, ending the game.

# WELCOME, JOSE MESA

It was Mesa's first save, the beginning of a sensational season in which he became the Indians all-time best reliever.

The victory also boosted the Indians to within a half-game of the first place Brewers.

But they fell back again to 1 1/2 games behind Milwaukee by fumbling to a 5-2 loss to the Twins the next day. The Indians committed four chargeable errors (two by Lofton and one each by Baerga and Belle) and several others of the mental variety, and never were in the game after Minnesota's first batter, Pat Meares, homered off Bud Black.

It also was during the Twins series in Cleveland that their ace reliever, Rick Aguilera, addressed speculation that the Indians had been - and were still at that time - trying to acquire him.

Aguilera pitched a perfect ninth inning against the Indians for his fourth save in four games, and said, "I have nothing against Cleveland, but I want to finish my career in Minnesota. I've made it clear that I want to stay with the Twins, and hopefully I will."

Aguilera did, but only temporarily, because of the inflated price tag the Twins put on him, as well as his exorbitant salary that would escalate from $3.8 million to $4.2 million in the event he would be dealt to another team.

Those two factors - Aguilera's unwillingness to leave the Twins, and his huge salary - proved to be a blessing in disguise for the Indians.

It led, out of necessity, to a greater reliance on Mesa, who came through sensationally.

And, as a footnote, despite Aguilera's stated preference for remaining with the Twins, he subsequently was traded to the Boston Red Sox and helped them win the AL Eastern Division championship.

After a postgame lecture by Hargrove in which he made clear his unhappiness with the Indians' poor execution of fundamentals, they bounced back the next day. They beat the Twins, 10-9, though it took 17 innings, eight pitchers and six hours and 36 minutes.

It was the longest game (by time) in franchise history, beating the club record of 6:30 set April 11, 1992, in a 19 inning, 7-5 Opening Day loss to Boston.

"It was a crazy game, I'm telling you," said Baerga, who was one of 47 players used by the two teams. Seventeen pitchers threw 581 pitches and allowed 44 hits.

The end mercifully came on hits by Ramirez, Levis and Lofton with one out. "I was so tired I didn't even want to run to first base," said Lofton.

Lofton was playing with a strained right hamstring that he originally injured in spring training and aggravated later. The leading base stealer in the major leagues the previous three seasons with 196, Lofton was thrown out in two of five attempts through the Tribe's first 10 games.

## MURRAY GETS NO. 462

Eddie Murray got four hits, including two homers, raising his career total to 462, one behind teammate Dave Winfield in 19th place on the all-time list. Murray also singled twice, giving him 2,949 hits in 18 major league seasons. Ramirez also homered, and Lofton and Belle each rapped four of the Tribe's 26 hits, with Poole, the eighth Cleveland pitcher, getting credit for the victory.

Mesa pitched 3 1/3 innings, blanking the Twins on two hits, before Poole took over in the 14th. Martinez started and was followed by Dennis Cook, Jason Grimsley, Tavarez, Paul Assenmacher and Eric Plunk, with Mesa stifling a Minnesota uprising in the 10th.

The Twins, who collected 18 hits, including homers by Marty Cordova, Puckett and Bernardo Brito, employed nine pitchers. The loss was charged to Mark Guthrie, a former college teammate of Belle.

Twenty four hours later the Tribe won again, this time beating up on Kansas City's Kevin Appier, one of the best pitchers in the game. Appier had won his first three starts and suddenly fans throughout the league - and especially in Cleveland - began to pay attention to the Indians.

After the 6-2 victory over Kansas City cut the Tribe's second place deficit to one game behind Milwaukee, Hargrove said, "To be honest with you, I think we caught Appier on an off night. But even on an off night, he's pretty tough."

It got even better the next night against Royals rookie Doug Linton.

Lofton led off the first inning for the rambunctious Indians with a home run, Vizquel walked and Baerga followed with another homer. Then Belle and Murray singled, Jim Thome and Ramirez walked, forcing in a fourth run, and Sorrento delivered the *coup de gras,* a grand slam into the right field bleachers for an 8-0 lead

It was easy thereafter for Hershiser as the Indians won, 10-0. It was Orel's first AL victory and boosted the Tribe to within one-half game of the Brewers, whose game against Detroit was suspended after nine innings with the score tied, 2-2.

Linton, who gave up two more runs in the second inning and was left in the game, said of the explosion triggered by Lofton, "It happened so quickly ... I guess you could say I was shell shocked."

## A RECORD TYING EIGHT RUN FIRST INNING

Sorrento's homer was his fifth in just 45 at-bats in the Indians' first 12 games, and the eight-run first inning tied a major league record for the most runs scored to start a game with nobody out. The record was originally set by the 1954 Indians, and tied by the 1960 New York Yankees.

"You just have a feeling that sooner or later this offense is going to have a big inning," said Sorrento. "No one wanted to be the guy who made the first out. I just didn't want to kill the rally." His slam was the first in the two season existence of Jacobs Field.

"I think we might have the best lineup in the league," said Baerga - and if there were any dissenters, they soon became believers.

The Indians pulled into a tie for first place in the AL Central the next day, May 10. They beat Kansas City, 3-2, while the Brewers were splitting a double header with Detroit (the Tigers' opening, 4-2, victory was a completion of the previous night's suspended game), giving Cleveland and Milwaukee identical 9-4 records.

Baerga's double and Ramirez's single with one out in the 10th inning won it for second reliever Eric Plunk, and was the third of what would be many last at-bat winning rallies by the Tribe in 1995.

Tony Pena solo homered in the third inning, and the Indians tied the game in the ninth against Royals relief ace Jeff Montgomery as Sorrento walked with one out, and Thome and pinch hitter Wayne Kirby singled back-to-back.

And then, almost as proof positive that 1995 would indeed be an Indian Summer to savor, the Tribe took over sole possession of first place on May 11, doing so without even taking the field.

By virtue of Milwaukee's 8-0 loss to Detroit the Indians - who had an open date in the schedule - moved a half-game ahead of the Brewers and never thereafter slipped from the top rung.

# 4

## No Place Like
## First Place

The Indians' battle cry in 1954 was, "There's no place like first place," and it was every bit appropriate again in 1995 for the more than two generations of baseball fans in Cleveland who had waited ... and waited and waited ... for another winner.

After taking over first place in the American League Central Division on May 11 without even playing a game that day, the Indians held the lead the rest of the season, for 142 consecutive days, clinching the championship on September 8 with a 3-2 victory over Baltimore.

It also was against the Orioles that the Indians won their first game - fifth in a row and ninth in their previous 11 - as the new leader of the AL Central on May 12. Changing the customary script, this time they relied on strong pitching and defense, while being held to eight scattered hits by Kevin Brown.

One of those hits was Jim Thome's second home run, a solo shot in the seventh inning that accounted for the winning margin. Afterwards, Thome, sounding more like a veteran than a second year player, said, "When you become a championship team, you have to do good things in the late innings. That's what we did tonight."

Indeed they did. Especially Jose Mesa, who earned his second save with a one-hit performance in the ninth.

Dennis Martinez, who had started his professional baseball career in the Baltimore organization in 1974, compiling a 108-93 record with the Orioles from 1976 through early-1986, pitched well into the seventh inning to win his third game without a loss.

It was Martinez himself who made a couple of key defensive plays in the seventh to shut down the Orioles, after their first two batters reached on singles. First he fielded Damon Buford's bunt and forced the lead runner at third. Then he knocked down Brady Anderson's liner with his bare hand and turned it into another force at third.

Though Martinez wasn't seriously injured, his hand became numb and he left the game. The Orioles cut their deficit to one run when Harold Baines solo homered off Jim Poole in the eighth, but Mesa held them at bay in the ninth.

Mike Mussina and the Orioles beat the Indians, 6-1, the next day, ending their winning streak, but Milwaukee also was beaten so the Tribe's half-game lead remained.

It was obvious, however, that the loss did not diminish the high regard in which the Indians suddenly were held by their former pitching coach, Phil Regan, who had been hired to manage the Orioles.

"Cleveland is so explosive that you never feel safe," said Regan. "Even in the ninth, when we had a five run lead, I was worried. That team can score four or five runs in a hurry."

Orel Hershiser and Charles Nagy pitched the Indians to victories in their next two games.

## MURRAY HITS NO. 463

Hershiser stopped the Orioles, 3-1, on a four-hitter, May 14. The big blow for the Tribe was Eddie Murray's fifth homer of the season and 463rd of his career, tying him with teammate Dave Winfield for 18th place on the all-time list.

Nagy was the recipient of a 15 hit outburst that featured homers by Albert Belle and Paul Sorrento (his sixth) to beat New York, 10-5, on May 16, while the Brewers were losing twice, to Toronto and Boston

The victory over the Yankees was the Indians' first in two years - they were 0-9 versus New York in 1994 - and also turned the tables on southpaw Jimmy Key. Going into the game Key's lifetime record against the Indians was 16-5, and it was the first time they'd beaten him since August 28, 1993.

"Last year is over," chortled Omar Vizquel. "That's why it was important for us to come here and show we can beat the Yankees. If we have to play a team like this in the playoffs, they know they're going to have to play hard to win."

That combination of two Cleveland victories and two Milwaukee losses boosted to 2 1/2 lengths the Tribe's first place margin - and it never got any smaller.

Though May 15 was an open date for the Indians, they were active in the front office. Ruben Amaro and Jesse Levis were demoted. General Manager John Hart made a minor league deal with Houston to acquire catcher Eddie "Scooter" Tucker (though he, too, would soon be gone) The moves reduced the roster to the required 25.

Despite being rained out in New York on May 17, the Tribe picked up yet another half-game in the standings to lead by three as Milwaukee lost a fourth straight game

The Indians might have suffered a degree of complacency going into Boston on May 18 as they proceeded to kick the ball around Fenway Park. The bull pen also faltered for one of the few times all spring, and the Red Sox won, 4-3.

Errors by Thome and Martinez provided Boston with two unearned runs in the first inning. Another miscue, this by Carlos Baerga, who dropped a throw from Vizquel nullifying a double play, gave the Red Sox a third run in the sixth. Martinez left with the score tied, 3-3, after seven innings, and Boston won on Mike Macfarlane's homer off Poole in the eighth.

Earlier, in the third inning, Kenny Lofton was easily thrown out trying to steal third with one out and the Tribe trailing 2-0. It obviously displeased Manager Mike Hargrove, though he snapped, "I have no comment on that," when asked his opinion of Lofton's unsuccessful dash for third.

There's no doubt, however, that Hargrove had something to say to, not only Lofton, but also, the entire team after the game.

Still, the loss didn't hurt the Indians in the standings as Milwaukee also was beaten that day for the fifth straight time.

It's probable that Hargrove's post-game remarks after the Indians kicked away that series-opener in Boston, had an effect on the way they played the next day.

## THE FIRST KEY VICTORY IN 1995

Which is the reason the game on May 19 should be circled as the first of several key victories by the Tribe in 1995 - though it didn't start out on a high note.

In fact, until the ninth inning, Baerga called it the "ugliest" game he ever played in. "We played bad," he acknowledged. "We made errors, hit into double plays with runners in scoring position, and didn't run the bases well."

And then he added, again accurately, "But in the ninth inning, that's when boys become men and Omar (Vizquel), a little boy, became a big man."

Going into the ninth the Indians trailed, 5-3, and the Red Sox had their ace closer, Ken Ryan, on the mound.

Manny Ramirez led off with a homer that apparently rattled Ryan, who then walked Wayne Kirby on four pitches, though he recovered his composure and struck out the next two batters, Thome and Tucker.

Kirby stole second while Tucker batted, leading Boston manager Kevin Kennedy to intentionally walk Lofton, who had three hits in his three previous at-bats.

It proved to be a huge mistake as Vizquel, batting under .200 at the time, lashed a single to right, scoring Kirby with the tying run. Then Baerga blooped a single to center for the go-ahead run, and Albert Belle, who was hitless in his previous seven trips to the plate, homered on an 0-and-2 pitch.

The 9-5 victory was credited to third reliever Julian Tavarez, his first of the season and third in his brief major league career, and Mesa hurled a perfect ninth inning on nine pitches, though it was not a save situation.

That dramatic comeback provided an emphatic indication of what the Indians' offensive lineup was capable of doing, and was repeated the next two days in Boston.

They rallied for four runs in the eighth inning to beat the Red Sox, 7-5, on May 20, this time abusing reliever Alejandro Pena. Belle led off with his fifth homer and, with one out, Ramirez, who earlier hammered his eighth homer, followed with a single.

Pinch hitter Paul Sorrento also singled and, after former teammate Derek Lilliquist replaced Pena, Thome homered for three runs.

Belle's four-bagger was a king-sized shot, as Assistant General Manager Dan O'Dowd commented later. "If Albert had hit that ball in Jacobs Field, it would have hit the Bob Feller statue on East Ninth Street," he said.

Eric Plunk got credit for the victory, and Mesa gave up a hit in the ninth, but struck out two for his fourth save in four opportunities.

It was more of the same the next day, May 21, as the Indians completed their destruction of the AL East leading Red Sox. They rallied in the eighth and ninth inning to overcome a 9-6 deficit and won, 12-10. It gave the Tribe a 6-2 record on the eastern trip, an overall 15-6 won-lost mark, and a five game lead over Milwaukee.

## PAUL SORRENTO: "THE NEW BABY RUTH"

The triggerman in this one was Sorrento, who hadn't played in five straight games because the opposition pitched a left-hander. He smashed two homers, his second of the game - and eighth of the season in 57 at-bats - was a two run shot that tied the score, 9-9, in the eighth inning.

"Paul Sorrento is the new Baby Ruth," said Baerga. "All he does is hit home runs."

But it also was Baerga's ground rule double that keyed the Indians' uprising that won the game in the ninth. Belle followed with a long fly to center that got Baerga to third. He waited as Murray was intentionally walked, and scored the tie-breaking run on a double by Thome. Then Ramirez singled for two more runs before the side was retired.

Hargrove rushed Mesa into the game and, though the fire-balling right hander was less than perfect on this occasion, the Indians' three-run lead was large enough to withstand Boston's last gasp.

Tim Naehring and Troy O'Leary greeted Mesa with back-to-back hits, and Naehring scored on a sacrifice fly before the next two batters were retired. It gave Mesa his fifth save without a failure.

In the four game Boston series the Indians scored 31 runs, 20 of them in the last three innings.

The Indians went home to face second place Milwaukee which had lost nine of its previous 12 games, but the Brewers reversed their losing ways - and the Indians' winning ways - in the opener of the series.

Ramirez hit another homer, his ninth, but the Brewers knocked Nagy out of the box in the sixth when they broke a 4-4 tie and continued their assault against reliever Dennis Cook, taking a 7-4 lead.

When Murray singled with one out in the ninth, his 2,962nd career hit, it appeared the Indians were mounting another of their last-ditch rallies. But it fizzled this time. After Thome walked, Ramirez drove in another run with a single, but the next two went peacefully and the Brewers prevailed to cut their second place deficit to four games.

"We were flat," Hargrove correctly assessed the Indians performance. "We were outplayed. We'll just have to come back and get them tomorrow."

## MARTINEZ'S RECORD CLIMBS TO 4-0

Which the Indians did, winning, 5-3, on May 23 as Vizquel and Thome homered, and Martinez's record climbed to 4-0. Mesa came through again with a perfect ninth inning in which he made 16 pitches, striking out two of the three batters he faced.

As Baerga remarked, "Jose is the man. If he keeps going like this, we don't need anybody else."

Mesa did keep going, though his teammates didn't. Especially not Mark Clark who, in spring training, had been penciled in as the Tribe's No. 2 starter after going 11-3 in 1994.

Clark was shelled by the Brewers in a 7-5 loss, his record falling to 2-2 with a bloated 10.65 earned run average. He was distraught after the game, as the Indians' lead over Milwaukee was cut back to four lengths.

"I'm being flooded with too much information," he lamented. "I need to forget about stuff that guys are telling me."

Maybe so, but it wasn't something that Hargrove and pitching coach Mark Wiley appreciated.

In his previous three starts covering 12 innings, Clark was shelled for 14 runs on 19 hits, and Hargrove and Wiley had good reason to be concerned.

"Mark's biggest problem is that, sometimes he is not aggressive enough," was all Hargrove would say.

The Brewers scored all their runs in the fourth inning, six of them charged to Clark and the other to reliever Jason Grimsley. Six pitchers worked for the Brewers, with the victory credited to second reliever Ron Rightnowar, who'd been a spring training replacement.

It was during the game that the Indians unveiled a banner in left field that counted down the number of hits Murray needed to become the 19th player in major league history to reach 3,000.

Murray went 2-for-5, giving him 2,965, but admittedly "embarrassed" the veteran first baseman-designated hitter.

"Most people would consider this flattering," Murray said. "I consider it a tad embarrassing. I'm just trying to do my job and trying to stay out of people's way."

## MANNY RAMIREZ: "THE BULL"

After an open date on May 25, the Indians took their sizzling offense on the road, to Toronto. Sorrento smashed two more homers, giving him 10, Ramirez, nicknamed "The Bull" by hitting instructor Charlie Manuel, also homered twice for a total of 11, and Vizquel, who had seven homers in six previous major league seasons, walloped his third of 1995 in a 7-4 victory in the SkyDome.

Hershiser was the beneficiary of the explosion, getting his third victory in four decisions. It was his best performance for the Indians, giving up six hits and three runs in seven innings, while striking out seven.

"This might be the best hitting team I've ever seen," said Hershiser, who spent his first 12 major league seasons with the Los Angeles Dodgers.

"But to try to compare (the Indians) to the Dodgers would be unfair. I've got to try to compare them to the best offensive teams I've ever seen," he said again.

On that same subject, Hargrove said, "In our first 10 games I may have been surprised by the number of home runs we hit. But not anymore. We've got big, strong guys on this team. And big strong guys can hit the ball a long way."

Especially those wearing Indians uniforms. In their first 25 games the Indians hit 46 homers.

Their power was shut off the next day, however, by Toronto southpaw Al Leiter and Darren Hall, to blank the Tribe, 3-0. All of the Blue Jays runs came on a seventh inning homer off Plunk by Lance Parrish, who caught briefly for the Indians in 1993.

"I read Mike Hargrove's quote about how a pitcher would eventually get worn down facing this lineup because there is no let up," said Leiter. "It's like the lineup we used to have a couple of years ago. I knew they could explode at any moment and not just for a couple of runs, but for a lot of runs.

"I just went from pitch to pitch, from moment to moment. When I faced Eddie Murray, I said I've got to throw this pitch at this time to get him out. The same with Manny Ramirez. It was more like, I've got to get this individual out because if you look at the Cleveland Indians lineup as a whole, there is no reprieve."

Three home runs by Thome, Tony Pena and Ramirez turned an otherwise ugly game for the Indians into a 5-4 victory over Toronto. Mesa struggled for the first time all season and was lucky this time to prevail.

## MESA GOES EIGHT-FOR-EIGHT

The Indians entered the ninth with a two run margin, with Mesa taking over as their fifth pitcher seeking to preserve Nagy's third victory, and to register his eighth save in eight opportunities.

It almost didn't happen as Roberto Alomar led off with a single, took second on a wild pitch, and scored when Joe Carter also singled. Another single by John Olerud advanced Carter to second, and both were sacrifice bunted into scoring position.

Mesa then walked Candy Maldonado, and escaped - but just barely - when Ed Sprague, who had struck out in his previous four at-bats, grounded into a double play.

While Hargrove breathed easier, Mesa smiled and said, "Saves like this are not all bad, you know. It's the first tough situation I've been in all year. To come out of that with a save will give me confidence. There's no doubt about it."

Mesa also took the opportunity to reflect on his being assigned to the relief corps.

"At first I was real mad when I was taken out of the starting lineup and put in the bull pen (in 1994)," he said. "I was mad mostly because no one told me it was going to be done.

"But I'm getting to like this now. Maybe four eyes (belonging to Hargrove and then pitching coach Phil Regan) were better than two. As a starter, you've got to pitch five, six, seven innings.

"In my case right now, I come in for one inning and that's it. I wish someone had done this to me sooner. I think it can do a lot in extending my career."

With nine victories in 14 games since taking over first place in the AL Central, the Indians returned home on May 29 for a four game series against the Chicago White Sox, who'd been a pre-season favorite to win the division.

In the opener, the Indians spotted the White Sox a 6-0 lead, but came back to win, 7-6.

Winfield, bothered with a sore left shoulder, and rusty because of a lack of playing time, made his biggest contribution to date with a three run, two out homer in the sixth inning when the Indians cut their deficit to 6-4.

They tied the score in the seventh, and doubles by Thome and Pena got the lead run home in the eighth. Mesa needed just six pitches to retire the White Sox in order in the ninth.

It was the Indians' 12th come-from-behind victory, and sixth in their last at-bat.

"I don't think I've ever been around a team that has come from behind as consistently as this one," said Hargrove.

Winfield's homer was the 464th of his career and raised his spirits considerably. "I feel like a weight has been lifted," he said. "I've seen this team come from behind so many times, to be able to contribute feels good."

It was a different route the Indians took the next night, May 30, though the result was just as good. It was another victory over the White Sox, 2-1, maintaining the Tribe's 4 1/2 game margin over Kansas City, which had taken over second place from Milwaukee.

## INDIANS WIN ON BELLE'S 45-FOOT NUBBER

In the eighth inning, with the score tied, 1-1, Albert Belle's 45-foot nubber along the third base line went for a single - but when White Sox pitcher Alex Fernandez picked up the ball and foolishly threw toward first base, it flew into right field for an error.

It allowed Wayne Kirby to trot home from third base, and Mesa stalked in from the bull pen to again put down the White Sox in order in the ninth for his 10th save in 10 opportunities.

The beat went on for the Indians the next day as Hershiser was staked to a 5-1 lead before he tired in the eighth. Paul Assenmacher and Mesa - yes, Mesa again - put the finishing touches on a 6-3 victory. The biggest blow of the game was Thome's sixth inning, two run homer, a 422-foot shot into the right field stands.

And then, on June 1, in the series finale, the Indians applied the finishing touches, beating the White Sox, 7-4, in front of another capacity crowd at Jacobs Field. More than 160,000 fans witnessed the Tribe sweep the team that was favored by many to win the AL Central in 1995.

Sorrento, Belle, Thome and Murray homered in the finale, as Bud Black won his first game for the Tribe with relief help from Julian Tavarez, Jim Poole and Plunk who got the save this time.

It gave the Indians a 22-9 record,. their best start since 1966, with five straight victories and 11 in their previous 15 games.

"I'm trying to downplay it, but this was a big series," acknowledged Hargrove. "Coming into the season we felt the White Sox were one of the teams we needed to beat, and it still remains true."

"I don't think anyone thought we'd sweep Chicago when this series started," said Thome. "But anytime you can take four against the Sox it's great. Now we've got to concentrate on our next series."

It also was a big day for Ramirez. After hitting .394 (39-for-99) with 11 homers and 27 RBI in May, he was named AL "Player of the Month."

When the White Sox came to Cleveland for the series, they were in fourth place, seven games behind the Indians.

## WHITE SOX FIRE GENE LAMONT

When they left they were 11 games out and their manager, Gene Lamont, was fired the next day.

Whether it was a matter of losing their concentration, or simply a case of too much Al Leiter again, the Indians were beaten the next night, 5-0, by the Blue Jays. It was the second time in six days they were shutout by the Toronto southpaw, though in this one Leiter needed - and received - eighth inning help from Mike Timlin.

Leiter and Timlin collaborated on a three-hitter, all singles by Lofton, Baerga and Murray, whose hit left him 29 shy of 3,000.

The next day was a special one for Martinez, the 40-year old Nicaraguan who pitched his 27th career shutout and raised his record to 5-0 with a 3-0 victory over Toronto.

It came 24 hours after the Indians had drafted Martinez's son, Dennis Jr., who's also a right handed pitcher, in the 42nd round of the amateur draft.

"I'm proud of him," Martinez said of his son. "When I look at it, he's got more potential than me when I signed in 1973, and I am going to do whatever I can to last as long as I can so maybe we can pitch on the same team."

The Indians had an option on Martinez's contract for 1996, and later exercised it, guaranteeing the veteran pitcher a $4.25 million salary next season.

Even greater proof that the Indians were indeed a bonafide contender surfaced in the finale of the Toronto series when they faced David Cone. The 1994 AL "Cy Young Award" winner was staked to a 7-0 first inning lead that climbed to 8-0 in the third.

But few among the crowd of 41,688 at Jacobs Field got up to leave, knowing how many times in the past the Indians had fought their way back from what seemed to be certain defeat.

They weren't disappointed this time either.

The Indians' comeback started with a run in the third, continued with two more in each the fourth and fifth, they added one in the sixth, cutting their deficit to two, and exploded with three in the ninth. The last two runs came with two out on the wings of a homer by Sorrento.

"It's like we are never going to lose again," said Baerga.

## THE TRIBE'S 15TH FINAL AT-BAT VICTORY

The victory was credited to Tavarez, his third without a loss, and was the 15th time the Indians won in their final at-bat in the two year existence of Jacobs Field. It also was their seventh comeback victory at home in 1995.

"If I had gone around and taken a poll with Cone on the mound for the Blue Jays, I would have said the game was over after the first inning," said Hargrove.

The following night, June 5, Hershiser made it look easy. He fired a six-hitter and struck out 10 in an 8-0 victory over Detroit for his 25th major league shutout. Lofton drilled two homers and Murray one, giving him a career total of 466.

It was the Indians' seventh victory in eight games, and gave them the best record - 25-10 - in baseball. It also was the franchise's best record after 35 games in 19 years.

"The Indians are the best club in baseball," said the Tigers' Sparky Anderson, who has been around 25 years, longer than any of his managerial colleagues. He's the third winningest in major league history, behind only the legendary Connie Mack and John McGraw.

"It's like what they said when John Wooden was at UCLA. The Bruins could lose if they were a little off and the other team played outstanding. That's the way it is with the Indians."

Then Anderson went a step further in his assessment of the Indians: "They'll have a seven year run here. They're going to win so much, they're not going to want to separate from what's going on."

At the time, not only were the Indians doing almost everything right, their string of successes had reached the point where the opposition began doing many things wrong.

The next night Tigers veteran second baseman Lou Whitaker unwisely attempted to turn a slowly hit ground ball by Kirby into a double play with one out and runners on first and third in the eighth inning.

Because the double play wasn't made, Alvaro Espinoza scored, giving the Tribe a 4-3 lead that Mesa protected with just five pitches in another perfect ninth inning for his 12th consecutive save.

## THOME'S 10TH HOMER IS GAME-WINNER

Then Thome completed the destruction of the Tigers the following night. He smashed a 10th inning, lead off home run, his 10th of the season, on a 3-and-0 pitch from Brian Maxcy. One report said the ball Thome hit would have flown completely out of the park, onto East Ninth Street, had the right field stands not been in the way.

"I kept looking into the dugout for a take sign, but Grover never gave it to me, so I just did what (hitting instructor) Charlie Manuel told me," said Thome.

What Manuel had been preaching to the 24-year old third baseman was this: "when ahead in the count, 3-and-0, 3-and-1 and 2-and-0, just try to hit the ball as hard as you can".

Thome did. So did Murray who whacked a second inning solo homer, his ninth of the season and 467th of his career. Nagy pitched well, scattering six hits, one of them Whitaker's two run homer that tied the game in the eighth, though Plunk got credit for the victory with two hitless innings in relief.

It was the 10th time the Indians won in their last at-bat this season, seven at Jacobs Field and five during the homestand that concluded with a 9-1 record.

And when the fireworks ended, most of the fans in the crowd of 36,363 remained in the park for about 40 minutes, yelling themselves hoarse and pleading for one curtain call after another.

The Indians' winning streak climbed to seven with victories in Milwaukee the next two nights, as Thome continued his hot hitting on June 8, and Baerga took over as the hero on June 9.

In the first game, won by the Tribe, 8-7, Thome clouted a two run homer in the ninth inning off Bill Wegman. It broke a tie, after Belle drove in two runs with a double, wiping out a 6-4 deficit. It was the 15th come-from-behind victory for the Indians.

Mesa pitched the ninth and, for one of the few times, struggled, giving up a run on two hits, but retired the last two batters to raise his perfect save record to 13.

Baerga's three-run homer in the fifth inning the next night wiped out a 4-2 deficit and led the Tribe to a 7-4 victory, its 18th in 23 games. It was credited to Chad Ogea, his first in the major leagues. Mesa - who else? - picked up his 14th save with a one-two-three ninth.

It boosted the Indians' first place margin to a season high 8 1/2 games over Kansas City.

## JUST LIKE TORONTO IN 1992 AND 1993

Baerga compared the current attitude of the Indians with that of the Toronto Blue Jays when they won back-to-back World Series in 1992 and 1993.

"The confidence level here is very high now," said Baerga. "It's like the Toronto teams from two and three years ago. They knew they were going to win every day, and you knew it was going to be hard to beat them. I think that's how other teams feel about us this year."

Maybe so, but 24 hours later the Brewers snapped the Tribe's winning streak at seven, 6-1, as Hershiser uncharacteristically surrendered three homers to the team that had hit only 23 - fewest in the AL - all season.

The culprits were Milwaukee's eighth and ninth batters, Dave Hulse and Jose Valentin (who homered twice). The Indians, who led the league with 67 homers, were choked into submission by Angel Miranda and Al Reyes, who combined on a three hitter.

To make matters worse, the Indians lost designated hitter Dave Winfield, who suffered an injury to his left shoulder. It was diagnosed as a strained rotator cuff, when he dived back to first base after stroking a single in the fourth.

Winfield subsequently was placed on the disabled list and replaced on the roster by rookie Herbert Perry, whose stay in the big leagues was supposed to be temporary, but became permanent.

Undaunted by the loss, the Indians started another winning streak, beating Milwaukee, 11-5, on June 11. They smashed 19 hits of assorted sizes, two of which were Thome's 12th and Baerga's eighth homers, as well as four singles by Murray, boosting him to within 16 of 3,000.

The offensive display, which gave the Indians an 8-2 lead after only four innings, made it easy for Black to hike his record to 2-1.

Returning to the friendly confines of Jacobs Field on June 12 for another homestand, this one nine games, the Indians' latest hero very nearly was a goat instead in a 4-3 victory over Baltimore.

In the third inning, Vizquel committed a rare throwing error that led to two unearned runs for the Orioles. Later he drove in two runs and the Indians prevailed, 4-3, with the bull pen making another major contribution.

Nagy went seven innings to get the victory, after Assenmacher pitched a scoreless eighth - his 11th appearance for the Tribe without giving up a run. Mesa retired the Orioles in order on 12 pitches in the ninth for his 15th save in 15 opportunities.

"Every day you wake up and pinch yourself to make sure what Jose has done is real," said Hargrove after the victory boosted the Indians record to 20 games over .500. "Jose fills a huge hole for us. If you don't have a guy like that to come in at the end of the game, it's like taking two steps backward every day."

But all the news was not good. After the game it was revealed that

Martinez was suffering a torn cartilage in his left knee that would bother him the rest of the season, though it would not prevent him from facing his old teammates the next night.

## THE LARGEST CROWD AT JACOBS FIELD

In front of the largest crowd - 41,927 - to see a game at Jacobs Field, Martinez coasted to his sixth victory without a loss, scattering eight hits and pitching his 28th career shutout, 11-0, over the Orioles.

Thome called Martinez a "gamer," and not only because of his sore knee. In the fifth inning Martinez was struck in the chest by a line drive off the bat of Brady Anderson. It staggered the pitcher, but he scrambled after the ball, threw out Anderson and remained on the mound to register his second complete game.

"My knee didn't bother me, but I was worried about my chest," said Martinez. "I was afraid my heart might stop beating. I kept breathing hard because I didn't want it to stop. I don't see anything wrong now, but the trainers said I'll be black and blue in the morning."

Belle hammered his ninth homer starting the second inning and the Tribe coasted. Thome smashed his 13th homer in the fourth, also off Orioles ace Mike Mussina, and the Indians went on to collect 14 hits.

Thome's homer, good for three runs, was another cannon shot, flying an estimated 440 feet into the right field stands. "I don't think I can hit a ball any better than that," he said - to which Mussina probably would have agreed.

Ogea made his second major league start on June 14, and it was another successful outing with the help of another rookie pitcher, Tavarez, who was establishing a reputation - and the nickname, "The Vulture" - for his effective work in middle relief.

Tavarez took over in the seventh with the Tribe ahead, 5-2, and held the Orioles scoreless until Mesa came aboard in the ninth with the predictable result.

Mesa walked a batter, but retired the Orioles on 14 pitches for his 16th save in 16 opportunities, and with Belle clouting his 10th homer, the Indians won 5-2, for a fourth straight victory.

After an open date, the Indians took a step backwards on June 16. The New York Yankees broke a tie with two runs in the ninth - no, not off Mesa - against Poole, Plunk, Assenmacher and Tavarez, to win, 4-2.

Hershiser started and pitched well through seven innings, but the loss was charged to Poole. He walked Don Mattingly to start the inning, and Plunk hit Jim Leyritz with a pitch. After a sacrifice bunt and an intentional walk, Bernie Williams singled off Assenmacher, and Mike Stanley got another run home on a sacrifice fly.

But the Indians didn't wait long to get back on the winning track. They beat the Yankees for the first time after nine consecutive losses, and the pace setter was Perry, the rookie who got a chance to play in the big leagues because of Winfield's injury.

## HERBERT PERRY HAMMERS TWO HOMERS

Perry crashed two homers, and Belle and Ramirez each hit one as the Tribe won, 7-4. Ramirez and Perry homered back-to-back in the fourth, triggering a four run uprising and erasing a 3-1 deficit that led Black to his third victory in four decisions.

Tavarez bridged the gap in the seventh and eighth between Black and Mesa who, despite yielding two singles and a walk, blanked the Yankees in the ninth for another save, his 17th.

"I was feeling some pressure after going 0-fer (the previous day), so (the two homers) really helped," said Perry. "If I'd had another 0-fer I would've gone batty.

"I think one of the hardest things a guy can do is join a first place team because you want to keep things going. You don't want to look back and think you might have thrown a monkey wrench into it."

As the Indians' won-lost record climbed to 34-12, 22 games over .500, former manager Birdie Tebbetts had an interesting comment about the fortunes of the team.

"It's almost time to take them seriously," said the 82-year old Tebbetts, who managed the Indians from 1963-66, as well as Cincinnati from 1954-58, and the Milwaukee Braves in 1961 and 1962.

"When I say *almost*, I mean, in my opinion it's too early to take any team seriously until it goes 25 games over .500. That's the way I felt in 1966, when everybody was getting excited about us (the Indians), and it's the way I feel now.

"It's good that the players are gaining confidence in themselves and their teammates, but the manager has to be realistic and keep everybody in check. It puts a lot of pressure on Hargrove, and I speak from experience. He can't get carried away, even if the fans are, and maybe the players, too. It's a tough thing to do.

"But I certainly wish the Indians well," added Tebbetts by telephone from his home at Anna Marie Island, Florida. "The fans in Cleveland deserve a winner."

When Tebbetts mentioned 1966, it was a reference to the fact that the Indians opened that season by winning 10 consecutive games, generating excitement - and pennant talk - throughout Cleveland.

Unfortunately, the Indians slumped after those first 10 victories, were overtaken by Baltimore, Tebbetts was fired on August 19, and the team finished in fifth place with an 81-81 record.

## INDIANS LOSE THEIR SECOND SERIES

It was the same old story for the Indians on June 18, in the wake of that first victory over the Yankees in 10 games.

They were beaten, 9-5, losing their second series of the season as Nagy faltered in the first inning. He gave up two runs because he was late covering first base on a potential double play and was sent to the showers after three innings with the Yankees leading, 5-2.

The Tribe attempted to mount a comeback in the eighth, when Ramirez batted with two on and two out and New York ahead by two runs. But the Yankees' ace closer, John Wetteland stalked to the mound and fanned Ramirez on a 3-and-2 pitch, ending the rally and, as it turned out, the Indians' hopes to win again.

Nagy's tardiness in covering first base in the first inning, he said, was because his feet "got all tangled up." It caused him to miss tagging the bag on Vizquel's return throw to first base. The Yankees went on to score twice, as Mike Stanley walked, and Don Mattingly singled and Danny Tartabull doubled, before Nagy retired the side.

"I was just horrible ... I didn't know where my pitches were going," he said. It probably was too harsh a judgment, though there was some truth to Nagy's self-criticism.

Hargrove was more lenient. "Sometimes a play like the one Charlie messed up hurts a pitcher's concentration," said the manager, "Obviously it hurt him."

It was Nagy's briefest performance as a starter since October 3, 1993, and the one-time ace of the staff saw his record fall to 4-3, though his teammates made it interesting late in the game - as usual.

Thome clubbed his 14th homer and Sorrento his 13th off winner Jack McDowell. The Indians closed their deficit to two, 7-5, in the seventh, only to have the Yankees put the game away with two more runs in the ninth off Plunk.

After the game Hart announced the promotion of Gregg Olson, who had been one of the best relievers in baseball with the Orioles in 1993, before he tore a ligament in his elbow. Olson had been signed as a free agent during spring training and at Buffalo recorded 13 saves with a 1-0 won-lost record.

To make room for Olson, southpaw reliever Dennis Cook was designated for assignment, and later was traded. Cook had pitched for the Indians in 1992 and 1993, then signed as a free agent with the White Sox, and was claimed on waivers by Cleveland on January 5, 1995.

The Indians got back on the winning track on June 19, using the same formula that had been so successful previously, but had failed them the night before.

Ramirez hit a laser beam home run into the right center field seats leading the 10th inning off Boston closer Ken Ryan - the same Ken Ryan the Tribe had abused on May 19 and 21 at Fenway Park.

It was the 12th time the Indians won in their last at-bat, eight of them at home, and raised their record in one-run decisions to 5-0.

## BAERGA: "THIS ISN'T A FLUKE"

"This isn't luck, and it's not a fluke," insisted Baerga, who probably was right. "We've got great talent on this team. That's how we're doing it." It was difficult to disagree with him.

Actually, Ramirez had failed in two previous opportunities to break the 3-3 tie, as he struck out on three knuckle balls from Tim Wakefield with runners on second and third in the fifth. He fanned again at the hands of Ryan with a runner on second and nobody out in the eighth.

Before Ramirez's heroics, the Indians got home runs from Thome (No. 15) in the fourth, and Belle (No. 12) in the fifth.

Martinez started for the Tribe and pitched well enough to win, though Plunk the third reliever, was credited with the victory. He came aboard with runners on first and third and one out in the top of the 10th, and struck out Tim Naehring and retired Mike Greenwell on a fly to right.

It was more - much more - of the same the next night as the Indians erupted for all their runs in the last four innings to overwhelm the Red Sox, 9-2. It gave Ogea his third victory in three starts since coming up from Buffalo to replace Mark Clark on the staff..

"This is the way it's supposed to be," said Hargrove, savoring the Tribe's 19th victory in its last 23 games.

"It's the first time in memory that it's worked this way around here, although, for the last couple of years we've been able to give our young starters like Ogea and Albie Lopez some breathing room in Triple-A. It's paying off."

As for Clark, whose record was 4-0 for Buffalo since his demotion, Hargrove said, "He's throwing the ball very well in Triple-A, and that's where he's going to stay."

Olson pitched the ninth, making his first appearance since joining the Indians, and gave up a solo homer to Chris Donnels, though it served only to cut the Red Sox's deficit by one.

Though the Indians were held homer-less, they collected 15 hits, including two doubles and a single by Baerga, who was leading the AL with 70 hits, and was batting .338

## VIZQUEL'S FIELDING GEM IS THE KEY

Still, it was a fielding gem by Vizquel that, in the opinion of Ogea, was the key to the Indians victory, their 102nd in the 162 games they'd played at Jacobs Field since it opened in 1994.

In the third, with the game scoreless, Mike Macfarlane and Luis Alicea singled with one out. Lee Tinsley followed with a grounder toward the hole at shortstop. Vizquel dashed over, backhanded the ball on the outfield grass and fired to Baerga for a force at second, Macfarlane stopping at third. Then Ogea retired John Valentin on a pop fly to end the inning.

After the game Ogea said, "To me, Vizquel's play won the game for us."

Whatever, it boosted the Indians' record to 36-13 - 23 games over .500, their largest margin since 1959 when that team finished 24 games over the break-even mark at 89-65 - and the significance of it wasn't lost on Vizquel.

"We have a great feeling on this club right now," said Vizquel, who'd spent the first five years of his major league career with the perennial loser

Seattle Mariners.

"I don't think there's a guy on this club who doesn't think we're going to go all the way this season. I know it's early, and you don't want to get overconfident, but sometimes it's good to feel like this. You have to feel like you're better than the other teams."

Which the Indians - and their fans - certainly had every reason to do.

# 5

## No June Swoon
## This Time

So often in years past, even when they'd gotten off to a promising start, Indians teams died - OK, *swooned* - in June, and by the All-Star break were not even close to being in contention.

So, when the Tribe lost four straight games, the first to the Red Sox, 3-1, and the next three to the revenge-minded White Sox, 12-5, 8-3 and 3-2, June 21-25, fans jumped to what they considered a logical conclusion based on historical proof, that the "June Swoon" had arrived again.

And though those four losses shrunk the Indians' first place lead from 8 to 5 1/2 lengths over runner-up Kansas City and their won-lost record was only 10-8 in the three weeks prior to the All-Star Game, the Tribe's margin was back to 12 by July 11 when the National League defeated their American League counterparts, 3-2.

But first ... not only was a Jacobs Field record crowd of 41,948 disappointed by a 3-1 loss to Boston on June 21, when Erik Hanson raised his record to 7-1, allowing the Tribe only four hits over eight innings, long suffering and cynical Cleveland fans found another reason for concern.

Orel Hershiser did not pitch well, yielding home runs to Mike Greenwell and Mo Vaughn in absorbing his third loss in eight decisions. Furthermore, he was forced out of the game in the fourth inning, complaining of "stiffness" in his lower back.

The ailment was later diagnosed as a strained ligament in the spinal column and Hershiser subsequently was placed on the 21 day disabled list.

## WELCOME BACK, MARK CLARK

Hershiser's misfortune turned out to be a break for Mark Clark, who had been demoted on May 25 to Class AAA Buffalo where his record was an impressive 4-0. When Hershiser went on the disabled list, Clark was recalled, but not immediately. Albie Lopez was because Hargrove and General Manager John Hart figured they might need a reliever prior to June 27 when a starter would be required to take Hershiser's turn.

Lopez made one appearance out of the bull pen, then was returned to Buffalo in exchange for Clark five days later.

"Of course we are concerned (about Hershiser)," said Manager Mike Hargrove, "although we have been assured by our medical staff that (the injury) is not serious, that it's only stiffness, and that all he needs is a little time off."

Boston's victory over the Indians and Hershiser was important for the Red Sox who had lost seven of their previous 10 games. Their lead in the American League East had shrunk to 5 1/2 games over Detroit, which then was one of the hottest teams in baseball.

"We needed to take a good look at ourselves ... when we played the Indians, we were kind of on a mission," said Hanson.

Prior to another loss by the Indians in their next game, 12-5, it was announced that only 200,000 tickets remained for the 44 remaining home games, thus assuring that the season attendance record of 2,620,627 set in 1948 would soon be broken.

"From our latest check, the Indians and Red Sox are the only teams in major league baseball who have increased in attendance from last year (when a strike by the players shutdown the game on August 12)," said Jeff Overton, vice president of marketing.

In losing to the White Sox, whom they had beaten four straight only four weeks earlier, the Indians were pounded for 20 hits, including six in the fifth inning when Charles Nagy was victimized and banished to the showers.

"It was bam, bam, bam, and all of a sudden they were leading, 5-1," said Nagy, whose ineffective outing in the wake of Hershiser's aching back compounded the fear that another June Swoon was in the making.

"The stars had to be aligned in a certain way for that to happen," said a shell-shocked Nagy. "It was a freak thing, and when Frank Thomas hit that homer, I knew I was gone." It was homer No. 16 for Thomas, and was a laser beam shot into the left field stands at Comiskey Park.

That loss cut the Indians' lead to six games over Kansas City, which was mounting a hot streak with seven victories in its previous 10 games.

## HARGROVE TO THE TRIBE: "BEAR DOWN"

The White Sox continued their assault on the Tribe the next day, June 24, with an 8-3 victory credited to Alex Fernandez - and blamed by some on Bud Black's pitching and Albert Belle's fielding.

Black was kayoed in the third inning on a yield of seven hits and seven runs, though only three were earned. The Indians committed four errors, two by Belle, and an overly generous official scorer could have charged them with a couple more.

Hargrove held a clubhouse meeting after the game. Though he wouldn't divulge what he told the players, there was no doubting his unhappiness.

When asked about the meeting, Hargrove snapped to reporters, "You watched the game so you can tell what I talked about." Enough said.

Omar Vizquel offered an enlightening comment. "I think the meeting was a good idea," said the slick-fielding shortstop. "We've busted our butts to get into first place, but we've played sloppy baseball the last two nights.

"There's no reason to panic, but we're not going to win games by five or six runs every night. We've got to learn to win games by closer scores, cut down the mental mistakes and keep playing hard."

Belle made no excuse for his misdeeds. "I'm pretty sure if I catch those two balls the outcome of the game is a lot different," he said.

Of Black's pitching problems, Hargrove said, "Some of the plays in the field didn't help Buddy, but for the most part he was his own worst enemy. He left a lot of pitches up over the heart of the plate."

Everything continued poorly for the Indians the next night and they lost again to the White Sox, 3-2. It was a fourth straight setback - the Tribe's longest losing streak of the season - and sixth defeat in nine games.

Dennis Martinez, pitching with a "tight" elbow and a torn cartilage in his left knee, and trying to raise his perfect record to 7-0, gave up only three hits in seven innings before turning a 2-2 tie over to Paul Assenmacher.

The White Sox proceeded to win it when Assenmacher walked Lamar Johnson leading the eighth, and Robin Ventura singled with two out.

The defeat elicited an interesting rationalization by Carlos Baerga.

"It's good this happened to us," he said. "We've got to realize that it's not going to be easy for us to win. Last month we swept Chicago at home and I think some of us thought we'd just come in here and sweep them again.

"But it doesn't work that way. I was reading the paper last week. When the Twins won the World Series in 1991, they were in fifth place in their division for a long time that season. Teams can come back, and we've got to understand that and keep playing hard everyday."

Baerga - as well as his teammates and Indians management - knew that it was necessary to reverse what had suddenly become a losing trend on the eve of a three game showdown in Kansas City that began on June 26..

## THE ROYALS GET CLOSE

The Royals had picked up a half-game on the Indians, cutting their deficit to 5 1/2, as they were rained out against Minnesota.

Kansas City manager Bob Boone was the first to admit the importance of the series. He said, "We're either going to get in the race, or out of it."

Boone was right - though what developed was not his choice.

The Indians, heeding the advice of Baerga and, undoubtedly, the scolding by Hargrove, held a players-only pre-game meeting. They righted themselves and swept the series, increasing their lead over the Royals to 8 1/2 lengths.

First, they beat the Royals, 2-0, with Jose Mesa getting his 18th save in his 18th opportunity, preserving a fourth victory without a loss for rookie Chad Ogea.

Kenny Lofton's infield single leading off the game, Baerga's double and an error by Royals right fielder Jon Nunnally, a former Tribe farmhand, got the first run home. An inning later Lofton singled again, driving in Jim Thome who had walked and stole second.

Hargrove was relieved. "It was huge," he said of the victory. "We needed to win. We needed to get back on the right track."

The next night, June 27, nobody would doubt they were, as Clark made his first start since returning from Buffalo - and first for the Indians since May 24, after which he was demoted for lacking aggressiveness. The big right-hander, nicknamed "The General," combined with Eric Plunk to pitch a five-hitter and a 7-1 triumph over the Royals.

Among the Tribe's 15 hits were three by Eddie Murray, snapping a 7-for-42 slump, boosting his career total of 2,996 and raising his average to .309.

Twenty-four hours later the Indians completed their destruction of the Royals with a 5-2 victory credited to Nagy, with Mesa picking up his 19th save.

Murray crashed a two-run homer off Kevin Appier who, until then, had won 11 games and five straight. But when reporters descended upon Murray for his reaction to climbing to within three hits of becoming the 20th player to join the exclusive 3,000 hit fraternity, he waved them away.

"Don't come over here asking about that," Murray responded to the obvious questions.

One who had plenty to say was Royals third baseman Gary Gaetti, whose homer off Nagy accounted for Kansas City's only runs. "If the Indians keep playing like that, nobody will catch them. It's a no-brainer. They've got too much talent," he said.

Appier also was impressed. "They're definitely loaded," he said of the Indians. "They have talent all the way through the lineup."

With their first place margin back up to 8 1/2 games over Kansas City, 14 over Milwaukee, and 14 1/2 over Chicago, the Indians moved on to Minnesota, which brought up the rear in the AL Central, trailing the Tribe by 22 1/2 lengths.

## MURRAY AT 2,999 AND COUNTING

Murray got his 2,998th and 2,999th hits in the Indians' series-opening, 10-5, victory on June 30, and again declined to talk about his impending accomplishment.

He homered in the first inning when the Indians jumped off to 3-0 lead, and singled in the second when they went ahead, 6-0.

Thereafter, with the fans in the Hubert H. Humphrey Metrodome on their feet each time he went to the plate, Murray struck out in the fourth and fifth innings, and grounded out in the seventh and ninth. The victory was credited to Black, whose record climbed to 4-2.

The game also marked the return of catcher Sandy Alomar Jr. from his sixth stay on the disabled list in five years, following a fourth operation on his left knee during the winter. Room on the roster for Alomar, who singled in three trips to the plate against the Twins, was made by selling Scooter Tucker on waivers to Atlanta. In 17 games for the Tribe, Tucker was 0-for-20.

Though Murray was still reluctant to be interviewed, Hargrove talked about the veteran first baseman-designated hitter.

"When Eddie struck out in the fourth, I think that was the only time he might have gotten anxious," said the manager. "He was up on the count, 3-and-1, and may have swung at some bad pitches."

Anxious or not, Murray reached his coveted milestone the next night, June 30.

He stroked a clean single to right field in the sixth inning against the Twins Mike Trombley in a 4-1 victory credited to Dennis Martinez, becoming the third player to get his 3,000th hit in a Cleveland uniform.

The others were Napoleon Lajoie in 1914, and Tris Speaker in 1925. Both were former player-managers.

Only the second switch-hitter to reach 3,000 - Pete Rose was the other - Murray also needed only 31 more homers to reach another exclusive milestone. Hank Aaron and Willie Mays are the only players to get 3,000 hits and 500 homers.

"That might be reachable, but I am not going to worry about it," said Murray, finally willing to talk about his achievement.

When he arrived at first base after getting the milestone hit, all the Indians - led by Dave Winfield - rushed onto the field to congratulate Murray. It was his only hit of the game as he walked in the first inning, lined to center fielder Rich Becker in the fourth, and then grounded out in the seventh.

The last player to get 3,000 hits was Winfield, who did so on September 16, 1993 when he played for the Twins.

## "THE WILDEST GROUP OF GUYS" - MURRAY

Murray was given a standing ovation by the 27,416 fans, and said of the Indians, "We've had a lot of fun in Cleveland. This is the wildest group of guys I've ever played with. The music in the locker room, and the jokes we play on each other, the reporters who come into our locker room must think we're crazy."

For Martinez, the victory raised his record to 7-0, but was only the second in his last five starts. Mesa pitched the ninth inning and relinquished a single, but struck out two for his 20th save. It gave the Indians the best record in the major leagues, 41-17, and kept them nine games ahead of Kansas City, equaling their largest lead of the season.

They also led the AL in batting average (.293), hits (607), total bases (1,122), and home runs (94), and their pitchers had the lowest earned run average (3.74) in the league.

But as Hargrove said, "There's more to it (winning) than being good ball players. They have to be winners. They have to be able to go out and compete every night."

He also admitted, "We have problems on our ball club, just like every other team. No way you can live with someone for eight months and not have problems. You have problems in your own family and you love them.

"But there are no petty jealousies on this club. Everyone is committed to winning. That's why I say it takes more than good players to have a winning club."

Apparently buoyed by his achievement of the night before, Murray went 3-for-4, including his 12th homer of the season and 470th of his career, but it wasn't enough to save the Indians. Their five game winning streak came to an end as the Twins won for only the second time in their previous 17 home games, 6-5, on July 1.

Ogea was roughed up and suffered his first loss of the season, and Manny Ramirez, despite hitting a two-run homer and a single, contributed to the Tribe's downfall with some weird base running.

It happened in the eighth inning after Murray's homer cut the Indians deficit to 6-5. Ramirez walked with one out, then took off for second as Paul Sorrento popped out to Minnesota third baseman Scott Leius. Ramirez was easily doubled, ending the inning and the chance to tie the score.

Earlier, in the fourth inning, Ramirez also committed a base running blunder. After leading off with a single, Ramirez raced around second and turned toward third on a routine fly ball to center by Sorrento.

When he realized the ball would be caught for only the second out, Ramirez tried to go back to first - but did it without re-tagging second - and was easily doubled, ending that inning.

As for Ogea, he was staked to a 3-0 lead, but yielded five runs in the second inning on three walks, two homers and a double.

The loss was not pretty, but it didn't hurt because the second place Royals also were beaten, allowing the Tribe to maintain its nine game first place margin.

## TRIBE'S LEAD UP TO 10

It climbed to 10 with a 7-0 victory over the Twins on July 2, but proved to be costly to the Indians as they lost the services of Murray.

The future Hall of Famer suffered two broken ribs in a third inning collision at the plate with Minnesota catcher Matt Walbeck. Murray was placed on the disabled list for only the second time in his 19 seasons in the big leagues.

Before he was injured Murray singled and doubled in his first two at-bats, the two-bagger scoring Albert Belle with a 3-0 Tribe lead in the third inning. Jim Thome followed with a single and Murray scored. However, as he slid past Walbeck, the catcher turned and his knee struck Murray on the left side.

Murray tried to stay in the game but, as he batted in the fifth, he swung at one pitch and couldn't straighten up. He left the field at that point and was replaced by Herbert Perry.

Hart, a former minor league catcher, said he understood how Murray was hurt. "Any play at the plate is dangerous," said the Indians general manager. "You've got a catcher protected by gear, and a guy sliding home at full speed. I don't think what happened was a dirty play. I think the catcher was just trying to make the tag."

Clark, starting and winning his second game since returning from Buffalo, also was injured, though not as seriously as Murray.

He left after five innings after being hit in the forearm with a line drive off the bat of Leius. Julian Tavarez completed the victory with four shutout innings, and the Indians' lead over Kansas City in the AL Central surged to a season high 10 games.

Ruben Amaro, who can play all of the outfield positions, second base and even catch in an emergency, and also can serve as a pinch runner and pinch hitter, was brought up from Buffalo to replace Murray.

## SIX INDIANS ON THE ALL-STAR TEAM

Despite the injury that forced Murray onto the disabled list, it was a good day - a *very good* day - for six of the Indians who were named to the AL All-Star team for the July 11 game at The Ballpark in Arlington, Texas.

They were starters Baerga at second base and Belle in left field, and reserve outfielders Lofton and Ramirez, and pitchers Martinez and Mesa. Lofton, who was fourth in the fan voting for outfielders, subsequently was named to start in center field in place of Seattle's Ken Griffey Jr., who was out with a broken wrist.

Six players on the All-Star team were the most for the Indians since 1955 when second baseman Bobby Avila, third baseman Al Rosen, outfielders Larry Doby and Al Smith, and pitchers Herb Score and Early Wynn were picked..

"That's the way it should be ... we should have our whole team on the All-Star team," said Mesa.

"We have the best record, so we should have the most players," said Lofton.

Hargrove said that Thome also should have made the team, and it was Hart's opinion that both Thome and Murray deserved to be on the squad. A case also could have been made for Vizquel, the Gold Glove shortstop.

Baerga and Belle were All-Stars for the third time, but never previously were they chosen by the fans as starters. Baerga's vote total was 1,152,652, ahead of Toronto's Roberto Alomar's 1,003,550, while Belle drew the second-most votes among outfielders, 1,056,134 to Griffey's 1,204,746.

Lofton was fourth behind Griffey, Belle and Minnesota's Kirby

Puckett, and Ramirez was fifth among outfielders; Murray finished second behind Chicago's Frank Thomas among first basemen; Thome was second behind New York's Wade Boggs among third baseman; Vizquel was third behind Baltimore's Cal Ripken and Texas's Benji Gil among shortstops; and Sandy Alomar Jr., despite spending most of the first half of the season on the disabled list, was second behind Texas's Ivan Rodriguez.

It cost the Indians nearly $1 million in bonuses and future boosts in contracts for the six players named to the All-Star team, though neither owner Richard Jacobs nor Hart expressed an objection.

"We don't mind doing this at all," the general manager said. "I'm happy to do it and I'm sure Mr. Jacobs is, too."

The increases amounted to $925,000 for Lofton, Belle, Martinez and Baerga. Ramirez and Mesa did not have All-Star bonus clauses in their contracts.

Lofton, Belle and Baerga each received $25,000 bonuses, and Martinez $50,000. Lofton also won a 1996 salary increase of $300,000 (to $3.5 million), and Belle's contract for the following year escalated from $5 million to $5.5 million for making the All-Star team.

## ALOMAR STEPS IN TO FILL A HOLE

Returning to the friendly confines of Jacobs Field on July 3 for seven games against the Rangers and Mariners, the Indians continued to pad their first place margin as Alomar stepped into the vacuum created by the injury-absence of Murray.

Before the opener of a three game series against Texas, Hargrove lamented the loss of Murray. "You don't replace a guy like Eddie," he said. "All you do is try to replace holes."

And Alomar, appearing in only his third game since undergoing arthroscopic surgery on his left knee on November 11, 1994, was the first to replace a hole.

He homered and doubled twice as the Indians beat the Rangers, 9-1. It was their seventh victory in eight games, and increased their lead to 11 lengths over the Royals, who lost to Boston, 12-5.

It also would have been the Indians' second straight shutout but for a ninth inning homer by Rangers catcher Ivan Rodriguez off Assenmacher, the second pitcher working in relief of Nagy, who won his second straight start, raising his record to 6-4.

Nagy blanked the Rangers on four hits through seven innings and compared his performance to the previous two. "Against the Yankees (on June 18) I was just horrible," he said. "Against Chicago (on June 23) I pressed. Tonight it just felt good to sit back and watch us score some runs."

Alomar homered in the second inning after Perry led off with a single. It provided Nagy with a 2-0 cushion. Alomar doubled to open the fifth and scored the Tribe's fourth run, and doubled again in the sixth, before being retired in his final at-bat in the eighth.

"What makes this club so special is that someone always seems to step up," said Alomar. "It's been a long, bumpy road for me. I know one game is not going to dictate what I do the rest of the season, but this is a confidence builder, that's for sure."

Another who stepped up against the Rangers, though it didn't show in the box score, was Amaro, who was batting .306 at Buffalo when he was recalled by the Tribe.

Starting for the first time in place of Lofton, who was nursing a recurring hamstring injury, Amaro made a sensational catch of a drive to left-center field off the bat of Luis Ortiz in the second inning.

"I just went to (the ball)," Amaro minimized his contribution. "I said to myself, 'I've got a chance to catch this ball.' I knew (Ortiz) hit it very well, but I also knew if I didn't get it, a run was going to score. I made contact with the wall, glove and ball. It felt great. Sometimes something like that feels better than getting hits."

## FIZZLED ON THE FOURTH

A step backward was taken the next day, however, as the Indians' bull pen, one of their strengths, fizzled on the Fourth of July. It was one of the few times Tribe relievers failed in the clutch, and resulted in a 7-6 loss to the Rangers.

"You would like to do it everytime, but you can't," Hargrove said of the inability of the Indians offense to generate another late inning comeback, and of the failure of Jason Grimsley, Tavarez and Assenmacher to protect a 6-4 lead.

It was only the second time in 24 save opportunities that the relievers were unsuccessful.

Baerga smashed his 11th homer, Thome his 17th, a three-run shot, and Amaro, his first, in the fourth inning when the Tribe scored all its runs off rookie Terry Burrows.

But the Rangers rallied against Grimsley, who replaced Black in the top of the fourth. They tied the score against Tavarez in the eighth, and scored the winning run off Assenmacher, also in the eighth, before Plunk came on to put out the fire.

Former teammate Dennis Cook blanked the Indians in the fifth and sixth, as did Roger McDowell, Ed Vosberg and Matt Whiteside the rest of the way.

The Tribe threatened in the ninth against Whiteside, who gave up a single to Baerga leading the inning, but retired Belle on a 400 foot drive to center, Ramirez on a pop fly, and Thome on a grounder.

Whiteside breathed a sigh of relief and said of the Indians, "Their whole team, one through nine, is solid and you have to make your pitches to stop them. You can't think about who is an All-Star or who isn't. You just have to concentrate. All I was thinking about was getting three outs for our team."

Black's failure - he was tagged for four runs on seven hits in 3 2/3 innings - and Grimsley's performance in the fourth and fifth, raised speculation that one or the other might be the odd man out with the return of Hershiser from the disabled list in two days.

As it turned out, both were given their walking papers. Grimsley was demoted and Black eventually was released, though he was kept on the payroll as a special scout.

The offense was still cold - except for backup catcher Tony Pena - the next night, but the bull pen recovered in a 2-0 victory over the Rangers on July 5. The game was interrupted twice by rain and an electrical power failure for a total of nearly three hours.

Pena, 38, had become Martinez's personal catcher after taking over when Alomar was sidelined in 1994. The victory raised Martinez's record to 13-2 with Pena behind the plate.

Before the first storm hit Jacobs Field, sending most of the 41,881 fans for cover, Pena slapped a two-run double off Kevin Gross in the second inning. It scored Ramirez and Sorrento, who had walked with two out.

## MARTINEZ'S BEST GAME

Martinez pitched perhaps his best game, until he was replaced in the seventh because his shoulder stiffened during the rain delays. He allowed only one hit, an infield single by Rusty Greer in the first inning, and went on to retire 16 consecutive batters through the sixth.

"I felt good until the last rain delay," said Martinez. "I was able to keep the ball down and change speeds, and I think that's what mixed them up. I could throw my changeup, curve and fastball for strikes whenever I wanted."

Jim Poole held the Rangers hitless in the seventh and eighth, and Mesa - that man again! - yielded a single to Otis Nixon with two out in the ninth. But he struck out Mark McLemore to end the game and earn his 21st save in 21 opportunities.

It was Martinez's eighth victory without a loss, and a career total of 227, putting him two behind Luis Tiant, whose 229 victories are second most by a Latin American pitcher. Hall of Famer Juan Marichal is first with 243.

The victory also boosted the Indians won-lost record to 44-19 - 25 over .500 - which solidly established them as bonafide pennant contenders, as Birdie Tebbetts had said it should.

The Indians' brief power outage ended the next night, July 6, as Ramirez clubbed two homers, his 17th and 18th, and Belle hit his 13th in support of Ogea's first major league complete game, a three-hitter for an 8-1 victory over Seattle.

Hargrove called it a "classic" Ogea performance. "He's not the guy who will come in and blow you away with his fastball, (but) his changeup is a major league out-pitch," said the manager.

"While none of his stuff is overly impressive to where it pops your eyes out, Ogea has won at every level he's pitched at, from Little League to now."

The only solid hit Ogea allowed accounted for the Mariners' only run, a homer by Tino Martinez in the fourth. Joey Cora was credited with a hit when his fly was dropped by Belle in the first inning, and Darren Bragg singled off Vizquel's glove in the second.

But after Martinez's homer, Ogea retired the next 17 batters in order, including eventual AL batting champion Edgar Martinez, who grounded out to end the game.

"It's fun and relaxing to pitch on this team. All it takes is one swing of the bat and we're right back in the game," said Ogea.

It was a reference to Ramirez's second homer, a three-run shot that broke a 1-1 tie in the fourth. It started the Indians en route to their 45th victory in 64 games, giving them the best record in baseball, a .703 winning percentage, and a 12 game lead over Kansas City.

Randy Johnson, already established as a leading contender for the AL Cy Young Award, cooled off the Tribe the next night.

## THE MARINERS' RESURGENCE

The overpowering southpaw struck out 13 - he would go on to lead the league with 294 - as Seattle won, 5-3. It began the Mariners' climb out of the basement of the AL West. At gametime Seattle's record was 32-34.

The loss was charged to Clark, his first after two victories since returning from Buffalo. For the second time in five days he was struck by a batted ball, narrowly escaping serious injury. This time he was hit by a line drive from Tino Martinez in the first inning.

"I'm starting to feel like a hockey goalie," quipped the pitcher.

Tino Martinez's hit went for a double and followed a two run homer by Edgar Martinez.

Clark's 1994 season was ended on July 21 when he was hit by a liner off the bat of Texas's Gary Redus and suffered a broken wrist.

The Tribe tied the score in the bottom of the first on singles by Lofton and Baerga, an error and fielder's choice. But the Mariners went ahead, 5-2, on three hits in the fifth when Clark was kayoed.

Perry got his second hit of the game, a double, and scored on a single by Alomar in the seventh, but Johnson was too tough as he hiked his record to 9-1.

"If the guy just threw fastballs you could get used to it," Perry said of Johnson. "What makes it even tougher is that he throws with no fast movement. He's so easy. And when he gets that slider over, he's real nasty."

Hargrove said it this way: "Johnson is 6-10 and when you're batting against him it looks like he is handing the ball to you."

Before the game the Indians honored Murray, which helped attract a sixth consecutive sellout crowd of 41,741.

Among those in attendance were 21 members of Murray's family and friends, including his 72-year old father, Charles, wife Janice and infant daughter Jordan Alexandra. .

## 'HE'S ALWAYS BEEN ABLE TO HIT'

The elder Murray said of his son. "He's always been able to hit. I've been with him all the way, starting in Little League. In those days I wouldn't work any overtime in the shop if Eddie and his brothers had a game. I'd go to the game instead."

Murray was given a commemorative crystal trophy, a bronzed bat and an oil painting of the 20 members of the 3,000 hit club, the exclusive fraternity that he had joined seven days earlier.

Nagy, who had struggled in his last couple of outings, showed signs that his troubles were behind him with a good performance on July 8. He shrugged off a shaky first inning, and a cut on his right ankle in the fourth inning that later required "four or five" stitches, to beat the Mariners, 7-3. Nagy gave up five hits, but only three from the second through the ninth in his first complete game of the season.

Jay Buhner homered in the first, when the Mariners took a 3-0 lead, but thereafter, as Hargrove said, "Charlie pretty much dominated the rest of the game."

It also was after the game that Seattle Manager Lou Piniella shook his head in wonderment and said, "Cleveland is the measuring stick for every other team in baseball."

Belle hammered his 14th homer in the second inning, the Indians tied the score with two more runs in the third, and went ahead, 4-3, in the fourth. They locked up the victory with three runs in the fifth, thanks to several misplays and errant throws by the Mariners.

The first half of the season ended the next day, July 9. It was marred by a 9-3 loss to Seattle, though hardly a discouraging word could be heard among the 41,897 fans who comprised the second largest crowd of the season at Jacobs Field.

## BEST RECORD IN BASEBALL

How could there be any complaints? The Indians' 46-21 record was the best in baseball, and they also were first in most offensive and pitching categories.

They had the best team batting average, .292; slugging average, .491; most homers, 104; hits, 682; total bases, 1,147; and their pitchers owned the best earned run average, 3.68; had the most shutouts, 7; saves, 23; allowed the fewest runs, 273; fewest earned runs, 248; and fewest walks, 205.

Their 12 game lead over Kansas City in the AL Central also was the largest in the history of baseball since the onset of divisional play in 1969. Milwaukee was in third place, 14 lengths behind the Tribe, Chicago was fourth, 17 1/2 off the pace, and Minnesota was last by 24 1/2.

Hershiser was charged with the loss in that first half finale. It was his first start since suffering a lower back sprain on June 21, and his rustiness was obvious. Hershiser worked five innings, giving up five runs on six hits, including a homer by Jay Buhner.

Black made his first relief appearance in five years, pitching the sixth and seventh innings, but was no improvement. He was charged with four more runs on three hits, one of them a grand slam by Tino Martinez, and it was the Mariners, rather than the Indians, who resembled baseball's best team that day.

"I don't know if I've ever been on a team with a 12 game lead at the All-Star break," said Hargrove. "But I'm going to treat it just like I did in the first half - like we're a half game out."

And Hart wondered, "If it's so big, why does a 12 game lead feel like a half game lead?"

Whatever, despite the lopsided loss to the Mariners in the first half finale, there was no more talk of a "June Swoon."

Instead, as the Indians took three days off for the All-Star break, fans began to figure their "magic number" for clinching a berth in postseason play for the first time in 41 years.

# 6

## The Midsummer Classic

"It took me a long time, but finally I made it," said Jose Mesa, who had become the Indians' ace closer - and the best in the major leagues - as he strode onto the field at The Ballpark in Arlington (Texas) the day before the 66th All-Star Game on July 11.

Not only was Mesa thrilled to be one of six Tribesmen among all the players in baseball considered to be the best at their positions, he also took the occasion to celebrate his third anniversary in a Cleveland uniform.

"The Indians made the deal to get me (from Baltimore) at the All-Star break in 1992, and it has made a world of difference in my career," said Mesa, who had logged 21 saves in 21 opportunities to earn his place on the American League team.

"The Indians gave me the opportunity, and I worked very hard for this honor."

There was no doubt that Mesa deserved the honor, as did the Tribe's other representatives in the "Midsummer Classic" - starters Kenny Lofton, who led off for the AL and played center field (in place of the injured Ken Griffey, Jr.), second baseman Carlos Baerga, who batted second; and left fielder Albert Belle, fifth in the order; as well as pitcher Dennis Martinez and outfielder Manny Ramirez, both of whom would get into the game as late inning substitutes.

Mesa, who was acquired in exchange for minor league outfielder Kyle Washington, never pitched exclusively as a closer until this year, though he recorded two saves for the Indians in 1994 when his won-lost record was 7-5 prior to the strike-shortened season.

The 29-year old right-hander from the Dominican Republic was originally signed at the age of 15 by Toronto, and pitched his first season of professional baseball in 1982 at Bradenton of the Class A Florida State League. He was traded to Baltimore in a minor league deal in 1987, and the following season injured his elbow and underwent the first of two operations that limited his pitching for two years.

Mesa made it to the big leagues briefly in 1987 with the Orioles, and to stay in 1990, but his inconsistency as a starter led to the deal that brought him to Cleveland. Through last season Mesa's major league record was 34-45 with a 4.89 earned run average in 149 games.

Mesa said of his sensational success with the Indians, "My control has gotten better and I've used the sinker to show what I can do." As for his selection on the All-Star team, he said, "There were some very good relievers who didn't make it, especially (Dennis) Eckersley.

"To be here with a pitcher like Dennis Martinez makes it even more special for me."

## Extra Special for the "Baby Bull"

It also was extra special for Ramirez, a.k.a. "Baby Bull." The 23-year old outfielder, playing only his second season in the big leagues, went into the break with a batting average of .320 that included 18 homers and 52 runs batted in. Only two players on the AL team had more homers, Mark McGwire of Oakland with 24, and Frank Thomas of Chicago with 21 (though McGwire was injured and remained at home).

"I never thought I'd have this good a start," said Ramirez, whose performance surprised a lot of people - but only because of his youth and limited experience. He was the Indians' No. 1 pick (13th overall) in the 1991 amateur draft.

Before the game Ramirez's only regret, he said, was that "I won't get a chance to face that Japanese guy," Hideo Nomo of the Los Angeles Dodgers, who was to start for the National League.

Martinez understood AL manager Buck Showalter's decision to start Seattle's Randy Johnson.

"Every pitcher would like to get a shot to start the All-Star Game," acknowledged Martinez. "I think they didn't want a guy from Japan (Nomo) and a guy from Nicaragua as the starting pitchers," he quipped.

In the pre-game "Home Run Derby," Thomas out-slugged Belle, 3-2, in the third and final round of the competition. Ramirez also represented the Indians in the contest, but didn't advance past the first round, which Belle won by going 7-for-10 while Thomas countered with 8-for-10.

But in the second round, Belle - who led the Indians to 12 victories in their last at-bat in the first half - hit seven homers to only four by Thomas, forcing a tie-breaking round.

When the "real" game was played the next day, it was the NL that displayed most of the power as Craig Biggio of Houston, Mike Piazza of Los Angeles, and Jeff Conine of Florida homered to beat the AL, 3-2. In fact, those homers were the NL's only hits.

Conine's homer was an eighth inning shot off losing pitcher Steve Otiveros of Oakland.

All six Indians representatives played and Baerga in particular accounted well for himself. He went 3-for-3. "I just tried to have fun," said the second baseman. "I was just trying to swing the bat well and get my hits. It was exciting, though I wish we had won."

## Fourth All-Star Game for Martinez

Martinez, appearing in his fourth All-Star Game, pitched the fifth and sixth innings. He retired the first five batters he faced, but was tagged for Biggio's homer that cut the NL's deficit to 2-1..

Ramirez batted for Minnesota's Kirby Puckett with one out in the seventh and the score tied, 2-2, and almost delivered a two-run homer. His drive off Montreal's Carlos Perez hooked around the left field foul pole at the last moment. Then Ramirez walked, and waited on base as Perez struck out the next two batters.

Ramirez remained in the game to play right field and made two catches as Mesa, needing only seven pitches, turned in a one-two-three ninth. He would have been the winner if the AL had rallied in the bottom of the final inning.

Lofton and Belle were a combined 0-for-6.

Baerga's first two hits, both singles, were from the left side of the plate, the first in the first inning off Nomo, the second in the fourth, off Atlanta's John Smiley. He was thrown out stealing after his first hit, but came home in the fourth on Thomas's homer, the only two runs scored by the AL. Baerga batted right-handed and doubled against southpaw Denny Neagle in the sixth, but died on base.

Also active during the All-Star break was Tribe General Manager John Hart, who tried to create an opening on the roster by trading one of three pitchers - Bud Black, Jason Grimsley or Gregg Olson - though nothing materialized.

Two days after the All-Star Game, both Black and Grimsley were dispatched and Albie Lopez and Alan Embree were called up from Class AAA Buffalo to replace them.

Black, a 37-year old southpaw who had a 121-116 major league record with five teams (including 4-2 with the Tribe in 1995 after being signed as a free agent in April) was released, while Grimsley was outrighted to Buffalo.

Lopez, 24, was 3-7 with a 5.32 ERA in 12 starts for the Bisons. Embree, 25, a southpaw reliever, had a 2-4 record with three saves and a 1.06 ERA in the American Association where batters were hitting .222 against him. He had not allowed a run in nearly two months, since May 16, a stretch of 21 1/3 innings.

Lopez was a 20th round pick in the 1991 amateur draft and pitched briefly for the Indians in 1993, going 3-1 in nine games, and 1-2 in four games in 1994.

Embree was a fifth round draft pick in 1989, and last appeared in a big league game in 1992, when he made four starts for the Indians, going 0-2 with a 7.00 ERA in 19 innings.

Embree's career was interrupted in June 1993 when he underwent surgery to repair a torn medial collateral ligament in his left elbow.

"With the two moves we've made, we've added power arms to the staff that weren't there before," said Hargrove.

However, the manager also said that one of the two newcomers, probably Lopez, would be returned to Buffalo when Chad Ogea was expected to be recalled on July 17.

It also was during the break that Hart laid the groundwork for the subsequent acquisition of veteran right-hander Ken Hill from St. Louis, after failing to swing a deal with Montreal for left-hander Jeff Fassero.

"Being in (the All-Star Game) was a great experience for our guys, and I'm glad they did well, especially Carlos and Jose," said Hart.

"But now we've got our work cut out for ourselves ... we've had a great first half, but we've still got a long way to go and we certainly can't afford to relax."

# 7

# Running Full Speed in the Second Half

Manager Mike Hargrove echoed General Manager John Hart's words of advice to the Indians - that despite their first half success, they couldn't afford to be complacent in the second half - as they returned to the "real" world against the Oakland Athletics at Jacobs Field on July 13.

With a 46-21 won-lost record the Tribe enjoyed a 12 1/2 game lead over Kansas City in the American League Central Division, with Chicago, the preseason favorite, 17 lengths off the pace at 29-38.

It meant that, if the Indians continued to play at a .687 clip, which would give them 99 victories by season's end, the Royals would have to win 67 of their final 79 games, an .848 winning percentage, to catch Cleveland.

It would be even tougher for the third place Brewers to win the division as they would be required to go 68-9 the rest of the way, while the White Sox could afford to lose only six of their 78 games to prevail.

If the Indians only won 39 of their final 77 games, for a .506 percentage, Kansas City would need to go 53-26 (.671) to win the division, Milwaukee would have to win 54 while losing only 23 (.701) to take over first place, and Chicago would be required to play at a .744 clip, by winning 58 and losing only 20, to prevail.

"We exceeded our expectations and we're in the driver's seat, no doubt about it - and I want to be sure we stay there," said Hargrove as the Indians prepared for a stretch of 18 consecutive games against AL West teams. The first six were at home against the Athletics and California, which was then tied with Texas for first place in their division.

It also was during the All-Star break that Rangers pitcher Bob Tewksbury popped off about the Indians being "undisciplined," which evoked angry responses from players on the team with the best record in baseball.

"You look at the Indians during batting practice and one guy's on the field with a blue top, the next guy's got a red top," Tewksbury was quoted as saying.

"One guy's taking infield with his hat off, and one guy walks to his position in left field, but nobody says a thing.

"There's a lot of talented people there, and they have a chance to succeed. But I like our professionalism, our workmanship."

## Belle Answers his Critic

Belle, who is not known for being particularly talkative, this time spoke out when Tewksbury's comments were reported. Belle, of course, was the player Tewksbury said "walks to his position in left field, but nobody says a thing."

"Baloney," or words to that effect, responded Belle, who took the greatest offense to Tewksbury's remarks.

"You don't go out there and have the best record in baseball without having a tremendous team concept. We've blended together well as a team. We come to the park early together, go out together, watch video together.

"And when I walk out to left field, I'm in the process of separating my offense from my defense," continued Belle. "I could see where the other side may pick up some bad vibes from that, but I'm not going to win every game with my bat. I may go 0-for-4, but I can still help us win by making four tremendous catches in the outfield.

"Everybody has had their own perception of Albert Belle since high school. But I'm just doing what it takes to keep our team in first place."

Despite Tewksbury's criticism, it was an especially good first half for several Tribesmen, particularly Dennis Martinez, whose 8-0 record and 2.37 earned run average was best in the league (though Seattle's Randy Johnson, at 9-1, had won one more game), and reliever Jose Mesa, whose 21 saves (in 21 opportunities) were one better than California's Lee Smith, and two more than Oakland's Dennis Eckersley.

## MESA FILLS THE "BIGGEST HOLE"

Of Mesa, Hargrove said, "Finding a closer was the biggest hole on our club and he filled it. I always felt Jose could do it, but in all honesty, I never thought he would dominate the way he did."

Jim Thome and Carlos Baerga were seventh and eighth in the batting race with .330 and .327 averages, respectively, behind Seattle's Edgar Martinez's league-leading .362; Manny Ramirez had 18 homers, fifth most in the AL, with Thome one behind him, as Boston's Mo Vaughn and Oakland's Mark McGwire were first with 24, while Belle - who would later go on a torrid streak - had 14 homers; Ramirez also was among the leaders in RBI with 52 for seventh place; Baerga had the most hits, 92, and Belle was fourth with 81; Belle had the most doubles, 27, and was tied for fourth in runs scored with 52; and Kenny Lofton was tied with Toronto's Robby Alomar for the most triples, seven.

Little wonder that Hart and Hargrove were pleased - and that they also wanted to be sure that there would not be a letdown in the second half.

The first three months also were good for the Indians at the gate as their attendance total for 35 home dates was 1,342,961, an average turnout of 38,370. Included were 20 crowds of 40,000 or more (the capacity of Jacobs Field is officially listed at 42,865).

Obviously, the Indians paid attention to their leaders, resuming the second half of the season just as they'd ended the first half. They beat Oakland in four consecutive games, the first two, 1-0 and 7-6, in a double header July 14.

The third was a 7-2 win the next night behind Orel Hershiser, recently returned from a three week stay on the disabled list, who previously had been the loser of three straight games.

And the fourth was a 5-4 victory in one of the most exciting comebacks in a season of comebacks by the Indians.

In that twin-bill sweep of the Athletics, Albie Lopez, Alan Embree, Julian Tavarez and Mesa collaborated on a five-hitter, with Baerga driving in the only run in the sixth inning to win the opener.

## "I SNEAKED IN A WIN" - EMBREE

The victory was credited to Embree, his first in the major leagues, after which he said, "I sneaked in a win ... I didn't want to give up any of Albie's runs and be the scapegoat. But Albie should have gotten (the victory), and would've if his leg had not cramped up."

Embree took over with two out in the sixth, after Lopez had allowed only two hits. Tavarez gave up two hits in the seventh and eighth, and Mesa - that man again! - yielded a harmless single but put the Athletics down on 11 pitches in the ninth for his 22nd save.

Except for Baerga's single that drove in Wayne Kirby, Oakland's Ariel Prieto was even better than the quartet of Tribe pitchers. Prieto relinquished only four hits.

Then in the nightcap, Charles Nagy struggled in the first two innings, giving up  four runs, but thanks to Hargrove's patience - and the offensive support of his teammates -  righted himself and held the Athletics at bay through the sixth. The Indians exploded for three runs in the first and four in the third to make it possible for Nagy to hang on.

Eric Plunk took over and pitched through the eighth, before Mesa did it again in the ninth, preserving the 7-6 victory.

This time the Indians' ace closer staggered - the Athletics scored an unearned run on two hits and an error by Alvaro Espinoza - but hung on to register his 23rd save.

Hershiser had not pitched well in the last game the Indians played before the All-Star break, and there was growing concern about his ability, considering his age, 37, and recent back problems.

But the former ace of the Los Angeles Dodgers, who is aptly nicknamed "Bulldog," pitched his best game in a Cleveland uniform, overcoming a two hour and 16 minute rain delay in the process.

In seven innings Hershiser produced 17 ground ball outs ... in the first inning alone, he retired the Athletics on three bounders back to the mound.

"That was one of my best performances in a long time," said Hershiser after giving up five hits and two runs while striking out three. Paul Assenmacher and Plunk finished up for Hershiser, whose record climbed to 6-4, and the Tribe's first place margin over Kansas City was hiked to 13 1/2 games.

Ramirez drove in three of the Indians' seven runs with his 20th homer and a double - but the best was to come 24 hours later, on July 16.

Take Eckersley's word for it.

The Indians and Athletics battled back and forth through 11 innings, after starters Martinez and Todd Stottlemyre had left the premises, and were tied, 3-3, with Embree on the mound against Oakland's fourth reliever, Carlos Reyes.

Embree, who had blanked the Athletics in the 11th, was greeted in the 12th by a double off the bat of Rickey Henderson, who went to third on a wild pitch, and scored on a sacrifice fly.

## WARNING: DO NOT LEAVE EARLY

It appeared that the struggle was ended as Eckersley came in to protect the Athletics' one run lead, and some - not many, but some - of the crowd of 41,767 started to leave Jacobs Field.

They soon learned their lesson.

As it turned out, Eckersley learned something, too.

First, Baerga singled to left, but Belle popped out. So did Thome. Lofton ran for Baerga and stole second, though it seemed to be all over as the youthful Ramirez approached the plate against the most experienced and celebrated relief pitcher in the league.

"I was mainly trying to relax myself," Ramirez said. after Eckersley fired two quick strikes for an 0-and-2 count. Eckersley's next two pitches were wide of the plate, evening the count at 2-and-2.

Then Eckersley, with 312 saves at that point in his career, fired again. This time it was a slider that stayed over the plate, thigh-high. Ramirez swung and the ball arched off his bat and flew majestically into the left field bleachers for a game-winning home run.

The television camera caught Eckersley watching the flight of the ball, then turning, and as he headed for the dugout viewers could see him exclaim, "Wow!"

Wow! indeed.

It might have been the most dramatic moment of the entire season.

Eckersley would have to agree. "It's phenomenal what's happening around here ... it's almost like it's meant to be," said the 40-year old righthander, who was drafted by the Indians in 1972, made it to the big leagues with them as a starter in 1975, and was traded to Boston on March 30, 1978.

It was the 13th game the Indians had won in their final at-bat, and gave them 24 come-from-behind victories.

It also boosted their lead over Kansas City to 14 1/2 games.

"I'd never faced (Eckersley) before, but I knew he is one of the best," said Ramirez after his 21st homer thrilled the Jacobs Field crowd of 41,767.

"I wasn't trying to hit a home run, I just wanted to stay back and try to hit the ball hard, the other way (to right field)." He did.

Embree, who became the winning pitcher because of Ramirez's blast, said, "I kept saying to myself, 'Manny, just drive that guy (Lofton) in from second base. Just get the score tied.' I wanted another chance to get out there, but instead, Manny gave me a 'W'."

Ramirez's homer and Embree's solid relief pitching gave the Indians their fifth series sweep of the season, fourth at home and first ever over the Athletics in Cleveland.

## WELCOME BACK DAVE WINFIELD

Embree's good work wasn't enough to keep him in the big leagues, at least not this time around. After the game the Indians announced the recall of Chad Ogea from Buffalo, and the activation of Dave Winfield from the disabled list.

To make room for Ogea and Winfield, on the roster, Embree was sent back to Buffalo, and Gregg Olson was designated for assignment (he subsequently was dealt to Kansas City).

Olson had appeared in three games for the Tribe, without registering a decision, though his earned run average was a bloated 13.50. He was battling back from an elbow injury that led to his release by Baltimore, and idled him most of 1994.

The moves also meant that Lopez would remain with the Indians for the time being as a spot starter.

Ogea's return, however, was not the kind he - or the Indians - had anticipated.

He started against California the next night, July 17, and was rocked by the then-rambunctious Angels, who were in first place in the AL West with a 44-30 record, two games ahead of Texas (while Seattle was tied for last place with a 35-38 mark, 8 1/2 games behind).

The Angels battered Ogea for four runs in the first two innings as J.T. Snow went 4-for-5 with a homer, and drove in four runs in an 8-3 victory over the Tribe. California scored four more in the seventh to make it easy for Brian Anderson, though he needed help in the bottom of the seventh when Sandy Alomar Jr. whacked his second homer of the season.

Anderson a 23-year old rookie southpaw who grew up in Geneva, Ohio, was the Angels' first round draft choice out of Wright State University in 1993.

"We just got our butts kicked," said Alomar after the Tribe's four game winning streak was snapped. "It was bound to happen sooner or later. Our offense simply didn't show up tonight." He was right. The Tribe was held to five hits, and nobody got more than one.

But the Indians didn't pitch well either. "You can see why the Angels score runs," said Hargrove. "They are a very good hitting club, and it's not a mistake where they are ranked offensively," which was, at the time, first in the AL.

"This was a big thing for me," said Anderson. "It was my first time in Jacobs Field, and facing the team I grew up loving. I had Albert Belle's poster over my bed in college."

Quickly, however, in a matter of only 24 hours, the Indians were off and running again. They constructed a seven game winning streak that was launched on the wings of another dramatic home run, a grand slam by Albert Belle in the ninth inning for a 7-5 victory over the Angels on July 18.

It was a colossal shot by Belle, a 425-foot laser beam into the picnic area beyond center field. It came off a pitch by Lee Smith, the major leagues' all-time saves leader.

Until the ninth, the Indians struggled behind Mark Clark, who surrendered eight hits and five runs - including homers by Tony Phillips, Jim Edmonds, and Garrett Anderson. They were losing, 5-3, to Mark Langston when Eric Plunk took over in the seventh.

## "BACK, BACK, 'WAY BACK"

The two run deficit was still in place when Smith trudged to the mound to start the ninth, seeking his 23rd save of the season, and 456th of his career.

Instead, Smith took his third loss in four decisions after pinch hitter Wayne Kirby singled to start the inning, and stole second with one out, went to third as Omar Vizquel singled, and waited as Baerga walked.

But not for long. Four pitches later, with the count 1-and-2, Belle drilled his grand slam, his 16th homer, fourth career grand slam, the Indians 25th come-from-behind victory, and 14th in their final at-bat.

"These guys have never known when it's time to fold the tent and go home, so nothing they do surprises me," said Hargrove.

It was credited to Assenmacher, and though Hargrove savored the victory that kept the Indians 13 1/2 lengths ahead of Kansas City, it was obvious he was concerned about Clark. It was the third straight time Clark failed to win and, though his record remained at 4-3, his ERA climbed to 7.47.

"(Clark) made three bad pitches and, unfortunately, they hit all three of them," said Hargrove in a reference to the homers by Phillips, Edmonds and Anderson.

"But we are not jumping to any hasty conclusions," added the manager, who had previously lost confidence in Clark earlier in the season and sent him to Buffalo "to get himself straightened out."

There were no late histrionics involved in the Indians' triumph the next night when they embarked July 19 on what could have been - but certainly wasn't - a disastrous western trip to play 12 games against the Rangers, Athletics, Angels and Mariners.

With rookie Herbert Perry, starting his first major league game as a designated hitter, and slump-ridden Paul Sorrento stepping into the limelight, the Indians started their journey with a 19 hit explosion and a 14-5 victory over Texas.

## SORRENTO'S SLUMP FINALLY ENDS

Perry went 4-for-5 and drove in four runs, and Sorrento delivered his first homer in 58 at-bats dating back to June 18, and was 3-for-4 also with four RBI, in the destruction of the then-playoff hopeful Rangers.

The Indians erupted for four runs in the first inning, and had an 8-1 lead before Nagy took the mound in the bottom of the third, as he coasted to his fifth straight victory.

The one who ignited this explosion was Wayne Kirby. He came off the bench to replace Kenny Lofton, who missed his sixth consecutive game with an injury to his right rib cage.

Kirby doubled to open the game, scored as Vizquel also doubled, and when Baerga followed with a run-producing single, the rout was in full swing, making it easy for Nagy.

"The deeper Charlie got into the game, the better he pitched," Hargrove said of Nagy, whose record rose to 9-4. Lopez pitched the eighth inning, and Tavarez the ninth, when the Rangers scored twice.

The Indians playoff express continued to roll the next day in the oppressive 102-degree heat at The Ballpark in Arlington, though it wasn't as easy for Hershiser as it had been 24 hours earlier for Nagy.

This time - with Lofton still sidelined with a rib cage injury, Eddie Murray still on the disabled list, and Winfield still nursing a sick bat - Alomar stepped to the forefront and assumed the hero's mantle.

## 'THE BEST NO. 9 HITTER'

Called by some "the best No. 9 hitter in baseball," Alomar socked two homers, the first in the third inning, the second in the seventh, as the Tribe beat the Rangers, 6-3.

Alomar's first homer tied the score at 1-1, and his second, his fourth round-tripper of the season, was a two-run shot that broke a 2-2 deadlock.

Hershiser succumbed to the heat and went to the showers after the Indians went on to score another run in the seventh for a 5-2 lead. Plunk gave up a run in the eighth, but Mesa blanked the Rangers in the ninth, raising his perfect saves record to 24, and Hershiser's won-lost mark to 7-4.

It also boosted the Indians' lead to 14 1/2 games over Milwaukee, which had taken over second place in the AL Central, and their record to 31 games over .500 (53-22).

Alomar was humble in accepting praise for his performance. "If we had a 10-man lineup on this team, I'd probably be batting 10th," he said. "Everyday somebody else does the job for this team. Today was my turn."

Hargrove said, "That's the thing about all the people we have in the bottom of the order. Late in the game they have a chance to hurt a pitcher because he's mentally tired from working his way through this lineup."

It was many players' "turn" the next night, July 21, in Oakland as Belle, Tony Pena and Ramirez homered, and Martinez pitched a six-hitter for his third complete game to beat the Athletics, 6-1. It was Martinez's ninth victory of the season, gave him a 2.35 ERA, and kept him unbeaten since July 31, 1994.

It also edged the 40-year old grandfather closer to the Cleveland franchise record of 15 consecutive victories at the start of a season, set by Johnny Allen in 1937. Barry Latman also started the 1961 season with a 9-0 record.

The three homers by Belle, Pena and Ramirez raised the Indians' total to 118 in 76 games. That put them on pace to hit 224 in the season's 144 game schedule, which would shatter the club record of 187, set in 1987 in 162 games. (As it would turn out, they finished with 207 homers.)

## ANOTHER "MONSTER" SHOT BY BELLE

Belle's homer, his 17th, led the second inning and was a monster shot, clearing the 400 foot center field fence by plenty. Belle also touched off a rally in the fourth when the Indians took a 4-0 lead on Ramirez's homer, his 22nd, only three fewer than AL leaders Vaughn of Boston and Frank Thomas of Chicago, and two behind McGwire of Oakland.

Pena, who was Martinez's "personal" catcher, at least until the playoffs, came through with his solo homer in the sixth. With Pena behind the plate, Martinez's record climbed to 14-2 since both joined the Indians in 1994.

It was during this western trip that speculation flourished that Hart, the Indians' aggressive general manager, was intent upon adding another pitcher to the starting rotation, and Ken Hill's name, among others, surfaced prominently.

In addition to Hill, then pitching for St. Louis, the Tribe also was primarily interested in the availability of the New York Mets Bret Saberhagen, Toronto's David Cone and Minnesota's Kevin Tapani.

Though both Hart and Hargrove were guarded in their comments, the manager conceded, "It wouldn't hurt us at all (to acquire another starter). If the opportunity presents itself to get a David Cone or a Bret Saberhagen, I certainly wouldn't tell John Hart, 'We don't want him.'"

## FIRST OBJECTIVE: WIN AL CENTRAL

Though Hart admitted, "There are seven or eight pitchers out there waiting to be had," he insisted no deal was "imminent."

"Sometimes the desire to improve the club and the reality of doing it are light years apart," Hart said. "So many factors come into play in making a deal like this (but) I will not mortgage our future for what may or may not get us to where we want to go.

"I'm in this for the long haul. One objective is to win a pennant, and a World Series. But first, we've got to win the division."

Six days later, on July 27, the Tribe traded three minor leaguers, including Class AAA infielder David Bell, the son of coach Buddy Bell, to St. Louis for Hill, whose record with the Cardinals was 6-7 with a 5.06 ERA.

If anybody doubted Hart's determination for the Indians to win their division before making a deal to strengthen the pitching staff, they would have become believers - or should have.

The *Plain Dealer* called the Tribe "a team that wins when it's supposed to win, and wins even more when it's supposed to lose."

That was in the wake of the Indians' 6-4 victory over the Athletics on July 22, the 12th consecutive time they'd beaten Oakland in a game they probably should have lost.

And again it was Eckersley, one of the all-time best relief pitchers in history, and major league baseball's premier closer for the last eight years, who was victimized. This time - only six days after Ramirez's homer beat him in the 12th inning in Cleveland on July 16 - Eckersley stalked to the mound to protect Oakland's 4-3 lead in the ninth.

On this occasion Eckersley was seeking his 315th save, and came within one pitch of getting it as he retired Belle for the second out after Vizquel singled and Baerga was hit by a pitch.

Eckersley went to a 3-and-2 count on Thome, who fouled off the next pitch, then slashed a double past first base to score Vizquel and Baerga with the tying and go-ahead runs.

The Indians almost added insult to injury by tacking on another run on a single by Sorrento, chasing Eckersley.

Mike Mohler came on to end the rally, but Mesa made sure the Tribe's two run lead was enough. He took over in the bottom of the ninth and struck out the three batters he faced on 15 pitches for his 25th save in 25 opportunities.

Eckersley was fuming after the game, though the object of his anger was umpire John Shulock, not the Indians.

"I threw about six strikes in a row, the kind of pitches I used to get," he complained about Shulock not calling Vizquel and Baerga out.

Instead, it was the Indians 15th victory in their last at-bat, and 27th time they'd come from behind to wipe out a deficit. "The feeling on this club right now is that we will not accept a loss," said Vizquel, who went 3-for-5 and scored three runs.

Belle, often the hero, very nearly was a goat this time as he dropped a fly ball in the eighth inning enabling the Athletics to overcome the Tribe's 3-2 lead.

It increased the Indians' first place margin to a season high of 15 1/2 games over Milwaukee, and gave them a winning percentage of .714 (55-22), which also was a 1995 high.

At the same time, however, the Indians lost - though only temporarily - the services of Lofton, who'd won the AL base stealing championship the previous three seasons (and would put on a blazing finish to repeat in 1995).

previous three seasons (and would put on a blazing finish to repeat in 1995).

## EMBREE'S ROLLER COASTER RIDE

Lofton, who'd been unable to start eight straight games while nursing a mysterious rib cage injury since July 14, was placed on the disabled list. Embree, whose season between Cleveland and Buffalo had resembled a roller coaster ride, was recalled again to fill the vacancy on the 25-man roster.

Lofton's absence had no immediate effect on the Indians, however, as they continued their domination of the Athletics with a 2-0 victory on July 23.

Clark, apparently back in control and, with his sinker sinking as it did so well in 1994, was the winner with late inning relief help from Plunk and (of course) Mesa. Both Tribe runs came in the fourth inning on singles by Belle, Ramirez and Sorrento.

Clark, whose early season inconsistency resulted in his being exiled to Buffalo in mid-May, pitched into the seventh, until he gave up a walk and a single with two out and was excused in favor of Plunk.

Plunk quickly retired Geronimo Berroa, to end the inning, pitched a scoreless eighth, and Mesa quickly retired the Athletics in the ninth on only 11 pitches. It was the Indians' 13th straight victory over Oakland since the start of 1994.

Hargrove sloughed off the Tribe's domination of the Athletics.

"No team is easy to beat," he said. "What we've done to Oakland over the last two years is more a fluke than anything. Oakland is a good ball club. They're fundamentally sound. And you know that any club managed by Tony LaRussa is going to be aggressive."

Fluke or not, Clark as well as Plunk, and especially Mesa, made it *look* easy.

"Last year everything that could go right, did go right for me," said Clark. "This year everything that could go wrong, has gone wrong."

At least until now, as Clark's record improved to 5-3, giving rise to the opinion that he would be an important contributor in the second half, even though his ERA was still a bloated 6.54.

The next night in Anaheim the Indians made it seven straight victories, 21 in 26 games, beating western division pacesetting California, 9-7, with another 10th inning rally, again against celebrated reliever Lee Smith.

It raised the Tribe's record to 11-1 since the All-Star break and, overall, to 57-22, a whopping 35 games above .500 for a .722 winning percentage and a 16 1/2 length lead over Milwaukee. The game was saved by another stellar performance by Mesa.

"I never thought about leading the division by that many games," said Mesa, after finalizing his 27th save without a miss, despite giving up two hits in the last of the 10th.

"But now that we do (have that large a lead), people have got to believe it, and in us."

Belle and Alomar homered for the Indians, though the Angels, who were at that time considered to be at least the *second best* team in the AL, had fought back from an early 6-1 deficit against Nagy.

They rallied for two runs and a 7-7 tie in the seventh on Edmonds' two run homer, after Tavarez had taken the mound.

Assenmacher bailed Tavarez out of trouble in the ninth, and was credited with the victory when the Indians scored twice in the 10th against Smith, on a walk, Ramirez's double and Sorrento's single.

## MESA: CY YOUNG CANDIDATE

Mesa's sensational work out of the bull pen established him as a bonafide candidate for the Cy Young Award, though four other AL pitchers, all starters, also were having exceptional seasons: the Indians' Martinez, who was unbeaten in nine decisions; Seattle's Randy Johnson, 10-1; Boston's Tim Wakefield, 9-1; and California's Langston, 9-1.

"Maybe so, but I am not thinking about that," said Mesa. "All I am thinking about is to keep winning."

When asked how long he can keep saving victories, Mesa replied, "Forever."

Perhaps. But complacency would not be a problem for the Indians the rest of the season, Hargrove insisted.

"It won't happen," he said. "This club has stayed so focused on what it has to do every day, that I can't imagine it happening."

Hargrove was right, although there were times that his confidence had to be doubted by Tribe fans who had been disappointed so often in the past.

For the past 41 years, in fact.

# 8

# The Pennant Express Gains Momentum

Okay, so they weren't complacent.

"You're damned right we're not," insisted Manager Mike Hargrove. "We just got beat. Give the other guys credit. Nobody around here is letting down, and they won't because I won't allow it to happen."

Hargrove's avowal - though it also could have been interpreted as an admonition - was issued in the wake of three consecutive losses, two to California and one to Seattle, July 25-27.

Many considered the series with the Angels to be a preview of the first round of the American League divisional playoffs.

The three defeats left the Indians with a 57-25 record, though they lost only one game in their American League Central Division lead and were still 15 1/2 lengths ahead of Milwaukee.

The first loss, 6-5, to the AL West Division leading Angels, was charged to Orel Hershiser, making his first visit back to Southern California since leaving the Los Angeles Dodgers for whom he'd pitched from 1983-94.

And credited with saving the victory for California's Chuck Finley was Lee Smith, baseball's all-time saves leader whom the Indians had beaten twice with ninth inning rallies earlier.

Only the night before the Tribe had rallied for two runs in the 10th inning for a 9-7 victory against Smith, who also was beaten on July 18 when Albert Belle smashed a grand slam in the bottom of the ninth for a 7-5 triumph at Jacobs Field.

Hershiser's loss ended his two game winning streak and was the first for the Indians after seven straight victories. It also was only their second setback in 13 games since the All-Star break.

As it was, Smith, recording his 23rd save of the season and 457th of his 16 year major league career, almost blew it again when the Indians came to life in the ninth. Sorrento singled with two out, but was retired trying to stretch the hit into a double.

"Paul represented the tying run, but you never want to make the first or third out of an inning at second base," Hargrove said of Sorrento's ill-fated dash that ended the game.

Actually, Sorrento reached the bag safely, but was called out by umpire Richie Garcia when his foot came off the bag and he was tagged by shortstop Gary DiSarcina.

Two innings earlier Jim Thome had whacked his 19th homer, but only his first in 11 games, cutting the Tribe's deficit to one run.

## FROM BAD TO WORSE

It was more of the same - and even worse - the next night as the Indians' best pitcher, Dennis Martinez, was scorched by veteran outfielder-designated hitter Chili Davis, who smashed a grand slam in California's 6-3 victory.

The loss was Martinez's first of the season after going 9-0 in his 16 starts - also his first since July 31, 1994 - and was all but finalized in the third inning when Davis unloaded his 12th homer.

"That pretty much was it," correctly assessed Martinez, who yielded all of the Angels' runs in six innings.

"The Angels showed they can compete with us offensively and defensively, although, pitching-wise, I don't think the five games we've played against them were a great matchup. Our pitchers gave up a lot of runs, and so did theirs. The hitters definitely took charge.

"But if we meet again in the playoffs, maybe it will be the pitchers who will take charge," added Martinez.

As for his winning streak coming to an end, Martinez was philosophical, saying, "I knew it was going to end sooner or later, but that doesn't mean I didn't want to keep it going."

The two victories by the Angels boosted their AL West record to 50-33, eight games ahead of Texas, 8 1/2 over Seattle, and 12 better than Oakland.

Sorrento and Thome homered for the Indians, but both were solo shots. They served only to cut California's lead to 5-2 in the fourth and 5-3 in the sixth, as Mike Harkey staggered to his fifth victory in 11 decisions with help from three relievers, including Smith, who pitched the ninth for his 24th save..

The next night, after losing a third straight game, this one in Seattle, 11-5, the Indians acquired pitcher Ken Hill from the St. Louis Cardinals in a trade for three minor leaguers - infielder David Bell, son of coach Buddy Bell, pitcher Rick Heiserman and catcher Pepe McNeal.

Hill was not setting the National League afire; his record was only 6-7 with a 5.06 earned run average, though he went 16-5 with a 3.32 ERA for

Montreal in 1994.

"He's healthy and our scouts say he has the same stuff as he did last year," said General Manager John Hart. "The best we can figure (Hill's lack of success with the Cardinals) is that his split-fingered fast ball is not as dominant as it was, for whatever reason, which we hope to find out.

"Then, too, the St. Louis defense hasn't helped him either," added Hart.

Hill brought with him a $4.375 million contract (of which the Indians were responsible for about $1.5 million). He would be eligible to become a free agent at the end of the season, and when asked if Hill would be signed for 1996, Hart evaded a direct answer.

"This is not a pitcher at the end of his career," said Hart. "(Hill) is young and strong, and a lot will depend on how he pitches for us the rest of the year. What kind of appetite will he have for Cleveland and playing in a new ballpark and on a pennant contender? And what kind of appetite will we have for him?"

## NOT MOTIVATED BY PANIC

Some thought the deal, coming in the wake of three straight losses, was a panic move, though Hargrove was quick to deny it.

"As the old saying goes, you can never have enough pitching," he said. "And getting another pitcher of Hill's caliber, definitely should make us a better team.

"We're hoping that a change of scenery will help get him back to being the pitcher he was last year."

The arrival of the 29-year old Hill cost Mark Clark his spot in the rotation, and Albie Lopez his place on the roster. Lopez was sent back to Buffalo for the second time; he was with the Tribe from June 23-27, and was again recalled on July 14 for what turned out to be a 14 day stay.

Bell, a seventh round selection by the Indians in the 1990 amateur draft, was hitting .272 with eight homers and 34 runs batted in for the Bisons. Heiserman was the Tribe's No. 3 pick in 1994 and had a 9-3 record and 3.74 ERA at Class A Kinston. McNeal, a fifth round choice in 1994, was batting .281 at Class A Burlington.

The deal for Hill beat by four days the July 31 trading deadline, as did others made by California for Jim Abbott (from the Chicago White Sox), the New York Yankees for David Cone (from Toronto) and Ruben Sierra (from Oakland), and Baltimore for Bobby Bonilla (from the New York Mets).

## FIVE HOMERS SINK THE TRIBE

As for the loss to the Mariners, it flew away on the wings of five homers - two by Mike Blowers and one each by Jay Buhner, Warren Newson and Dan Wilson.

It was the 11th time in 13 games dating back to August 26, 1992, that the Tribe had lost in the Kingdome.

The Indians scored all their runs in the first two innings, four in the first on Ramirez's grand slam, his 23rd homer giving him 69 RBI for the season. Dave Winfield homered in the second inning, his second of the season and 465th of his career.

Both Tribe homers were struck off Tim Belcher, who somehow righted himself and went on to pitch a complete game while his teammates were abusing Chad Ogea, Lopez (which might have hastened his exile to Buffalo), and Jim Poole.

Hargrove had little to say after the beating - as did beat writers traveling with the team. "What could you possibly ask after a disaster like that?" said Hargrove.

Omar Vizquel was more talkative, but only slightly. "We learned we aren't invincible," said the Gold Glove shortstop.

Hargrove wasted no time seeing what Hill could do, starting him the next night, July 28, against the homer-happy Mariners and, though the newcomer didn't win, the Indians did, 6-5.

Hill pitched six so-so innings, yielding two runs on six hits and four walks while striking out four. He left with a 5-2 lead that Julian Tavarez couldn't protect.

The Mariners erupted for three runs off Tavarez in the seventh. The Indians broke the tie in the eighth, on behalf of Eric Plunk, when Thome led off with his fourth hit in four at-bats, was sacrificed to second and scored on Ruben Amaro's single.

Then Jose Mesa did it again, recording his 28th save in 28 opportunities, although this one didn't come easily for the 29-year old Dominican. The Mariners loaded the bases on singles by Newson and Blowers, and a walk to Wilson. Then, with two out, Mesa fanned pinch hitter Luis Sojo.

While Hill did not get credit for the victory, Hargrove praised him for a solid outing. "I thought he threw the ball very well," said Hargrove. "I was very encouraged, very pleased. He threw strikes, and when he missed, he was just off the plate."

Hill acknowledged, "There has been a lot of talk this year that I've lost my fast ball, but I haven't, and I wanted the Indians to know it. I've just had some mechanical problems where I've been throwing across my body and letting my arm drop to the side. It felt good to go out there and throw like I know I can."

## TWO NEW CAUSES FOR CONCERN

Two aspects of the game were distressing, however, despite the victory and Hill's "encouraging" performance.

First, catcher Sandy Alomar Jr. had to leave after eight innings because of soreness in his right leg. It also was Tavarez's third straight appearance in which he was hit hard.

But Hargrove was not among the cynics. At least not publicly. "I just think Julian is going through one of those stages," said the manager. "Even the stock market makes a correction now and then."

As for Alomar, Hargrove shrugged and said, "It's just a little tightness in his quadriceps (thigh muscle)."

The Indians split the next two games in Seattle, losing, 5-3, on July 29, and winning, 5-2, on July 30, concluding a grueling 12 game western trip.

They won eight games, but only two of their last six before returning to Cleveland with a 59-26 record and a 17 1/2 game lead over Kansas City in the AL Central.

Though Charles Nagy wasn't the pitcher of record in the loss to the Mariners, he was a victim - again - of the Kingdome jinx, where he had never won in six starts. This time Nagy took a 3-3 tie into the sixth inning, when he was replaced by Alan Embree, and the Mariners rallied for two runs in the seventh to win.

In those starts in the Kingdome, Nagy was 0-5 with a 6.82 ERA.

"I'm just not comfortable in here, but that's all I can tell you ... I don't have any other reason," Nagy said of his lackluster performances in the Kingdome. Going into the game Nagy had won five straight for a 9-4 record since his last defeat at the hands of the White Sox on June 23.

The Indians' only runs came on Belle's 19th homer off Chris Bosio in the third, after Vizquel walked and Carlos Baerga singled with one out.

The Mariners' go-ahead and insurance runs in the seventh were unearned because of an error by Baerga that preceded a walk by Embree. After Tavarez took over with one out, the Mariners scored one run on a fielder's choice and another on Newton's double.

Hershiser, along with Ramirez and Sorrento, made sure the trip ended on a positive note the next night when they played key roles in beating the Mariners - Hershiser with seven strong innings backed by Ramirez's 24th homer, and Sorrento's 18th.

"I had no idea about this team's history in the Kingdome," said Hershiser, whose record climbed to 7-5. "Maybe they didn't want to tell me because they didn't want to worry me."

Going into the game the Indians were 9-21 in the Kingdome in the 1990s, and 13-29 since 1988.

After the game Sorrento explained it this way: "When we stunk we didn't play well here, and it's the same now that we're good. We were lucky to come out of here with a split (of the four games)."

Whatever, except for the third and seventh innings, Hershiser was at his best. Buhner solo homered in the second, cutting the Cleveland lead to 2-1. Blowers smashed a bases-empty homer in the seventh, pulling the Mariners to within two of the Tribe, 4-2.

## MESA: 29-FOR-29 AND COUNTING

But Plunk blanked the Mariners in the eighth, and Mesa did the same in the ninth for his 29th save in 29 opportunities.

When it was over and the Indians were packing to return home,

Hargrove breathed a sigh of relief and said, "I'm glad we don't have to come back here again this season."

Little did he know what would happen. At the time, the Mariners, with a 43-44 record, were third in the AL West, 11 games behind California.

The Indians returned to the friendly confines of Jacobs Field - and so did Eddie Murray and Kenny Lofton from the disabled list - on August 1, when the Minnesota Twins came to Cleveland to open a six-game homestand.

Lofton went on the DL on July 27 with what subsequently was described as "torn cartilage" in his right rib cage. Murray had been sidelined since he suffered two broken ribs on his right side while sliding home in a game against the Twins on July 2.

"We've done very well with Eddie and Kenny out of the lineup, but their absence is beginning to show," said Hargrove. Without Murray in the lineup the Indians' record was 17-8, and 13-4 without Lofton.

Their return resulted in a demotion to Buffalo for Embree, and a trip to the disabled list for Amaro, who was said to be suffering a strained left hamstring.

But Murray and Lofton couldn't prevent the Twins' Chuck Knoblauch from blasting a solo homer with two out in the ninth inning. It gave Minnesota a 6-5 victory in front of 42,033 fans who comprised the largest crowd in the two year history of Jacobs Field.

It also was the 22nd of what would become 52 consecutive sold out games through the end of the season at Cleveland's new ballpark.

Knoblauch hit his homer off Tavarez, who had had three shaky outings in a row. Still, Hargrove would not complain about the rookie reliever.

"He's been very good for us all year," the manager said of Tavarez. "Am I worried about him? No. He's got good stuff. The Julian we saw pitch until the last three outings is the Julian we know. He will come around."

## MARTINEZ: "MR. NO-DECISION'

It was another unrewarded good start for Martinez, who began to refer to himself as "Mr. No-Decision." He left after six innings with a 5-3 lead in quest of a 10th victory in 11 decisions. Instead, Martinez got nothing to show for his efforts as the Twins tied the score with three hits off Plunk in the seventh.

It stayed that way until Knoblauch spoiled it in the ninth, and the Indians' last gasp fell short after Thome and Ramirez walked with one out.

Scott Wadkins replaced Pat Mahomes and his first pitch was popped up by Alomar. Then Dave Stevens came in and fired a called third strike past pinch hitter Herbert Perry, ending the game.

Despite the loss, the *Plain Dealer* came up with what had to be considered the epitome of positive thinking.

Despite the fact that 58 games remained on the schedule, Ohio's Largest Newspaper introduced the Indians' "Magic Number" for clinching the division title.

It was 42 on the morning of August 2.

It meant that any combination of 42 Indians' victories and losses by the second place team - on this date Milwaukee and Kansas City were tied, 17 1/2 games behind Cleveland - would clinch a place in the postseason playoffs for the Tribe for the first time in 41 years.

If anybody feared that the PD's mention of the "magic number" would jinx the Indians, they blasted the superstition the next night, mauling the Twins, 12-6. Sorrento hit his second grand slam of the season, Belle blasted his 21st and 22nd homers, giving him three in two games, and Lofton drove in three runs with three hits, two them triples.

And, for good measure, Clark, who forfeited his place in the starting rotation when the Indians acquired Hill, relieved Ogea in the third inning with the score tied, 5-5, and held the Twins to one run on five hits in 5 1/3 innings.

Then Hill, the man who replaced Clark, won his first game in the AL the next night, August 3, beating Minnesota, 6-4, though it did not come easily. The Indians battled back from a 3-1 deficit with four runs in the sixth inning for their 29th comeback victory of the season.

"The guys in the dugout kept telling me, 'Just hold 'em right there and we'll get 'em back,'" said Hill. "When a pitcher knows he is going to be supported by an offense this talented, it lets him relax."

Plunk gave up a run but clung to the lead in relief of Hill in the seventh and eighth. Then Mesa made it look easy in the ninth when his fast ball was clocked by radar guns at 98 miles per hour. He struck out two and retired the Twins in order on only 10 pitches to remain perfect with a 30th save.

Twenty-four hours later, upon the arrival of the now all-but-beaten and demoralized *former* pennant-favorite Chicago White Sox to Jacobs Field, Nagy could have added an "amen" to Hill's endorsement of the Tribe's never-quit, awesome offense.

## NAGY WINS 16-HIT LAUGHER

With their AL Central Division lead now up to a season-high 18 1/2 games over Milwaukee and Kansas City, the Indians walloped the White Sox, 13-3, dumping them 23 games off the pace, and only 8 1/2 lengths out of the basement.

Ramirez led a 16-hit laugher on behalf of Nagy, who hadn't lost in six weeks, winning a sixth straight decision to boost his record to 10-4.

Ramirez drove in five runs with a grand slam, his 25th homer, and a single, and Sorrento also homered as the Indians assaulted two Chicago pitchers and an outfielder - yes, outfielder Dave Martinez who took the mound in the eighth.

Actually, Martinez was the White Sox's most effective pitcher, holding the Indians hitless (though he walked two) in his one inning stint. He came aboard when starter Jason Bere was banished in the third inning, after giving up eight runs, six hits and three walks.

Bere's successor Ron Bolton was no improvement as the Indians scored all their runs in the first five innings. In addition to their 16 hits, they also took advantage of seven walks, two wild pitches, a passed ball and one hit batter.

It was ugly, the kind of game the Indians used to lose.

"I thought it was beautiful," quipped Nagy, whose most difficult task was to stay focused. "The offense gave me such a big lead that even I couldn't screw it up. I tip my hat to our lineup. They've been doing it all year."

They had been doing it especially for Nagy. In his last eight starts the Tribe had scored 67 runs, an average of 8.4 per game.

And while Hargrove preferred to "not pay any attention" to the "Magic Number" that was posted daily by the *Plain Dealer*, the fact is, it shrunk to 38 after beating the White Sox.

Proving there was no favoritism involved, the Indians' muscle-men regally supported Hershiser the next day, August 5, bashing a season high 21 hits and six homers. Two round-trippers were slugged by Belle, and one each by Lofton, Baerga, Murray and Sorrento in an 11-7 victory that was close until the eighth inning.

Then, after the White Sox had cut their deficit to 8-7 against a still-shaky Tavarez with two runs in the seventh and one in the eighth, the Tribe erupted. It ensured a victory for Hershiser, whose record climbed to 9-5.

It also boosted the Indians lead in the AL Central to 19 1/2 games.

Though Mesa gave up a hit in the ninth, he blanked the White Sox on only seven pitches, but because of the Tribe's four run lead, it was not a save opportunity for the hard-throwing reliever.

## BELLE OFF ON A HOT STREAK

Belle, whose two homers gave him 24, ignited a three run eighth inning uprising that provided the Tribe's four run cushion.

Those two homers by Belle also gave him five in five games, launching a torrid streak of sensational power hitting that would continue through the final two months of the season. He would go on to hit 14 homers in August and 17 in September, the latter tying a record held by Babe Ruth.

Murray's homer, No. 13 and the 471st of his career, and the one by Lofton was the first for each since coming off the disabled list five days earlier. Sorrento's was his 19th, a career high for the first baseman who was regularly benched against left-handed pitchers.

The Indians' domination of the White Sox, that led to the firing of manager Gene Lamont when they lost four straight in Cleveland from May 29-June 1, came to a screeching halt on August 6.

After their pitchers had been battered unmercifully for 24 runs and 37 hits, including eight homers, the White Sox finally managed to retaliate with a 5-1 victory on August 6.

It ended the Tribe's six-game homestand, during which 251,405 fans spun the Jacobs Field turnstiles. They swelled season attendance to 1,803,066, fifth most in the 95-year history of the franchise, with 25 home dates remaining.

Though the loss hardly dented the Indians' first place margin - they still were ahead by 18 1/2 lengths over Milwaukee and Kansas City - it did provide one cause for concern for the future, if not the present.

As Martinez, who suffered the loss, his second in 11 decisions, said after the game, "I'm going to learn how to be a left-hander and pitch to this club (the Indians). I guess it's something psychic. Any left-hander seems to become Sandy Koufax against us."

It was an exaggeration, of course.

But there also was some validity to his comment.

The White Sox winner was veteran southpaw Dave Righetti, who pitched five innings, allowing only one run, though three right-handed relievers - Bryan Keyser, Matt Karchner and Roberto Hernandez - pitched the final four frames, preserving the victory.

Actually, the Indians' record against left-handers, 16-13 (.552), wasn't all that bad until it was compared to the success they had enjoyed against right-handers, 47-15 (.758). Southpaws were even more troublesome in 1994 when they beat the Tribe 19 times in 33 decisions.

Righetti's presence motivated Hargrove to drastically change his lineup, benching Thome, despite his having reached base 19 times in his last 24 plate appearances, and Sorrento, who had three homers in the previous four games.

Alomar was another regular who was benched, this time for two reasons.

## ALOMAR'S PROBLEMS CONTINUE

As had been the case all season, Tony Pena was considered Martinez's personal catcher, which some feared would cause a problem when the Indians got into postseason play. Even if that were not the case, however, Alomar continued to have leg problems and was nursing a sore left knee.

"I'm not 100 percent, and I know I won't be until the off-season when I'll have a full four months to let the knee recuperate," said the catcher, who was one of only five players remaining from the 1991 team that lost a franchise record 105 games. The others were Baerga, Belle, Kirby and Nagy (though Belle and Kirby spent part of that awful season in the minor leagues).

The Indians were presented an excellent opportunity to take the lead in the sixth inning, but this time they couldn't mount what would have been their 30th come-from-behind victory.

Trailing 2-1, Vizquel walked and Baerga singled with nobody out. That's when Keyser was rushed to Righetti's rescue and struck out both Belle and Murray. Then, after walking Ramirez, Keyser also struck out Sorrento.

The White Sox added three runs in the ninth, two off Martinez and the third off Plunk. Karchner and Hernandez blanked the Indians in their last chance.

After a day off to rest and revitalize themselves, the Indians embarked on an eastern trip that some considered would be a stern test of their mettle. They would face the Red Sox in Boston for two games, the Yankees in New

York for five, and the Orioles in Baltimore for three.

All three AL East teams had loaded up for the stretch run in hopes of making the playoffs as a division winner or wild card representative. The Red Sox acquired relievers Rick Aguilera and Mike Stanton, and infielder Dave Hollins; the Yankees picked up DH-outfielder Darryl Strawberry, in addition to Cone and Sierra; and the Orioles got pitcher Scott Erickson along with Bonilla.

The Red Sox, with a 54-39 record, led the AL East by 5 1/2 games over the Yankees (48-44), and were nine ahead of Baltimore (45-48).

As Thome said, "This may be the biggest time of the year for us. If we go on this trip and play well, Boston, New York and Baltimore are going to say, 'These guys can play.' That's important with the playoffs coming up. We've got to go into these games as if we're playing California."

Thome's reference to California was based on the fact that the Angels appeared to be running away with the AL West title, and were expected to be the opponent for the Indians in the first round of the divisional playoffs.

There also was concern on the part of Hargrove and the coaching staff because Tavarez and Plunk, the two set-up pitchers for Mesa, were still struggling.

Tavarez faltered in several of his previous seven appearances, during which he blew three save opportunities while allowing seven earned runs, 14 hits and two walks in 11 1/3 innings. The last three times Plunk was called upon, he yielded four earned runs on six hits in three innings, and also blew one save.

## INDIANS SPLIT 10 IN AL EAST

And though Hargrove was reluctant to speak for the record, he left no doubt about his unhappiness with the outfield play of Lofton, Ramirez and Belle, all of whom had been guilty recently of committing the fundamental mistake of overthrowing cutoff men.

The eastern swing proved to be a difficult journey for the Indians as they managed to merely split the 10 games, though the five losses - two in Boston, two in New York and one in Baltimore - only cost them a half-game in the AL Central standings.

When they left Cleveland on August 8 the Indians led Milwaukee and Kansas City by 17 1/2 games. When they returned to open a homestand on August 17 they were 17 lengths ahead of Milwaukee.

The Red Sox, who had won five in a row, stretched their streak to seven against the Indians as Tim Wakefield raised his record to 13-1 with a 5-1 victory. The next day Erik Hanson and Aguilera combined on a six-hitter for a 9-5 triumph.

Wakefield, establishing himself as an early candidate for the AL Cy Young Award, stymied the Tribe with his unpredictable knuckleball, though Tribe hitting instructor Charlie Manuel was unimpressed.

"Yeah, he beat us," acknowledged Manuel, "but we hit some shots off him that went right at their guys. I'll betcha he won't do it again if we meet the Red Sox in the postseason."

Wakefield didn't fool Murray in the second inning when the veteran DH whacked his 14th homer for a 1-0 Tribe lead.

Thereafter, however, it seemed everybody in the Cleveland lineup was puzzled as Wakefield hurled a complete game, six-hitter. "It was moving all over the place," Vizquel said of Wakefield's freak pitch.

Clark, who earned a return to the rotation with a good performance in relief six days earlier, was hit hard in 6 1/3 innings and took the loss.

After the game it was announced by Hart that the Indians had picked up the 1996 option on Martinez's contract, although a portion of his $4.25 million salary would be deferred over a 10 year period starting in 1997.

The Indians will pay Martinez a total of $4.125 million, but $1 million of that will be deferred in annual payments of $100,000 from 1997 through 2,007.

"Dennis has been one of the better pitchers in baseball over the last two years, and we want him back," Hart said of Martinez, whose two season record at that point was 20-8 in 43 starts since joining the Tribe in 1994.

Still undecided was Murray's future in Cleveland. His $3 million contract would expire at the end of the 1995 season. "We've got time to decide what to do," is all that Hart would say on that subject.

Plunk failed again the next night in the Indians' third straight loss and second to Boston. Plunk entered the game in the eighth inning after Hill left with the score tied, 5-5.

What transpired next was ugly. Plunk allowed four runs on two hits, three walks and a wild pitch. He struck out the first batter, Jose Canseco, but walked Mike Greenwell and Troy O'Leary.

"That set up the whole inning," said Hargrove. It sure did.

A wild pitch advanced the runners and eliminated an opportunity for a double play, then pinch hitter Matt Stairs singled to break the tie. Chris Donnels tripled for two more runs, and Luis Alicea's sacrifice fly got Donnels home.


## NOT THE TIME TO PANIC - WILEY

"We're not going to panic," pitching coach Mark Wiley said of Plunk's problems, as well as those experienced recently by Tavarez. "They've pitched too well for us to jump to a conclusion. We're just going to do what we can to get them back on track."

Neither Plunk nor Tavarez was given an opportunity to get back on the track the next day when Hargrove went to the bullpen four times - for Poole, Paul Assenmacher and twice for Mesa - as the Indians struggled, but swept a double header from the Yankees.

First, they exploded for five runs in the ninth inning against John Wetteland for a 10-9 victory that Mesa saved despite yielding two hits in the bottom of the ninth. It was the 17th time they won in their last at-bat, which took some of the luster off a three home run performance by New York catcher Mike Stanley.

Stanley unloaded in the fifth and sixth innings, the latter a grand slam, against Nagy (who was tagged for 11 hits and seven runs in 5 2/3 innings), and in the eighth off Poole.

Then the Tribe broke a 2-2 tie with a run in the seventh and two in the eighth to beat New York, 5-2. Mesa again blanked the Yankees in the ninth, this time in one-two-three order on 13 pitches.

Those two saves gave Mesa 32 in as many opportunities.

"We needed that after the way we played in Boston, and we've done this time and time again," said Hargrove, sounding like a modern day Yogi Berra. "This team has an attitude that the game is never over until it's over."

Of Mesa's performance, Hargrove said, "You've got to be a horse to save both ends of a double header, and that's what Jose is."

Tavarez was given a chance to redeem himself, and did, the next night as the Indians rallied again - for a 32nd comeback victory, and 18th in their last at-bat - to beat the Yankees, 5-4, on Lofton's 11th inning RBI double.

There was plenty of fireworks early in the game as Hargrove and Vizquel were ejected by plate umpire Darryl Cousins in the fifth inning for arguing a called strike on the shortstop.

"I deserved to get thrown out, no doubt about it," Hargrove said of his first ejection of the season. It also was Vizquel's first. "Cousins said Omar was thrown out because he threw his helmet and I thought that was unfair," added Hargrove.

It caused a drastic revamping of the Tribe infield, as Thome already was sidelined with a bruised right hand. Thus, third baseman Alvaro Espinoza moved to shortstop, Herbert Perry went from first base to third, and Sorrento came off the bench to play first.

Until then Hershiser was cruising along with a 1-0 lead. He retired 12 batters in order before running into trouble with one out in the sixth. Suddenly, the Yankees loaded the bases on singles by Wade Boggs and Bernie Williams, and a walk to Paul O'Neill.

Sierra followed with a grand slam, New York's second in two days, making it necessary for the Indians to stage another comeback, which they did in the eighth against starter Andy Pettitte and reliever Bob Wickman.

## A VICTORY FOR TAVAREZ

Back-to-back doubles by Baerga and Belle started it, followed by Ramirez's single and another double by Murray before Wickman could put out the fire. That cut the Tribe's deficit to 4-3 and set the stage for the ninth inning rally that tied the score on two walks and Baerga's single.

Tavarez, who was the Indians' fourth reliever to follow Hershiser, worked out of a jam in the 10th inning.. He became the pitcher of record when the Tribe scored in the 11th as Espinoza singled, was sacrificed to second and scored on Lofton's double off Steve Howe.

And then, of course, Mesa came on again to stop the Yankees cold on 12 pitches, striking out two, and getting his 33rd save, still without a failure.

"That man (Mesa) has been amazing this season," Hargrove said without fear of contradiction.

He could have said the same about Lofton, who was batting .429 on 21-for-49 since returning on August 1 from the disabled list where he'd been since July 21.

"I'm glad now we placed Lofton on the DL when we did because it gave Kenny the time he needed to get over his injury," said Hargrove.

The Indians dropped the next two games in Yankee Stadium, losing to Jack McDowell, 3-2, on August 12, and the next day to Cone, 4-1.

Martinez was McDowell's victim and, while the Tribe right-hander pitched well enough, scattering six hits, his record fell to 9-3, to 0-3 in his last four starts, and overall against the Yankees to 2-12.

O'Neil solo homered for New York in the fourth, but the Indians rallied for two runs in the sixth, though the 2-1 lead didn't last long. Bernie Williams homered leading off the bottom of the sixth, and it also was Williams who broke the tie in the eighth. He singled to score Boggs, who had doubled with two out.

The game was played on the anniversary of the date the players went on strike, aborting the 1994 season. Nobody had much to say about the strike, although Hargrove commented, "I don't look back at it ... nothing was solved, it was totally useless, worthless."

At the time the players walked off their jobs, the Indians were 66-47 and trailed the White Sox by one game in the AL Central. They almost certainly would have won a wild card berth had the playoffs taken place.

Alomar argued that what the players did was not a matter of greed, as had been charged.

"It's not that we wanted more money," said Alomar, "we just wanted our benefits and our pension plan to stay the way it was. I lost a lot of money. I've never seen greed lose a lot of money."

But the fact is, as Hargrove said, one year after the strike began, and more than four months after it ended, nothing was settled. There was no basic agreement between the owners and players.

And, perhaps most significant, with the exception of a couple of cities - including Cleveland, where the turnstiles clicked merrily for Tribe games - attendance was down throughout baseball as fans continued to resent the action taken by the players a year earlier.

## TRIBE LEADS AL CENTRAL BY 18

After the loss to McDowell that left the Indians with a 66-31 record, but did not reduce their 18 game lead in the AL Central, Winfield was placed on the disabled list with a sore left shoulder. It was diagnosed as a rotator cuff injury.

He was hurt on June 10 while diving back to first base. Off season surgery would be required that might end the 43-year old outfielder's outstanding, 22-year major league career.

Winfield, a certain Hall of Famer five years after his retirement, was hitting only .198 (19-for-96) with two homers and four RBI.

Replacing Winfield on the roster was southpaw reliever Alan Embree, who was called back from Buffalo for a third tour of duty with the Indians.

Cone's victory the next day came at the same time that the death of Mickey Mantle was announced, and followed a tribute to the former New York star by 45,866 fans in Yankee Stadium.

Cone won his fourth game in five starts since being acquired by the Yankees from Toronto prior to the July 31 trading deadline. He admitted to being moved by the outpouring of affection by the fans for Mantle, but said he was determined to keep himself focused for the task at hand.

Namely, "To get ahead of them by throwing first pitch breaking balls for strikes, because the Indians are the best fast ball hitting team in the league. They may also be the best fast ball hitting team I've ever seen, especially on the first pitch."

Obviously, Cone had a good memory. Two months earlier, on June 4 when he was a member of the Blue Jays, he was handed an 8-0 lead against the Indians in a game at Jacobs Field. "I got real aggressive and started challenging them with fast balls," he said.

It was not a wise thing to do. The Indians chased Cone with six runs on 13 hits in 5 2/3 innings, and won the game, 9-8, with a two-run, two-out homer by Sorrento in the last of the ninth.

"It was one of the toughest games of my career, and I learned a lesson from it," Cone said.

In this one, Cone was staked to a 2-0 lead in the first inning on a two run homer by Paul O'Neill off Clark, the Tribe's starter and loser. The Yankees added a run in the fourth when the Indians failed to make a routine double play, and Clark gave up another run on three hits in the sixth before he took a shower.

Belle's solo homer, No. 26, in the sixth was the Tribe's only run.

The second straight loss to the Yankees sliced a game off the Indians' Central Division lead, but they still were 17 lengths ahead of Milwaukee, and the major concern was who they'd meet in the playoffs.


## HILL CONTINUES TO STRUGGLE

The hoped-for rejuvenation of Hill resumed the next night, August 14, in Baltimore but, while the game's bottom line was good - a 9-6 victory over the Orioles - the former St. Louis pitcher continued to struggle.

Hill was tagged for three home runs, by Palmeiro, Bonilla and Chris Hoiles, among 10 hits in 5 1/3 innings.

"He's gotten into some bad habits, like throwing across his body," said Hargrove. "But he didn't get like this overnight, so it's going to take a while to get him straightened out."

Hill received plenty of help from his teammates - Ramirez and Espinoza homered - as the Indians overcame deficits of 4-0 and 6-5. They won the game for Assenmacher with three runs in the ninth. It was their 19th victory in their last at-bat, and the 33rd time they'd come from behind to win.

Their three runs in the ninth came on Lofton's leadoff single, an intentional walk to Baerga with one out, Ramirez's two out single for one run and Sorrento's double for two more.

Assenmacher took over in the eighth, when the Orioles threatened with Plunk on the mound, and Mesa pitched another perfect ninth against his former team for his 34th save in 34 opportunities.

They were two shy of the record for consecutive saves set by Dennis Eckersley in 1992, and were more than 24 major league teams had in total. Mesa had not allowed one earned run in his last 30 appearances, and when he pitched, the Indians' record to date was 42-1

It was Nagy's turn to get rocked by the Orioles the next night, and suddenly some questions surfaced about his status.

The one-time ace of the staff was kayoed in the first inning in an 8-3 loss on August 15, lowering his record to 10-5 with a 4.81 ERA, though the Indians' lead remained 17 games over Milwaukee.

Nagy retired the first two batters, but Palmeiro doubled, Bonilla singled, Cal Ripken and Harold Baines doubled, Hoiles walked, Jeff Huson singled, Bret Barberie walked, and Curtis Goodwin singled, after which Nagy was mercifully replaced by Ogea.

By then the Orioles were ahead, 6-1, and coasted behind Erickson.

Hart admitted, "Nagy is a little bit of a concern. Not a big one, though I think he'll come around.."

As for Hill, who was manhandled by the Orioles 24 hours earlier and also had to be the cause of at least "a little bit of a concern" to the Indians, Hart said, "There's a long way to go. There's a lot to get done before we can even think about the playoffs, and who will pitch them for us."

## CONCERN ABOUT NAGY

Hargrove was more candid in his evaluation of Nagy.

"We sure need to examine our options on what it is that Charlie is doing. After I took him out I talked to the umpire (Tim Tschida). He said that, against the first two batters, Charlie looked sharp and then, all of a sudden, his pitches flattened out.

"We've got to find out why. Balls that are down in the strike zone should not be hit that hard, unless there is no movement.

"He has not pitched one game this season with the consistency that I associate with Charlie," added Hargrove.

Nagy did not hang around to be interviewed after the game, though later he spoke briefly of his problems without shedding much light on whatever might be wrong.

"Am I concerned?" he repeated the question. "No. I'm not concerned."

When asked the cause of his problems, Nagy said, "I have no idea. I do know they are not mechanical. You can draw your own conclusions."

The next night, finally, the difficult trip through the eastern division strongholds was completed, and it was Ramirez, the 23-year old burgeoning star, who ended it on a positive note.

Despite a couple of fielding lapses that helped the Orioles fashion a tie in the fifth inning, Ramirez atoned for his misdeeds with a three run homer that helped provide the Tribe and Hershiser with an 8-5 victory.

It was Hershiser's 10th in 15 decisions, and gave the Indians a 68-33 record, maintaining their 17 game lead over Milwaukee in the AL Central.

Ramirez's homer, his 27th of the season, gave him 88 RBI, and was a shot into the left field seats. It put the Indians ahead, 8-3, and proved to be the difference as the Orioles rallied for two runs in the eighth on a home run by Hoiles off Embree, who had relieved Hershiser an inning earlier.

## MESA'S STREAK UP TO 35-FOR-35

Once again Mesa marched out of the bull pen, retired the Orioles in order on 17 pitches in the ninth, and was rewarded with his 35th save.

Despite winning, Vizquel, for one, expressed concern about the way the Indians played on the 10 game, nine day trip.

"We're not going to score five or six runs every game, and sometimes you've got to bear down and play the game right," he said. "That's the only thing that worries me about this team. We get sloppy in the field some times because we always think we're going to score five or six runs."

Vizquel knew, as did others, that the Indians had grown careless at times in the execution of basic fundamentals. He did not mention anybody by name, though there was no doubt that Ramirez and, on occasion, Lofton and Belle again were the principals.

It was a matter that Hargrove discussed several times in clubhouse meetings, though he did not speak out publicly on the subject.

Hershiser also alluded to it as he praised Ramirez as one of the game's best young hitters. "It's pretty clear that Manny isn't tied up in big games and big situations," said the pitcher.

"We've all seen him forget the count four or five times this season, but he's an awesome hitter. I'm sure his goals are to win a Gold Glove in right field, but right now he just loves to hit."

Hershiser also commented on the 5-5 split on the trip through Boston, New York and Baltimore. It was the first one this season that the Indians failed to finish on the plus side.

Hershiser, who played on three National League pennant-winning teams and in one World Series, said, "Most championship teams would be happy to play .500 on the road.

"But for us, it's a little disappointment."

# 9

## Amazing and Absolutely Wonderful...Finally

Returning home to play Milwaukee on August 17, the Indians discovered - thanks to the confidence of the *Plain Dealer* - that their magic number for clinching the American League Central Division championship had shrunk to 27, after a 5-5 trip through Boston, New York and Baltimore.

The Brewers spoiled the homecoming, however, in front 40,505 fans who comprised the 28th consecutive capacity crowd in Jacobs Field.

"It's hard to get motivated," acknowledged Omar Vizquel, in the wake of the Indians' 7-3 loss to Milwaukee, cutting their lead over the Brewers to a still-comfortable 16 games.

Still, Vizquel remained upbeat in his comments, saying, "Actually, what's happening to us now is a good thing. It should start to make us think differently. Everything was so easy for us for so long. We'd come from behind in so many games. We hit the ball great. All the pitchers threw strikes. For awhile, it looked like a dream.

"It's true, we have a comfortable lead. But we need to play better ball. All teams go through this. Maybe we're just tired. Whatever, it's good that we go through something like this now, instead of later."

Dennis Martinez failed for the fifth time to record a 10th victory, and it was the third time in the last four games that a Tribe starter was treated rudely. He yielded three homers, to Dave Nilsson, Jose Valentin and John Jaha, and was charged with five runs on seven hits in seven innings.

It definitely was not a good sign, giving greater rise to ongoing speculation that Martinez's sore left knee and right elbow were causing more trouble than he was willing to admit.

Despite the loss, Martinez reached two career milestones. It was the 521st start in his major league career, tying him with Hall of Famer Jim Palmer for 30th place on the all-time list. And Kevin Seitzer became

Martinez's 2,000th strikeout victim in the first inning, moving him into 45th place, one ahead of Billy Pierce.

## REPLACEMENT PLAYER WINS

The Brewers erupted for four runs in the second inning on Nilsson's and Valentin's homers, and the Indians couldn't come from behind for what would have been the 34th time to prevail.

It was the first major league victory for Milwaukee rookie Jamie McAndrew, who was 0-2 going into the game. A former replacement player who was re-signed by the Brewers after the strike ended on April 1, McAndrew scattered seven hits in eight innings. The Indians threatened in the ninth, but the rally fell short after they scored twice against reliever Mike Ignasiak.

Twenty-four hours later, on August 8, the amazing Jose Mesa tied the major league single season record by registering a 36th save in his 36th opportunity as the Indians continued their runaway in the AL Central Division race, beating Milwaukee, 7-5.

He did it with 11 pitches - one of which was lashed for a single by B.J. Surhoff with two out - in the ninth inning, enabling Mesa to equal the mark established by future Hall of Famer Dennis Eckersley in 1992.

While accepting congratulations for another splendid performance, Mesa praised two of his set-up relievers, Jim Poole and Eric Plunk, who held the Brewers scoreless in the seventh and eighth.

"I owe a lot to those guys," said Mesa. "It makes my job so much easier knowing that I'm only going to pitch one inning."

Albert Belle was another who kept his hot streak going. The Indians left fielder led off a three-run fourth inning with his 27th homer, and ninth in the last 21 games, dating back to July 28. During that stretch Belle batted .405 (34-for-84) and drove in 20 runs.

Disconcerting, despite the victory, was the fact that Mark Clark was hammered early in the game, giving up five runs in the second inning before settling down and holding the Brewers scoreless through the sixth.

The Indians rallied to tie the game in the fourth, and went ahead to stay in the fifth after Vizquel beat out a bunt single and came around to score on throwing errors by Surhoff and Joe Oliver.

"Omar is a very daring, very aggressive base-runner," Manager Mike Hargrove said, giving a large share of credit for the victory to Vizquel. "When you've got a guy out there with larceny in his soul, those kinds of things - wild throws - can happen."

Then it became Eddie Murray's opportunity to step into the spotlight.

The veteran first baseman-designated hitter whose bat had cooled off since getting his 3,000th hit on June 30 and spending four weeks on the disabled list, smashed a home run leading off the ninth inning to provide the Tribe with a 4-3 victory over the Brewers.

It was the Indians' sixth game ending homer, and was the 20th time they'd won in their last at-bat, but only the first at home since July 18. Earlier in the season, Manny Ramirez hit two game-ending homers, and one each by

Paul Sorrento, Belle, and Jim Thome.

## NO COMPLAINTS BY HARGROVE

"I'm sure the fans enjoy these late inning heroics a lot more than we do," said Murray. "We'd like to win these kind of games a little earlier."

So would Hargrove, though he made it very clear, "I'm not complaining."

Neither were Ken Hill, Alan Embree, Julian Tavarez, Paul Assenmacher and Eric Plunk - especially Plunk, who got credit for the victory.

Hill pitched well through the first six innings, surrendering two runs on six hits, one of them a solo homer by Jaha in the third. The Brewers' other run was a homer by Surhoff off Assenmacher in the eighth, nullifying the 3-0 lead the Indians took in the first inning.

Embree bailed out Hill in the seventh, after Milwaukee had loaded the bases with one out, and induced Valentin to line into a double play. Then it was Tavarez's turn. He came on, walked Jeff Cirillo to re-load the bases, but got out of it unscathed by getting Seitzer on a fly to Ramirez.

After Surhoff greeted Assenmacher with a game-tying homer leading the seventh, Nilsson grounded out and Plunk stalked to the mound, He retired five batters in order, three on strikes, through the ninth, setting the stage for Murray's homer off Bill Wegman on a 2-and-0 count leading off the bottom of the ninth.

The brief homestand against Milwaukee, the Indians' closest competitor in the AL Central, came to an end on August 20 with another victory - and another contribution by Mesa to the team's highlights film.

Mesa saved his 37th game in this, his 37th opportunity, breaking the major league record he'd shared with Eckersley, as the Indians beat the Brewers, 8-5. It was another come-from-behind victory, their 35th of the season and 21st in their last at-bat.

Mesa's record was all the more remarkable when it's remembered that he did not register save No. 1 until May 12, in the Tribe's 14th game. Prior to that Mesa had been credited with only four saves, two in the major leagues, in a professional baseball career that began in 1982.

## MESA: "PEOPLE LOVE ME HERE"

"It's probably the most improbable thing anyone could imagine," is the way Hargrove marveled about Mesa's record.

Mesa exulted in the attention heaped upon him. He said, "People love me here," and he was right.

But Mesa was only partly right when he added, "The fans are not cheering for me, they're cheering for the team."

The Indians won it with five runs in the bottom of the eighth, wiping out a 5-3 deficit. The uprising was triggered by Carlos Baerga who led off with a triple. Belle reached on a fielder's choice when the Brewers tried but failed to retired Baerga at the plate. Murray struck out, but Jim Thome walked, loading the bases.

Then, after Ramirez flied to right for the second out, Paul Sorrento, in an 0-for-18 slump, came through with a double that tied the score and sent Thome to third.

Rob Dibble replaced knuckleballer Steve Sparks on the mound and was greeted by pinch hitter Wayne Kirby, who singled for two more runs. Then Vizquel said hello to second reliever Angel Miranda with a single for the Tribe's fifth run of the inning and eighth of the game.

Mesa walked a batter, but struck out two in the ninth for the record-setting save. It provided Tavarez with his eighth victory in nine decisions after he pitched a hitless, two-strikeout eighth inning.

Belle continued his torrid hitting in the game, going 2-for-4, including his 28th homer, extending his consecutive game streak to 14, a career high. Ramirez also smashed his 28th homer.

Still, there was a downside to the game. Charles Nagy struggled again, yielding five runs on 10 hits in 6 2/3 innings, leaving with the Indians trailing, 5-3.

When asked what was wrong, Nagy replied, "I'm fine. I've just got to stop reading the newspaper."

But nobody else was grumbling. When the Indians flew to Toronto the next morning, they owned a 71-34 record for a season-high 37 games over .500, a 19 length lead - also a season high - over the Brewers, and their magic number was down to 21.

That night, August 22, it got even better.

Sorrento hammered a homer off Edwin Hurtado, becoming the fourth Tribesman to hit 20 (Belle, Ramirez and Thome were the others), and the Indians won, 7-3, boosting Orel Hershiser's record to 11-5

Sorrento, who only played against right-handed pitchers, also doubled for a run in the second inning, when the Indians took a 4-0 lead, and though he was hitting only .244, his 20 homers and 68 RBI were career highs.

It all came undone for the Tribe the next night as, first, Martinez left the game with an aching elbow and, then, Thome committed a throwing error in the bottom of the ninth to snatch a defeat from the jaws of victory.

The Indians lost, 5-4, when Joe Carter beat out an infield single with one out. With two out, Tomas Perez grounded to Thome, whose throw to first base was wild. It allowed Carter to score from first base, costing Tavarez, the Tribe's third reliever, a second loss in 10 decisions..

## MARTINEZ TRIES AGAIN

It was a tie game before Thome's costly error, but as he said, "Who knows what might have happened. I could have gotten the guy out and we would have gone into extra innings, and we could have scored some runs with the power we have.

"I just didn't do the job," added a crestfallen Thome, who had entered the game as a pinch hitter for Alvaro Espinoza in the top of the ninth.

Martinez, seeking for the seventh time his 10th victory after going 9-0, remained stuck at 9-4. He pitched six innings and left with a 4-2 lead that the Indians fashioned against Al Leiter.

Vizquel delivered his fifth homer of the season - only two fewer than he hit in six previous major league seasons combined - and Ramirez took over the team lead with his 29th homer. It broke a tie with Belle, who went 0-for-3, snapping his 15 consecutive game hitting streak.

Of the strained ligament in his right elbow, Martinez said, "I felt it, but it wasn't too bad ... I'll be able to make it through September. Everything will be all right."

The loss to the Blue Jays left the Indians' record at 15-13 since July 25, their worst stretch of the season. "They don't call these the dog days for nothing," said Hargrove. "It's hard to kick yourself into gear sometimes."

However it happened, somebody kicked the Indians into gear there-after as, after that 5-4 loss to the Blue Jays, they embarked upon a nine game winning streak between August 23 and September 1. It boosted their record to 81-35 - 46 games over .500! - and a 21 1/2 length lead over Kansas City.

It also trimmed their magic number to eight.

First, they beat the Blue Jays, 6-5, as the Indians' bullpen again came through in the clutch to rescue Clark, still struggling to regain his 1994 form.

Jim Poole, Tavarez, Alan Embree and Mesa combined to hurl 4 1/3 scoreless innings, with Poole getting credit for the victory and Mesa increas-ing his open-end record by racking up his 38th save in 38 opportunities.

It gave the relief corps a combined 26-11 won-lost mark with 42 saves.

"If these guys aren't the best, somebody will have to prove to me that there is a better bullpen in baseball," said pitching coach Mark Wiley.

With the Indians trailing, 5-3, in the sixth, Belle led off with his 29th homer off rookie right-hander Giovanni Carrara, who proceeded to load the bases on two walks and a single by Thome.

The next two batters, Sorrento and Tony Pena, swung at first pitches and popped both of them up, setting the stage for a gift by umpire Durwood Merrill.

Kenny Lofton sent a grounder up the middle. Second baseman Roberto Alomar dashed to his right and made a diving stop of the ball, flipping it back to shortstop Tomas Perez covering second.

Television replays clearly showed that Perez stepped on second forc-ing Ramirez for what should have been the inning ending third out. But Merrill called Ramirez safe, allowing Murray to score the tying run.

Moments later reliever Paul Menhart flung a wild pitch that enabled Thome to race home with the go-ahead and, as it turned out, deciding run.

"Everybody in this game is human," said Baerga. "Players make mis-takes, umpires make mistakes. Umpires have a second to call you safe or out. Manny (Ramirez) did a good job of hustling down there because he knows Robby (Alomar) has good range." The Indians failed to score after they loaded the bases in the seventh, but it didn't matter because the Blue Jays got only one hit off the quartet of Tribe relievers the rest of the way. Mesa walked one batter, but needed only 11 pitches to wrap it up.

## SWEEPING THE TIGERS AND JAYS

It brought the Indians home where they swept Detroit in three games, 6-5, 6-2 and 9-2, and the Blue Jays in four, 9-1, 4-1, 4-3 and 6-4, then ran their winning streak to nine with a 14-4 trouncing of the Tigers in Detroit.

It was obvious by then that nothing would stop the Indians, at least not until they got into postseason play, though Hargrove continued to insist, "We haven't won anything yet ... we've got to keep going."

And keep going they did - although Mesa finally faltered, proving that he is, after all, only human. Not super human.

It happened on August 24, in the opener of the Detroit series at Jacobs Field in front of 41,676, the 32nd consecutive capacity crowd, raising the Indians' season attendance total over the two million mark for only the third time in franchise history, to 2,010,740.

After Belle celebrated his 29th birthday by bashing two more homers, giving him 31, and a single, the Indians took a 5-3 lead into the eighth inning when Assenmacher replaced starter and apparent winner Hill.

In 25 games in August, Belle batted .426 (40-for-94) with 12 homers and 24 RBI. He also became the first Tribesman to hit 30 or more homers in four consecutive seasons, and the 32nd in baseball history to do it.

Assenmacher struck out Bob Higginson, the only batter he faced, and Plunk was called in to face right-handed hitting Travis Fryman, who promptly homered, cutting the Indians' margin to one. When Cecil Fielder singled, Plunk was lifted in favor of Embree, who gave up another hit, but managed to prevent further scoring.

Which set the scene for Mesa in the ninth. He got Milt Cuyler to pop out, and John Flaherty to fly out, but couldn't retire Chad Curtis, who lofted Mesa's first pitch into the right field stands, tying the game at 5-5.

It was the first time in 38 opportunities that Mesa failed to protect a lead and earn a save.

When Mesa retired Higginson, his night's work was finished, though the Tribe's wasn't.

Tavarez pitched the 10th and 11th innings, retiring all six batters he faced, and got credit for the victory, his ninth in 11 decisions, when Alomar socked his homer with one out in the bottom of the 11th off Felipe Lira.

It was the Indians' 22nd victory of the season in their last at-bat, and the 37th time they came from behind to prevail.

After spoiling Mesa's perfect record, Curtis said of the pitcher, "He throws hard enough that if the ball hits my bat it could go out ... and it did."

It was only the second home run allowed by Mesa this season, the first earned run against him since June 8, and ended his streak of 18 1/3 scoreless innings.

"I hated to see his streak come to an end, though we all knew it would end sometime," said Hargrove.

"Nothing Jose does surprises me anymore, and if you had told me during spring training that, on August 25, Mesa would have 38 saves, I would have said that you are crazy."

After the game, with the Indians magic number down to 17 and only 35 games left in the regular season, the club was given permission by the American League to print postseason tickets for the first time since 1959.

## BLAME THE MESSENGER

Nagy, who claimed he was going to "stop reading the newspaper" in order to correct his pitching problems, might have done so - though a meeting he held with Hargrove probably had more to do with his success against the Tigers in a 6-2 victory on August 26.

The two principals acknowledged the session, but neither would reveal what took place behind the locked doors of the manager's office.

"I don't want to elaborate," said Nagy. "It helped me out a great deal, but that's all I want to say."

"It's a state secret ... I could tell you, but I'd have to kill you," quipped Hargrove. It was easy to make light of the meeting after Nagy struck out a career high 12 batters, including Cecil Fielder twice, and scattered nine hits over 6 2/3 innings, hiking his record to 11-5.

So what was wrong with Nagy in the past - aside from the fact that he was reading the newspaper too much?

Pena, the veteran catcher who was behind the plate for Nagy, said: "You could see Charlie was confident and in command. He threw more fast balls, which made his breaking ball and split finger (fast ball) better. He's always had a good breaking ball, but he was throwing it too much."

Said Nagy, who was 7-1 in his previous 12 starts and had a 5-0 lead after four innings, "In the past, I'd get behind hitters and try to make the perfect pitch, but I'd usually end up walking them.

"Today I just said, 'If I fall behind a batter, I'm going to throw my fastball. If they hit, they hit it.'"

They didn't, and the rampaging Indians' magic number shrunk to 16 - except that Hargrove didn't want to know about it, and he didn't want it posted on the scoreboard.

"Not until I give the OK," said the manager.

And when might that be? "I'm not going to say," Hargrove told Tribe publicity director Bart Swain. "It bothers me when things like that are mentioned too soon. As far as I'm concerned, there is no 'magic number.'"

Another sparkling performance by Hershiser followed, and John Hart's decision to sign the free agent pitcher last spring looked better every outing.

This time Hershiser, a.k.a. "The Bulldog," gave up two runs on four hits, and struck out four in six innings.

The only negative aspect was that he walked six, though it didn't matter as the Indians surged to a 7-0 lead in the first three innings, and were ahead, 9-0, before the Tigers scored twice in the sixth.

Hershiser's 12 victories matched the most he'd won in six years, since he was 12-4 for the Dodgers in 1993. "When we got guys like Orel and Dennis (Martinez), the idea was for them to keep us in games, which is exactly what they're doing," said Hart. Sorrento drilled his 21st homer in the fifth inning. Poole, who struck out five of the six batters he faced, and Assenmacher blanked the Tigers from the sixth through the ninth in what turned out to be a laugher for the Tribe, completing the three-game sweep.

It was another laugher the next night, August 28, when the Indians erupted for a 9-1 victory over the Blue Jays. The beneficiary pitcher in this one was Chad Ogea, starting in place of Martinez, who needed more rest because of his ailing elbow and aching knee.Ogea, the rookie right-hander spent most of the first half of the season at Class AAA Buffalo,

Other highlights of the one-sided victory over the once-strong Blue Jays:

* Lofton went 4-for-4, scored two runs, stole a base, giving him 32 for the season, and made an outstanding catch in center field to steal an extra base hit from Paul Molitor in the fifth inning.

* Ramirez became the second youngest Indian to hit 30 homers in a season (Hal Trosky was 21 when he hit 35 homers in 1934).

* Ogea held the Blue Jays to one run on seven hits in 5 2/3 innings, raising his record to 7-3.

* Murray got three hits in four at-bats, including his 16th homer of the season, and 474th of his career, one behind Stan Musial and Willie Stargell in 18th place on the all-time list.

Sorrento also homered, No. 22, for the Tribe.

"Consistency is the mark of a championship team, and we've been consistent," said Lofton.

## MAGIC NUMBER 13 AND COUNTING

And, whether Hargrove wanted to know about it or not, the Indians' magic number shrunk to 13.

Clark, trying desperately to ensure, not only his place in the starting pitching rotation, but also, a spot on the 25 man playoff roster, took a giant step in that direction on August 29, leading the Indians to a sixth straight victory.

Hurling the Tribe's first complete game since July 21, Clark fired a three-hitter to beat Toronto, 4-1.

"This was probably the best command I've ever had of all my pitches since I've been in the major leagues," said Clark, who broke into the major leagues with St. Louis in 1991. "It's the best I've felt since last year. I know this is no time to slack off."

The victory, which was the Indians' 12th in 15 games and would be the first of four in a row over Toronto, impressed Blue Jays' slugger and former Cleveland outfielder Joe Carter.

"Right now," he said after the game, "these guys (the Indians) can do no wrong. This team just seems destined. You can't stand in their way."

Molitor, on the other hand, said he was "surprised" that the Indians were doing so well, and gave most of the credit for their success to the discovery of Mesa as the AL's premier closer.

"I believed the Indians could be a contender, but for them to be 40 (actually 43) games over .500 and the best team in baseball is a surprise," he said. "Mesa is the guy who got them over the hump. I'd love to see an Atlanta-Cleveland World Series just because of Atlanta's pitching."

The victory also boosted the Tribe's lead over second place Milwaukee to 20 1/2 games, largest of the season.

In addition to Mesa, another of the reasons for the Indians' success - for their seemingly being "destined," as Carter said - might have been what happened before the game.

Hargrove ordered the players to report to Jacobs Field at 4 p.m., an hour earlier than usual "to work on fundamentals - relays, cutoffs, bunt situations, and a few other things," he said.

Why? "Because I thought it was necessary," was Hargrove's terse response. Clark, whose record climbed to 8-5. was competing against Hill for the fourth and final spot in the rotation for the postseason. Ironically, Hill also was acquired from the Cardinals. He came to Cleveland in a July 27 trade for three minor leaguers. The other three places in the rotation were filled by Orel Hershiser, Dennis Martinez and Charles Nagy.

Hargrove acknowledged that the choice between Clark and Hill would be difficult. "He (Clark) has forced us to do a lot of thinking on it," said the manager. "It is hard to decide, but that's the way I'd rather have it. Mark needed to have a strong game, and he did."

## THE INDIANS: A TEAM OF DESTINY

The Blue Jays' only run was Molitor's 13th homer with one out in the ninth. Then Clark got Robby Alomar to ground out, and struck out Carter to end the game.

The only other hits allowed by Clark were singles by Carter in the second, and Green in the eighth.

Toronto's Juan Guzman, activated from the disabled list prior to the game, was almost as good. The Indians scored an unearned run in the fourth, two in the seventh when they were helped by another Toronto error, and added one in the eighth as Murray and Thome each got two hits.

There was a negative aspect to the victory, however. Sorrento suffered a hamstring injury during a play at second base in the eighth inning and was forced out of the game.

Carter's words - saying that the Indians appeared to be "destined" to win, were even more prophetic the next night when Belle delivered again, this time with his 32nd homer of the season. It came with two out in the 14th inning off Tony Castillo to beat the Blue Jays, 4-3, ending a four hour, 52 minute marathon.

It gave the Tribe a 10-0 record in extra inning games and was the team's 23rd victory in its final at-bat.

"The more improbable it gets, the more they do it," Hargrove said of his players. Again, he was right.

The Indians gave up a tie-breaking run in the top of the 14th off

Assenmacher, but rallied for two in the bottom of the inning. The tying run came around after Lofton led off with a double, was bunted to third and scored on a sacrifice fly. Four pitches later, with the count 2-and-1, Belle homered, the ball flying into the bleachers in left-center field.

The victory added another game on the Indians' all but mathematically-insurmountable lead in the AL Central - with Milwaukee falling into a second place tie with Kansas City, they trailed the Tribe by 21 1/2 lengths with 30 games remaining.

Assenmacher was the fifth pitcher to work in relief of Martinez, who failed again - despite working seven strong innings - to win a 10th game and first since July 21. Pitching with seven days rest, Martinez gave up two runs, only one of which was earned, on six hits in seven innings.

He left with a 2-2 tie and the Blue Jays were blanked by Plunk, Embree, Tavarez and Mesa, before Assenmacher entered in the 14th.

"We made it clear to Dennis that the first sign of tightness or any kind of change in his arm that we were going to get him out of there," said Hargrove. "But the reason we took him out was that he'd made 105 pitches and, under the circumstances, we felt that was enough."

When Hargrove talked about what appeared to be the "improbability" of winning, it wasn't totally in praise of the Indians, as they committed several base-running blunders without which the victory could have been achieved much earlier and easier.

"We weren't too smart on the bases tonight, but then, neither was Toronto, so I guess it was kind of a wash," said Hargrove, pleased to have won the game, but obviously unhappy about the mistakes that made it more difficult.

Twenty-four hours later Belle did it again to the Blue Jays. His two-run homer in the 10th inning broke another tie and enabled the Indians to sweep the series with a 6-4 victory credited to Mesa.


## "ALBERT CAN DO ANYTHING"

It was Belle's third game-ending homer of the season, 17th in the month of August, and was a shot, off a 1-and-1 pitch from Jimmy Rogers. The ball flew deep into the plaza beyond the left field wall.

"Nothing Belle does surprises me ... but you'll have to ask him if he went to the plate trying to hit a home run," said Hargrove. But nobody did as this was one of those times that Belle did not feel like talking to the media after the game.

Others did. As Baerga remarked, "When Albert gets hot, he can do anything ... and he's very hot right now."

It was Baerga who had been given the night off, but came on as a pinch hitter in the ninth to send the game into overtime with a sacrifice fly that scored Kirby with a run that tied the game.

Kirby was running for Ramirez, who started the inning with a single off Danny Cox. Alomar followed with a double and, with one out, Baerga batted for Alvaro Espinoza and lofted a deep fly to center field off Castillo, who'd replaced Cox.

The Indians also were aided by the erratic pitching of Toronto's Ed Hurtado, and some equally erratic work behind the plate by his catcher, Sandy Martinez.

Hurtado flung four wild pitches, the last of which enabled the Tribe to tie the game at 3-3 in the sixth, and Martinez was charged with two passed balls.

Hill, hoping to convince Hargrove that he should be the Tribe's fourth starter in the postseason, started and pitched nine strong innings. He yielded all of Toronto's runs, three on four hits in the third, and the fourth on Mike Huff's double and Martinez's single that put the Blue Jays ahead again by one in the seventh.

After Baerga's sacrifice fly tied it, Mesa made a rare appearance in a game in which the Indians were not ahead and retired the Blue Jays on 11 pitches in the 10th. That set the stage for Belle, who also stroked his 42nd double of the season and raised his RBI total to 94.

It put the finishing touches on a sensational streak by Belle, who was named the AL's "Player of the Month" for August during which he hit .381 (45-for-118) with 14 homers and 30 RBI.

He was the second Tribesman to win the award as Ramirez was the AL's "Player of the Month" for May.

As for the Indians' amazing propensity for last at-bat theatrics that had now accounted for 24 victories, almost a third of the team's total, and 11 in extra innings, Alomar admonished, "Don't call it luck."

"We expect to win every time because we believe in ourselves. A lead of a couple of runs is not enough against us."

Then Alomar suggested, "Maybe they should make Major League III and, this time, use real players."

And Hill, who a month earlier came from the downtrodden St. Louis Cardinals, said, "It's crazy. I've never seen anything like this. As a pitcher I just try to keep the score close because I know something is going to happen."

The victory was the Indians' eighth straight and ended their seven game homestand in front of 41,746 fans who comprised the 38th consecutive capacity crowd at Jacobs Field and boosted season attendance to 2,259,193, second most in franchise history with 14 home dates remaining.

It also maintained the Indians' 21 1/2 game margin over Kansas City, which had taken possession of second place in the AL Central, and reduced their magic number to nine.


## WINFIELD AND AMARO RETURN

After the game the Indians announced the 25 players they were making eligible for postseason play. Conspicuous by his absence from the list was future Hall of Famer Dave Winfield.

However, as Hart pointed out, Winfield, as well as Ruben Amaro - both of whom would be activated from the disabled list the following day, September 1, when rosters would be expanded to 40 - could be added to the playoff roster if somebody was injured in the final month.

Hart also was busy up until the August 30 midnight deadline trying to make a deal for an experienced right-handed batter to strengthen the Indians against left-handed pitchers.

Mentioned most prominently were Alan Trammel and Juan Samuel of Detroit, Molitor of Toronto, and switch-hitter Rickey Henderson of Oakland, though their price tags were higher than Hart was willing to pay.

As Alomar said the night before, it wasn't luck propelling the Indians to their first pennant in 41 years, to which the Detroit Tigers would have agreed in the wake of a 14-4 loss to the Tribe on September 1.

It came about after the Tigers had taken a 4-0 lead in the fourth inning against Nagy, the eventual winner.

Again, it was Belle who swung the most potent bat, with a grand slam and a double, as the Indians went ahead, 5-4, in the fourth, and turned the game into a laugher with two runs in the fifth, five more in the eighth and two in the ninth.

It was following Thome's 22nd homer of the season leading off the fourth inning that seemed to ignite the Tribe, as Tigers right-hander Jose Lima threw a high and tight pitch that hit Belle on the wrist.

Belle took a couple of menacing steps toward the mound and shouted at Lima, then took first base - but didn't wait there for long.

Murray and Ramirez followed with singles, and Alomar blasted his homer following a wild pitch by Lima, who was then excused for the night.

As it turned out, nobody was any better for the Tigers as four relievers were treated equally rudely by the rampaging Indians who finished with 21 hits, including four by Espinoza, who filled in at second base for Baerga..

Finally the Indians pennant express was slowed - not stopped - by the Tigers on September 4, after nine straight victories and 15 in 18 games. Felipe Lira and John Doherty combined on a five-hitter to beat the Tribe, 3-2, despite another good outing by Hershiser.

Hershiser lost for only the first time since July 25, during which he'd won five games - but probably didn't pitch as well in any of them as in this one. Hershiser called it "one of my best starts in the last five or six," but added, "There's no way you'll catch me complaining about this team."

## VIZQUEL IN THE MIDDLE

Vizquel played a prominent role in the game, cracking his eighth home run - one more than he'd hit in five previous major league seasons put together - and drove in the Tribe's first run with a sacrifice fly.

But the Gold Glove shortstop also committed a costly first inning error, only his eighth of the season, that led to an unearned run that proved to be the margin of difference for the Tigers.

Vizquel also was the focal point of an argument between the Tigers and Indians that almost turned into a brawl. He was accused of trying to "show up" Fielder on a play in the seventh inning and was challenged by Fryman.

Both benches emptied and there was a lot of gesturing, but cooler heads prevailed, order was soon restored, and the Tigers were able to cling to the lead they produced an inning earlier on a walk and Flaherty's two out double.

And though the Indians lost, their magic number to clinch the AL Central title shrunk by one to seven, and their lead over second place Kansas City remained at 21 1/2 as the Royals were beaten by Texas.

Mesa proved once again - or the Tigers did on September 3 - that he is only human, though the end result was still good for the Tribe.

For only the second time all season Mesa blew a save opportunity, both of them at the hands of the Tigers, as he served a grand slam to former Tribesman Ron Tingley in the ninth inning.

It wiped out Detroit's four-run deficit and tied the game at 8-all, though Ramirez and Vizquel took Mesa off the hook an inning later, making him and the Indians a 9-8 winner.

Obviously unaccustomed to committing such a dastardly deed, Mesa was uncommunicative after the game, though his silence might have been motivated by things Hargrove said to him.

"I'm not talking to reporters anymore," said Mesa. "I'm not mad at them, I'm mad at myself."

It was Hargrove's opinion that Mesa didn't throw his best fast ball to Tingley and, in effect, scolded the ace fireman for taking Tingley lightly.

"There's nothing physically wrong with his arm ... I'm not worried, but it is a concern," is the way Hargrove summarized his thoughts on Mesa. "Let's just say it was an unfortunate pitch selection."

With the exception of home runs by Fielder, No. 28 in the fourth inning, and rookie Phil Nevin, his first in the eighth, Lopez was pitching well. He was en route to what would have been his first victory in 1995 and fifth in parts of three seasons with the Tribe.

The Indians staked Lopez to a 4-0 lead in the first, two of the runs coming on Belle's double, giving him 100 RBI for the fourth straight season. The Tribe's margin climbed to 5-0 in the third before the Tigers got on the board with three runs in the fourth. Belle cracked his 35th homer leading the fifth, and the Tribe added two more in the seventh for an 8-3 cushion.

After Nevin's solo homer in the eighth, Lopez gave up a single and two walks with one out in the ninth, which signaled the entry of Mesa.

His second pitch jumped off the bat of Tingley - who'd hit six homers in parts of seven previous seasons with four other teams in the major leagues - and flew into the right field stands, tying the score.

## HARGROVE'S HUGE GAMBLE

The Tigers didn't stop there, re-loading the bases on two singles and an intentional walk, although Mesa and the Indians survived the threat to win in the 10th, thanks to a good play by Thome.

The intentional walk brought Fielder to the plate in a huge gamble by Hargrove. "Cecil doesn't run well ... I knew if he hit the ball anywhere on the ground we'd have a chance to turn two," said the manager.

Hargrove proved to be right, but not before Fielder - or Mesa, take your choice - provided one more reason for concern.

The count went full on the Tigers' mammoth first baseman. Another pitch outside the strike zone would be ball four and Fielder would walk, forcing in the winning run for Detroit.

Instead, Fielder swung at the 3-and-2 pitch and bounced it toward third. Thome backhanded the grounder, fired to Baerga to force Fryman at second, and Baerga's relay to first arrived in plenty of time to double Fielder.

It ended the uprising, and gave the Indians another chance to win, which they did as Ramirez doubled and Vizquel singled with two out.

But Mesa and the Indians still weren't home free. Tony Clark and Bobby Higginson led the Tigers' 10th with back-to-back singles, and finally - *finally* - Mesa reverted to form, again with the help of his infielders.

He struck out Nevin, then induced Samuel to ground to Vizquel who started a 6-4-3 double play that ended the game, allowing Hargrove a huge sigh of relief.

The pesky Tigers won the next night, 3-2, behind rookie right-hander Clint Sodowsky, but it served only to delay the inevitable, which by then, with the Indians' magic number down to five, even Hargrove was willing to concede.

Despite the loss, Clark turned in another good performance, hurling a four-hitter for his second consecutive complete game, strengthening his bid to be included on the four-man starting rotation for the postseason playoffs.

Except for one inning, Clark was nearly perfect, though his record fell to 8-6. All the hits he allowed were delivered in the fourth - a leadoff double by Chris Gomez, Fielder's one-out single, Tony Clark's triple for two runs, Higginson's sacrifice fly for a third run, a walk and Scott Fletcher's single before the inning ended with two runners aboard.

Clark went from there to retire the final 13 batters in order as efficiently as he had set down the 10 Tigers who preceded the uprising.

But his teammates couldn't help this time. They were held to three hits - their lowest offensive total of the season - by Sodowsky and four relievers.

Both of the Indians' runs came in the third on a walk, Baerga's double, an error, and fielder's choice.

"It was strange, what happened (in the fourth inning)," said Clark. "I started flying open in my delivery. Then (pitching coach) Mark Wiley told me to keep driving toward the plate and when I did, everything was all right again."

## MARTINEZ FINALLY WINS AGAIN

The next stop on the Indians pennant express was Milwaukee. There they defeated the Brewers twice, 7-3, as Martinez finally got his 10th victory, and 12-2, as Hill all but matched Clark's last two performances in their head-to-head battle for the final place in the postseason pitching rotation.

By beating Milwaukee in the first game on September 5, Martinez won for the first time in eight starts, officially eliminating the Brewers from the AL Central race, and cutting the Indians' magic number against Kansas City to four.

Hargrove called it "a typical Dennis Martinez game ... he was as sharp as he's been in awhile." It also helped that the Indians supported Martinez with 15 hits, including four - for four RBI - by Murray. Martinez was 0-4 with a 4.40 ERA in his previous seven starts.

"The runs made a difference," said Pena, who continued as Martinez's personal battery mate. "I don't know if his elbow is 100 percent, but one thing sure, you didn't see him hang as many breaking balls as he did the last few starts."

It was the 229th victory of Martinez's career, tying him for second place with Luis Tiant among Latin American pitchers. Only Hall of Famer Juan Marichal (243-142) won more. It also made Martinez the only pitcher in the major leagues to win at least 10 games a season for the last nine years.

A 13 hit attack that helped produce a 7-1 lead in the second inning also made it easy for Hill the next night. Belle hammered another homer, his 36th, and Ramirez hit his 31st.

Though neither Hargrove nor Wiley would indicate their plans, if indeed they'd already been made, Hill was confident he would be the choice over Clark to fill the fourth position in the postseason pitching rotation.

"I feel I'm one of the four," said Hill, whose record with the Indians was 2-0. "I know they didn't trade for me to pitch in the bullpen, although, if that's my role, I'll do it to the best of my ability. I'll do anything I can to help this team win."

Hill also was confident that he and Wiley had found the flaw that had caused his early season problems with the Cardinals, for whom his record was 6-7 before the July 27 trade that brought him to Cleveland.

"We've got it corrected," he said, without explaining what it was. "Mark Wiley and I have been working hard at it. When I get into a rut now, I know what I'm doing wrong."

Hargrove didn't sound so sure that Hill was out of the woods. "He did not pitch that well tonight, but he pitched well enough to win," said the manager. "That's why we got him. To win."

The Indians, of course, would like nothing better than to be sure Hill could continue to be the kind of pitcher he was in 1994, when his record for Montreal was 16-5, rather than the 6-7 (with a 5.06 ERA) pitcher he was for St. Louis.

Hill's contract was to expire at the end of the 1995 season, and he would become a free agent if the Indians didn't re-sign him.


## BACK HOME FOR THE PARTY

Needing only a combination of two victories or losses by Kansas City, the Indians returned to Jacobs Field on September 7 to play a makeup game against Seattle which, by then, had become a contender in the AL West.

The Mariners, who had a sub-.500 record most of the season, had fought back and were taking advantage of California's collapse to advance to within 5 1/2 lengths of the Angels with 22 games remaining.

It was appropriate, then, that Nagy, whose season appeared to be going down the drain as recently as a month earlier, would beat the Mariners, 4-1, to place the Indians on the brink of their first championship since 1954.

"All I've been trying to do, and which I did tonight, was go to the mound and have some fun," said Nagy, who won his third straight start giving him the best record, 13-5, on the Tribe staff.

"There were a lot of things going wrong (a month ago), which I could take all night to talk about. But I finally decided to just let it all go and not worry about anything else."

Whatever, the results indicated that Nagy's method was good.

Nagy gave up five hits and a run, Jay Buhner's 28th homer, in seven innings before Embree and Tavarez pitched the eighth, and Mesa hurled a perfect ninth on 14 pitches for his 39th save in 41 opportunities.

It also was appropriate that the Indians' hitting star of the game was Baerga, who went 2-for-3, including his 16th homer.

Nagy and Baerga each played their first full season in the major leagues in Cleveland in 1991, when the Indians lost a franchise-record 105 games and finished 34 lengths out of first place.

The victory gave the Indians an 85-37 record for a whopping 48 games over .500, and their largest first place margin - 22 1/2 games - of the season over Kansas City.      The end of a long, *very long* wait was only 24 hours away.

Finally, after 6,422 games - 3,332 of them losses - since the Indians were swept by the New York Giants in the 1954 World Series, they would be champions again, with one more victory (or one Kansas City loss).

What's more, by winning 16 of their final 22 games they would become only the ninth team in this century to finish with a .700 percentage.

Amazing, and absolutely wonderful ... finally.

# 10

## A Dream Comes True
## Another One Begins

It was exactly 11:02 p.m., September 8, 1995, when the moment arrived that Indians fans had waited for all season - actually, for *41 seasons.*

Baltimore Orioles third baseman Jeff Huson swung at a Jose Mesa fast ball and popped it into foul territory along the third base line.

Jim Thome jogged over to where the ball would come down and 41,656 fans in Jacobs Field, all of whom already were on their feet, began to cheer in joyful expectation.

Mesa punched the air and let out a yelp as Thome reached up with his gloved hand and grabbed the foul, then leaped high in exultation as the ghosts of Chico Salmon and Leon Wagner and Ernie Camacho and, yes, even Rocky Colavito were final exorcised.

The Cleveland Indians had finally won a championship, for the first time in 41 years, since 1954, when they set an American League record with 111 victories, but were swept in the World Series by the New York Giants.

"I cried," admitted catcher Sandy Alomar, as the American League Central Division championship banner was run up the flagpole at the center field corner of the scoreboard.

As the flag was hoisted, the public address system played Garth Brooks' song, "The Dance," which had a special meaning to the Tribesmen.

It was the favorite of Steve Olin, the former ace reliever who died with teammate Tim Crews in a tragic boating accident during spring training in Winter Haven, Florida in March 1993.

"I cried, thinking about Ollie, and all we'd gone through to get where we finally were," said Alomar, one of only four players wearing Cleveland uniforms in 1991 when the Indians lost a franchise-record 105 games.

Albert Belle, Carlos Baerga and Charles Nagy were the others.

Belle, the oldest Tribesman in point of service - he played his first game for the Indians in 1989 - said it this way:

"We've been through a lot of hard times here, but the front office made some great trades and drafted some tremendous players. And then, when we got our new ballpark, everyone wanted to play here."

Baerga said, "I still can't believe that we've won this. A couple of years ago we lost almost every game, but this year it was a special team and we came to the park knowing that we were going to win every game."

Baerga also paid tribute to the fans. "I saw so many people crying," he said. "They've been waiting so long. Fans in Cleveland are different. They supported us during the strike, they supported us when we came back from the strike.

"They love baseball in this town. They love the sport and they wanted a winner this year. I am so happy we were able to give them one."

General Manager John Hart, architect of the team that clinched the division with a 23 1/2 game lead over second place Kansas City, might have been the happiest person in the park.

"Imagine!" he marveled. "Clinching on September 8th with a lead of 22-some games. This is Joe Hardy and 'Damn Yankees' all over again. I'll sign on for this every year."

Happiest of all the Tribesmen might have been coach Luis Isaac, who has worked for the club for 30 years in one capacity or another, though never as a major league player. Only Mel Harder, a member of the Indians for 36 years as a pitcher and coach, served the franchise longer.

"This is super special to me," said the 49-year old Isaac. "I've seen bad times and good times around here - but mostly bad."

## A FIRST FOR CLEVELAND

It was the second-earliest clinching since Major League Baseball went to divisional play in 1969. Only the Cincinnati Reds, who won the National League West Division on September 7, 1975, did it faster than the Indians.

And prior to the advent of division play, the 1941 New York Yankees won the AL pennant on September 4, for the earliest clinching of all-time.

It was the first championship of any kind for a Cleveland team since the Browns beat the Baltimore Colts, 24-0, for the National Football League title in 1964.

Actually, the only suspense involved in the clinching was the date. The Indians took over first place on May 11 and by the time of the All-Star break, they had a 12 1/2 game lead over Kansas City, and had been making playoff plans ever since.

When Thome caught Huson's pop foul, it finalized the a 3-2 victory, the Indians' 86th in 123 games, fourth in a row and 14th in 16 games, and gave them a 40-16 record since the All-Star break.

It also was a 13th victory in 19 decisions for Orel Hershisher, the most for him since 1989, before he suffered a shoulder injury that required reconstructive surgery in 1990.

"I wanted this game to be pressure-packed," said Hershiser. "I treated it like a Game 7, a do-or-die game. I wanted to simulate what's going to happen later this year. I think the guys on the bench did the same. They were quiet and tense."

Then, added Hershiser, "Besides, no one wanted to wait up all night to see if Kansas City lost to Seattle."

The latter was a reference to the fact that, had the Indians lost, they could have "backed in" to the title if the Royals also lost - which they subsequently did - to the Mariners.

What would happen later in the season, as Hershiser said, was that the Indians would go into a first round, best-of-five divisional playoff against either the winner of the AL East or AL West, with the best-of-seven AL Championship Series to follow for the winner, and then the World Series.

It also was appropriate that the "save" in the AL Central clincher against Baltimore was credited to Mesa, whose professional career began in the Orioles organization. It gave him 40 saves in 42 opportunities, the first of which didn't present itself until May 5, making his record all the more remarkable.

"I love this," said Mesa, who'd been a starter - though not a very good one - for the Orioles before he was acquired by the Indians on July 14, 1992, in a trade for minor league outfielder Kyle Washington. It will be remembered as one of Hart's best deals.

"I liked being a starter, but I love being a closer, and I love this team," said the 29-year old right hander, a native of the Dominican Republic.

Lost in the euphoria of the division-championship clincher was Baltimore shortstop Cal Ripken Jr. playing in his 2,132nd consecutive game, two more than the record set by Lou Gehrig from 1925-39.

## RIPKEN GOES HITLESS

Ripken went hitless in the game as the Indians scored all their runs, taking a 3-0 lead against Kevin Brown in the third inning on hits by Kenny Lofton, Baerga, and Murray, a hit batter, walk and sacrifice fly.

Hershiser allowed only four hits, giving up single runs in the fourth and seventh, when he was replaced by Paul Assenmacher, who was relieved by Julian Tavarez. Mesa stalked to the mound in the ninth and, though he walked a batter, needed only 13 pitches to put the Orioles down and clinch the victory and, in effect, the AL Central championship.

## THE AL CENTRAL CLINCHER

### Indians 3, Baltimore 2

| Baltimore | AB | R | H | BI | | Cleveland | AB | R | H | BI |
|---|---|---|---|---|---|---|---|---|---|---|
| ByAnderson lf | 4 | 0 | 0 | 0 | | Lofton cf | 4 | 1 | 1 | 0 |
| CGoodwin cf | 3 | 1 | 1 | 0 | | Vizquel ss | 1 | 0 | 0 | 1 |
| a-Bass ph | 1 | 0 | 1 | 0 | | Baerga 2b | 4 | 1 | 1 | 0 |
| 1-Brown pr-cf | 0 | 0 | 0 | 0 | | Belle lf | 2 | 0 | 0 | 0 |
| R Palmeiro 1b | 3 | 0 | 1 | 0 | | Murray dh | 4 | 0 | 3 | 2 |
| Bonilla rf | 4 | 0 | 0 | 0 | | Thome 3b | 4 | 0 | 0 | 0 |
| CRipkin ss | 0 | 0 | 0 | 0 | | MRamirez rf | 4 | 0 | 0 | 0 |
| Baines dh | 4 | 1 | 1 | 0 | | Kirby rf | 0 | 0 | 0 | 0 |
| Hoiles c | 3 | 0 | 0 | 0 | | Sorrento 1b | 4 | 0 | 0 | 0 |
| 2-Hammond pr | 0 | 0 | 0 | 0 | | SAlomar | 2 | 1 | 1 | 0 |
| Huson 3b | 3 | 0 | 1 | 1 | | | | | | |
| Alexander 2b | 1 | 0 | 0 | 1 | | | | | | |
| Barberie 2b | 1 | 0 | 0 | 0 | | | | | | |
| **Totals** | **31** | **2** | **5** | **1** | | | **29** | **3** | **6** | **3** |

| | | | | | |
|---|---|---|---|---|---|
| **Baltimore** | 000 | 100 | 100 - 2 | 5 | 1 |
| **Cleveland** | 003 | 000 | 00x - 3 | 6 | 0 |

**a:** singled for Goodwin in the 8th.
**1:** ran for Bass in the 8th. **2:** ran for Hoiles in the 9th.
**E:** Brown (2) **LOB:** Bal 6    Cle 8 **2B:** Baines (14), Huson (1), Murray (19)
**RBI:** Huson (10), Vizquel (47), Murray 2 (70) **SB:** SAlomar (1) **SF:**Vizquel
**GIDP:** Bonilla, Baerga **Runners left in scoring position:** Bal 2 (ByAnderson, Barberie):
Cle 5 (Lofton, Murray,Thome 2, Ramirez. **Runners moved up:** Thome **DP:** Bal 1
(CRipken and RPalmeiro); Cle 1 (Sorrento, Vizquel and Sorreto)

| Baltimore | IP | H | R | ER | BB | SO | | Cleveland | IP | H | R | ER | BB | SO |
|---|---|---|---|---|---|---|---|---|---|---|---|---|---|---|
| Brown L, 7-9 | 6-2/3 | 6 | 3 | 3 | 4 | 0 | | Hershiser W | 6-2/3 | 4 | 2 | 2 | 3 | 5 |
| Lee | 2/3 | 0 | 0 | 0 | 0 | 1 | | Assenmacher | 1 | 1 | 0 | 0 | 0 | 0 |
| Benitez | 2/3 | 0 | 0 | 0 | 0 | 0 | | Tavarez | 1/3 | 0 | 0 | 0 | 1 | 0 |
| | | | | | | | | Mesa S, 40 | 1 | 0 | 0 | 0 | 1 | 0 |

**Inherited runners-scored:** Lee 2-0, Assenmacher 1-0, Taverez 1-0
**HBP:**by Brown (SAlomar)
**Umpires:** H-Garcia; 1-Ford; 2-Young; 3-Reilly **T:**2:55 **Attendance:** 41,656

## THE TRIBE'S COASTER RIDE

Everything that followed for the Indians was a coaster ride - not a *roller* coaster, simply a coaster - because, by then, it was only a matter of getting ready to go on to bigger and better things.

"We don't care who we play ... the important thing is that we are going to play somebody for the right to win the pennant and go to the World Series," said Baerga.

"What we have to do is keep our intensity," said Hargrove, guarding against the possibility of a letdown as he did three months earlier when cynics feared a repeat of the infamous "June Swoon" that had destroyed so many Indians teams in the past.

Obviously, Hargrove guarded well. The Tribe won 14 of its final 21 games, including two more against the Orioles on September 9 and 10, giving them six in a row.

The day after the division-clinching celebration, during which the players showered themselves with 10 cases of champagne and 10 cases of beer - but drank very little of either - Hargrove employed a makeshift lineup to beat the Orioles, 2-1.

Chad Ogea, Alan Embree and Mesa collaborated on a two-hitter. Ogea's record climbed to 8-3 on seven solid innings, and Mesa picked up his 41st save. The Indians runs came in the second inning on a walk, Thome's triple and Alvaro Espinoza's sacrifice fly.

If anybody was hungover from the night before, it didn't show, and nobody reported it. "If somebody didn't show up, I didn't want to know about it," said Hargrove.

"I put the whole thing in a positive way," said Ogea. "I figured, 'If nothing else, we'll all be relaxed.' That was a big burden we got out of the way by clinching the division.

"But the guys on this team know it's only one step. They know we can't just roll over and take it easy because we won the division."

The Tribe completed the sweep of the Orioles the next day, beating them, 5-3, on Alomar's three run homer with one out in the eighth inning.

It was the Indians' 43rd comeback victory, the 10th time one of them hit a last-at-bat homer, and second by Alomar. He also homered in the ninth inning to beat Detroit, 6-5, August 25.

"You don't really expect it, but it's happened so often for us this year, I've come to anticipate it," said Hargrove.

And Espinoza, who filled in at shortstop for Omar Vizquel, made it clear that anyone who anticipated a letdown because the Indians had clinched their way into the division playoffs was wrong.

As he said, "The name of the game is to win. Even if it doesn't really matter, who wants to lose?"

It was the Indians' 14th consecutive victory at Jacobs Field, and boosted their won-lost record to a season-high 51 games over .500 (88-37) with a .704 winning percentage.

## TAVAREZ BECOMES THE "VULTURE"

Since 1900, only eight teams have played .700 baseball an entire season. "It's something we believe we can do, but it's not a conscious thought," said Hargrove.

"It also would be nice to finish with 100 wins, but all we're trying to do is keep the intensity, to win as much as we can without setting any goals."

Alomar's homer was a shot off Armando Benitez and followed a double by Belle and Murray's walk. It came an inning too late to make a winner of Mark Clark, who pitched well into the seventh, when Jim Poole bailed him out of a jam.

Tavarez, earning the nickname, "The Vulture," picked up the victory with nine pitches in a scoreless eighth, and Mesa got another save, his 42nd, with a one-two-three ninth.

Those two victories over the Orioles were followed by two sobering losses to the New York Yankees, 4-0 and 9-2, the next two nights, September 11 and 12.

Jack McDowell blanked the Tribe on four hits to keep the Yankees' wild card hopes alive. They were second in the AL East by 11 1/2 games to Boston, and their 65-61 record tied them with Seattle for the best among the also ran teams, as California was still ahead by five lengths in the AL West.

It was only the second time the Indians were shutout in the two years they've played at Jacobs Field. It also ended their six game winning streak and was their first loss in 15 games at home.

Dennis Martinez, a.k.a. "Mr. No-Decision," got the decision this time, a loss, though he again pitched well enough to win, yielding five hits and three runs in seven innings. For Martinez, who was 9-0 in his first 16 starts, the loss was his fifth with one victory in nine starts.

Alomar was behind the plate for Martinez for the first time all season despite Martinez's oft-stated preference for working with Tony Pena.

When asked about the switch, Martinez chose his words carefully, fueling speculation that he was less than pleased about pitching to Alomar instead of Pena. "I don't want to get into any type of controversy," he replied, "so I'd rather not say anything."

And that which Alomar did not say also spoke volumes. "To me, it was like catching any other pitcher. (Martinez) did a good job. He pitched seven innings and allowed three runs. That's all I've got to say about that."

Despite what seemed to be obvious - that Martinez felt more comfortable with Pena behind the plate instead of Alomar - Hargrove said, "I would hate to go into the postseason, especially a best-of-five series, with my No. 1 catcher on the bench for two of the five games," he said.

## McDOWELL TOO TOUGH AGAIN

McDowell became the only pitcher to go 3-0 against the Indians in

1995, and pitched only the second shutout for a visiting team at Jacobs Field. Al Leiter and Mike Timlin combined to beat the Tribe, 5-0, on June 2.

It was worse the next night as Ken Hill, still competing with Clark for the No. 4 place in the starting rotation for the postseason, was victimized by a season high five errors by Lofton, Baerga, Manny Ramirez and Paul Sorrento, who committed two.

"This team doesn't take embarrassment lightly," said Hargrove, "and tonight was embarrassing for all of us. It was the worst game we've played in a couple of years.

"I don't know if you're ever due for a game like this. Hopefully, it's only one of those things that comes along once in awhile. But if it happens again, it will be a concern for me."

It was a concern for Hill, who - as Clark did his last time out - pitched well enough to win with decent support in the field and at the plate. He worked five strong innings, and left in the sixth after giving up hits to the first two batters.

Embree took over and, though the Yankees scored a run, the Tribe only trailed 3-2, before the roof collapsed on Tavarez in the ninth. Paul O'Neill's homer, a double, three singles, two walks and errors by Ramirez and Sorrento produced six runs.

"That's the first time I've seen something like that happen with this team since I've been here," said Hill.

Then, answering what would have been the next question before it could be asked, "I don't think we've let down. I think it's a case of not getting timely hits."

Nagy made sure that only one "timely" hit - combined with Lofton's strong legs - was necessary the next night, September 13. Nagy pitched a three-hitter for his fifth career shutout and first since August 8, 1992, winning his fourth consecutive start for a team best 14-5 record.

The only run Nagy needed was produced by Lofton and Vizquel before the Yankees and their new ace, David Cone, retired a batter. Lofton led off the Indians' first inning with a walk, stole second and third, and waltzed home on Vizquel's double.

Ramirez got Vizquel home with a two-out single, and Belle cracked his 37th homer with the bases bare in the third for more than enough runs that Nagy needed. Belle's homer tied him with Boston's Mo Vaughn for the American League lead.

Nagy's performance provided a welcome boost in Hargrove's disposition. "Charlie threw the ball as well as he's thrown all year," said the manager. "That was a very good (Yankees) team he shut down."

The game started on an alarming note, however, as Nagy walked Bernie Williams with one out and Mike Stanley with two down, bringing Darryl Strawberry to the plate in his first ever appearance in Cleveland.

## NAGY HALTS THE YANKEES

With the crowd of 41,708 taunting the troubled outfielder who was coming off a suspension because of drug abuse, Strawberry struck out, ending the threat. Nagy also fanned Strawberry in the fourth, and retired him on a weak pop-up in the seventh.

The only hits Nagy allowed were singles by O'Neill in the fourth and Dion James in the fifth, and a double by Don Mattingly in the seventh.

It was Orel Hershiser's turn the next night to stymie AL East leader Boston, equaling Nagy's victory total of 14. Hershiser, 7-1 in his last nine starts, beat the Red Sox, 5-3, holding them to four hits in 8 2/3 innings

It hiked the Tribe's lead over Kansas City to 25 games but, more important to Hershiser, "I was just out to fine-tune myself for the playoffs," he said. "I want to be mechanically sound and healthy. That's the key. I feel real good about myself, about my performances, about the club."

Hershiser was working with a four-run lead on a three-hitter going into the ninth. With two out he walked Jose Canseco and was tagged for a homer by Mike Greenwell. That signaled the entry of Mesa, who needed only two pitches to retire Tim Naehring, for his 43rd save, tying the club record set by Doug Jones in 1990.

Ramirez, who turned 23 on May 30, also entered the record book. He drove in two runs for 101 on the season, to go with his 31 homers, thus becoming the 25th player in major league history to exceed 30 homers and 100 RBI at the age of 23 or younger.

Mel Ott was the first to do it in 1929 when he was 20, and former Indians slugger Hal Trosky did it twice, in 1934 when he was 21, and again in 1936.

After the game it was announced that about 20,000 tickets for the divisional playoff series would go on sale the next morning by telephone. It would prove to be a fiasco, and even cause a breakdown of the telephone system.

The Red Sox, who had lost six of their previous seven games but still led the Yankees by 10 1/2 in the AL East, snapped out of their lethargy the next night to win, 6-3. They erupted for five runs in the eighth against Embree and Poole as the Tribe bullpen collapsed after Ogea pitched seven strong innings.

More interesting - if not necessarily more important - than the final score was the matchup between Belle and Vaughn of Boston, the AL's two leading competitors for the Most Valuable Player award.

Belle, on a hot streak since the beginning of August, homered twice and singled, and had three RBI, while Vaughn smashed a three-run homer and singled twice.

Belle's performance gave him a .315 average with a league-leading 39 homers and 108 RBI. He also was No. 1 in the AL with 49 doubles, 321 total bases, and 80 extra base hits, and was among the leaders with 157 hits, 103 runs, batting average and slugging percentage.

Those 39 homers by Belle were the most for the Indians in a single season since 1959 when Colavito blasted 42.

Vaughn's average was .297 with 38 homers and 117 RBI, most in the AL. He also ranked among the league-leaders with 93 runs, 293 total bases, 65 extra base hits, and slugging percentage.

Hargrove made clear his support of the enigmatic Belle. "I'm partial, of course, but I believe Albert is ahead, though I don't have a vote and my opinion doesn't count for much," said Hargrove.

The first of Belle's homers led the fourth off Erik Hanson. His second greeted Rick Aguilera, who had taken over in the ninth after the Red Sox had rallied an inning earlier. Eddie Murray followed with his 17th homer, but that's all the Indians got as Aguilera retired three of the next four batters.

Vaughn's homer was a cannon shot off Embree after the rookie southpaw had walked the first two batters he faced in the eighth, breaking a 1-1 tie.

## SEVEN FARMHANDS RECALLED

It also was a big night at the box office as 41,833 fans surged through the gates - the 46th consecutive sellout at Jacobs Field - boosting the season attendance to 2,634,139, breaking the franchise record of 2,620,627 set in 1948.

Afterwards, the Indians announced the recall of seven farm hands from Class AAA Buffalo - outfielders Brian Giles and Jeromy Burnitz, infielder Billy Ripken, catcher Jesse Levis, and pitchers Joe Roa, John Farrell and Paul Shuey.

They were available after the Bisons lost the American Association championship to Louisville in the fifth and deciding game of that league's playoffs.

Shuey was a last minute addition because Eric Plunk was suffering tendinitis in his right shoulder that prevented him from pitching since September 6.

No sooner did the recallees arrive than three of them were pressed into service and made contributions in the Tribe's 6-5 victory over Boston ace Roger Clemens. The deciding run came on Thome's 23rd homer, a two-run shot in the third.

Giles played right field and went 1-for-4, Levis caught and singled in his only official at-bat and drove in a run with a sacrifice fly, and Ripken took over at second base and was 1-for-4.

Two others who spent time at Buffalo earlier in the season, first baseman Herbert Perry and pitcher Mark Clark, also were factors in the victory that boosted the Indians' 91-40 record to within nine of 100 with 13 games remaining.

But it was an "old" hand, Mesa, who finalized the victory, registering his 44th save (in 46 opportunities), wiping out Jones' club record with a perfect ninth inning, enabling Clark's record to climb to 9-6.

It was Clark's third straight solid performance, although in each of them - including this one - he had one shaky inning.

Mesa for some reason declined to be interviewed, but said in a statement prepared by the Indians public relations department: "I was lucky. God helped me do this. He gave me the talent and now I'm using it. It feels great to break the record. When I came to spring training I had no idea I'd be the closer."

When Hargrove was asked to compare Mesa with Jones, the manager grinned and replied, "It's like the tortoise and the hare. The one thing they do have in common, though, is that when they do come in with the game on the line, they do not get rattled."

## SHUEY CONTINUES TO STRUGGLE

Shuey, regarded as the closer of the future since his first round selection (second overall) in the 1992 amateur draft, did not fare as well as his former Buffalo teammates when the Indians closed their second last homestand in a 9-6 loss to the Red Sox on September 17.

Taking over as the Tribe's fourth pitcher in the seventh inning of a 6-6 game, Shuey - due partly to two errors by Espinoza - was charged with two hits and two runs in the eighth when the Red Sox broke the tie.

The game was played in a steady drizzle, which was the reason, Hargrove said, that he replaced Martinez after the first inning, during which the Red Sox took a 2-0 lead.

"I didn't want Dennis slipping around on the wet ground and taking a chance on aggravating his bad (left) knee," said Hargrove.

"We should not have even started the game," grumbled Martinez. "I was worried about my knee."

As for his aching elbow, Martinez underwent a Magnetic Resonance Imaging (MRI) test two days earlier and was told, "There is nothing wrong with the ligaments or bones," he said. "It's just something from pitching a lot of innings. I need to strengthen it with exercises and weights."

Sorrento's activities also were limited. He was still limping with a strained right hamstring dating back to August 29, and a pulled muscle in his rib cage that he incurred in batting practice a couple of days earlier.

It was Sorrento's injuries that gave Perry an opportunity to play first base, which he did very well and was batting a very solid .338 (47-for-139)

Shuey was disappointed, but felt he threw the ball well until the errors compounded the situation. He blanked the Red Sox in the seventh and was replaced by Embree in the eighth.

"I want to come up here and do some of the things that I need to get done and hopefully prove that I can pitch up here," he said.

The victory reduced the Red Sox's magic number to two for clinching the AL East championship.

Embarking on their final trip of the season for nine games in Chicago, Kansas City and Minnesota, the Indians blasted the White Sox, 11-1, on September 18, as Belle hammered two more homers.

They raised his season total to 41, two fewer than the franchise record set by Al Rosen in 1953, and gave Belle 22 in 48 games since August 1, and 27 since the All-Star break.

Belle's homers and another by Pena (who went 4-for-4) were the biggest blows in the Tribe's 13 hit attack. They made it easy for Hill to win his third game in four decisions since being acquired from St. Louis eight weeks earlier. He fired a six hitter and struck out eight.

"I know I haven't hurt the club since I came over here," said Hill, in a reference to the Tribe's 8-2 record in games he has started. "I want to get the critics off my back, and help this club. I know, over there (in the National League), they said I'd lost my fast ball. I hope I'm proving that I haven't."

## THREE MORE FOR BELLE

The next night, September 19, Belle got even hotter, hammering three homers - in the same park where he was accused in 1994 of using a corked bat - as the Indians beat the White Sox again, 8-2.

Belle's homers, giving him five in two games to tie a major league mark, also gave him 44 for the season, one more than Rosen's club record.

"The only other guy I can remember hitting home runs like that was Don Mattingly when he hit about eight in nine games one year," said veteran Dave Winfield, who was Mattingly's teammate with the Yankees.

"Other than that, I've never seen anybody as hot as Belle is now. He's got a grooved swing and he's making fierce contact."

The homers by Belle came in the sixth, eighth and ninth innings, all were leadoff shots, and all traveled more than 400 feet.

It raised to 13 the homers Belle had hit in his last 21 games, and to 25 in 49 games.

After his power display, however, Belle declined to be interviewed.

Hargrove marveled at Belle's accomplishment. "I don't think I've ever been around anybody who has not missed a pitch like Albert has these last two days," said the manager.

"I'm sure glad he's on our side."

Nagy was, too, though the veteran right-hander who struggled earlier in the season was, in his own way, as hot as Belle, causing Hargrove to say, "I'm also glad Charlie is on our side."

Nagy surrendered one run, a homer by Barry Lyons in the seventh inning when the White Sox were trailing, 3-1. He left after the Indians broke the game open with four in the eighth, eliminating a save opportunity for Shuey, who hurled a perfect ninth on 12 pitches. It raised Nagy's record to 15-5.

Belle's bid for a fourth consecutive homer in his first at-bat the next day, September 20, failed as he flied out to center fielder Tim Raines in the first inning. He went 0-for-5 as the Tribe's makeshift lineup was beaten by the White Sox, 4-3.

And while Belle finally was halted by Jason Bere and five relievers, a key member of the White Sox, Frank Thomas, the AL's MVP the last two years, was convinced of that which members of the Baseball Writers Association were still contemplating.

"Three or four weeks ago the media asked me who I thought was this year's MVP," said Thomas. "I said Albert Belle. I told them his numbers weren't great yet - and they weren't at that time - but he's the kind of guy who gets hot late in the year. I knew he was capable. He's on a mission.

"Nothing Albert does surprises me. I saw him do the same thing in college. Right now he's as dominant in the big leagues as he was at LSU (Louisiana State University).

"One more thing," continued Thomas. "I don't think Albert's relationship with the media should affect the voting, but I think it will. I hope it doesn't because at this point of the season he's the MVP."

## HART'S MVP CANDIDATES

Hart agreed with Thomas that Belle deserves consideration for the award, but also - perhaps for diplomatic reasons - suggested that Mesa does, too.

"They've certainly been two impactful players," said the Indians Chief. "If I had to vote for the MVP of our team, I'd have to give them co-MVP awards.

"Mesa came in and filled a gaping hole for us at the start of the season. For me, he's the reason we had so much success early in the year.

"And there certainly can be no minimizing of Belle's contributions. Just look at his numbers. He's had a remarkable season ... he is a very focused, driven player."

Roa, who won 17 games at Buffalo, started in place of Hershiser, who was scratched at the last minute because the field conditions were so bad and a light rain fell through most of the game.

Roa pitched six innings, giving up all the White Sox runs on nine hits. The teams were tied 1-1 after one inning and 2-2 after two, before Chris Snopek hit his first major league homer of Roa in the fourth. Thereafter the Indians were held at bay, except for Ripken's solo homer in the sixth.

After an open date on September 21, the Indians pennant express rolled into Kansas City where they all but finished off the Royals' hopes for a wild card invitation to the playoffs.

Hershiser won his 15th game as the Tribe beat the Royals, coming from behind and then hanging on for a 5-3 victory, their 94th of the season with eight left to play.

It ensured Hershiser of his best year since 1988 when he went 23-8 for the Dodgers, pitched them to the pennant and world championship, winning the NL Cy Young award in the process. The following season, while going 15-15, Hershiser hurt his shoulder, requiring reconstructive surgery, which he underwent in 1990.

"The surgery keeps paying off," said Hershiser, 10-2 since the All-Star break. He limited the Royals to six hits and three runs in seven innings. "My breaking ball is getting sharper and sharper, and I'm throwing two to three miles per hour faster than I did last year.

"The human body is a wonderful thing if you take care of it. Right now I'm getting paid back for all those workouts following the operation."

And so were the Indians.

The biggest blow off Hershiser was Joe Vitiello's solo homer in the fourth inning, but the Indians retaliated with single runs in the seventh, eighth and ninth.

The loss was charged to Gregg Olson, the reliever who had started the season with the Tribe's Class AAA club in Buffalo, spent a couple of weeks with the parent club, and was designated for assignment on July 17, at which time he went to the Royals.

## LOFTON VERSUS GOODWIN

An off-beat mini-drama also was part of the game, involving Lofton of the Indians and Tom Goodwin of the Royals.

Lofton, who won the AL base-stealing title the previous three seasons, but had been slowed by several injuries most of 1995, was running second to Goodwin, 46-43, when the Tribe arrived in Kansas City for three games, September 22-24.

And finally, Lofton was ready to meet Goodwin's challenge, he said - and then did.

"This is the time to set my game to where it should be," Lofton said. "The playoffs are coming, and it's time to start doing the things I can do to help this team win. I know I haven't been doing that."

With that, Lofton proceded to rap two hits, steal two bases and score two runs, while Goodwin swiped one. It left Goodwin two ahead, 47-45.

Lofton declined to talk about that race after the game, though Hargrove did. "I think (winning another stolen base title) is something Kenny wants very badly," said the manager. "to be honest with you, that's why he's played so much in the last 10 to 15 days," despite not being 100 percent healthy.

And just as Lofton was back on track, so was Belle the next night.

Two more homers jumped off his bat in a 7-3 rout of the Royals, who were out of the wild card race and fell to 27 games behind the rampaging Indians.

"The man is amazing," said Baerga without fear of contradiction. "I said it before and I'll say it again. I would not be surprised by anything Albert does."

What Albert did this time was crush a 3-and-1 pitch from Mark Gubicza for a two run homer in the first inning, the ball traveling an estimated 416 feet over the left field fence.

Then in the fifth, against Gubicza again, Belle pulled a 3-and-2 pitch into the left field stands, giving him seven homers in 20 at-bats in his previous six games, and 46 for the year.

It was Belle's sixth two-homer game, as well as one three-homer game, all of them coming since August 2. In his last 24 games he'd hit 14 homers, and 26 in his last 52.

And suddenly, 50 homers, which seemed impossible in a 144 game season, was within Belle's reach with seven games remaining.

Lost in the excitement created by Belle were the deeds of Martinez, Lofton and Murray.

Martinez, still nursing a sore elbow and aching left knee, registered his 230th career victory, making him the second winningest Latin American pitcher in baseball history. Hall of Famer Juan Marichal is No. 1 with 243.

It was, however, only the second game Martinez had won since the All-Star break, raising his record to 11-5.

Alomar caught him for the third time, instead of Pena, and after the game Martinez said, "Sandy is starting to get the feel of the pitches I throw. Sometimes I've got to talk to him, but in this game he was really with it. He's gotten more reliable.

"When I check (shake) him off, Sandy used to think it was because he called the wrong pitch. But I told him it might be the right pitch, but I wanted to throw a pitch even if it was the wrong one. I think that made Sandy feel better.

"But it really doesn't make that much difference to me who my catcher is, as long as I can stay with one guy. Then he (the catcher) knows the sequence of your pitches."

## TWO MORE FOR LOFTON

Alomar said he didn't care. "Dennis is going to call his own game and it doesn't matter if it's Tony or me catching him. I feel I can catch any pitcher on the staff. i don't lose any sleep over this. You guys (in the media) are the ones who make a big deal out of it."

Lofton stole two more bases, giving him 47 for the season, one fewer than Goodwin, who swiped one. Lofton had a chance to tie Goodwin, but was thrown out trying to steal third base in the fourth inning.

And Murray drove in his 1,812nd run with a ninth inning single, tying him with Frank Robinson for 13th place.

Belle's impact on the Tribe might have been best illustrated the next day, September 24. He asked for, and received a day off - "I was more than happy to say yes," said Hargrove - and the Indians lost, 4-2, to Kansas City.

There were held to five hits, only three in 7 2/3 innings by starter Kevin Appier, who always has been difficult for Belle. In 35 career at-bats against Appier, Belle had only six hits for a .173 average.

The only hits Appier allowed were a double and single by Thome, and another single by rookie Burnitz. The Tribe's only runs were scored in the ninth on another single by Burnitz and a two out, pinch hit homer by Giles off reliever Jeff Montgomery.

Clark, still trying to win the fourth spot in the postseason pitching rotation, did not help his chances. One of the nine hits he yielded in 5 2/3 innings was a two run homer in the third inning by Keith Lockhart, who'd been a spring training replacement player.

"Everything was working well for me, but I just left that pitch up," Clark said of the hanging slider that Lockhart hammered for his sixth homer of the season. "If I'd gotten that pitch down, (Lockhart) probably would have rolled a ground ball to second base."

As for the competition between Lofton and Goodwin, neither stole a base, but would go head-to-head again in the final series in Cleveland, September 29-October 1.

In the meantime, in the Indians' quest for their first 100 victory season since 1954 and second in franchise history - they needed to win five of their final six games - resumed in the Hubert H. Humphrey Metrodome, a.k.a. the "Homerdome," against the Minnesota Twins on September 26.

Of even greater interest to several of the players, however, concerned the Indians' plans for the postseason playoffs that would begin with the AL Division Series on October 3..

Rosters had to be reduced to 25 by midnight October 2, the day after the regular season would end. The critical decisions came down to a choice among three pitchers who were on the bubble - Hill, Clark and Ogea - and keeping either Winfield or Ruben Amaro.

Though neither Hargrove nor Hart would reveal the club's plans until being required by the AL to do so, it was generally conceded that Hill would be kept and employed as the fourth starter, leaving the last vacancy on the staff to be filled by either Clark or Ogea.

And because Ogea had shown better ability to pitch despite long periods of inactivity, he seemed to be favored over Clark.

As for the decision to keep Winfield or Amaro, it appeared that Amaro would be the chosen one because of his versatility, as well as Winfield's still-aching left shoulder, an injury he suffered in July and had plagued him ever since.

## SWEATING IT OUT

All the players involved did their best to shrug off the pressure they most certainly were feeling.

"I've basically forgotten all about it," said Clark, whose record was 9-7 with a 5.38 ERA. "They're going to take who they think can do the job. I feel I've pitched pretty well the last month and a half, and we'll just see what happens."

"I've pretty much put it out of my mind, too," said Ogea, 8-3 with a 3.08 ERA. "There's really no reason to talk about it. When you let something like that affect you, it shows up in your performance."

Winfield, maintaining - as he had all along - that he was healthy, would not discuss the situation. He was hitting .183 (30-for-109) with two homers and four RBI.

Amaro, batting .164 (9-for-55) with one homer and five RBI, was not so reticent.

"This is a hard situation," he acknowledged, "but I can't control what happens. I've got to live with whatever decision they make. I hope I get a chance to help the team in the playoffs. I think I can, but again, it's not my decision."

Belle, after two days off because of the open date prior to the start of the series in Minnesota, clubbed his 47th homer, but the Indians lost to the Twins, 13-4, as Nagy - who hates to pitch in a domed stadium - was routed. It lowered Nagy's record to 15-6.

"I just don't feel comfortable pitching indoors," he said. "It's just something I've got to deal with."

Otherwise, Nagy did not offer any excuses. "They hit everything I threw up there."

Though it had no effect on the Indians' standing, it was a distressing loss for Nagy, whose record in 13 starts since the All-Star break was 9-1. In the Metrodome, however, he was 0-4 with a 6.75 ERA.

Adding to Hargrove's concern was that Nagy's record in the Seattle Kingdome was even worse, 0-5 with a 6.82 ERA, and indications were that the Mariners - who made a remarkable comeback in the AL West - might be the Indians' opponent in one of the postseason playoff series.

"I can't tell if Charlie's (poor) record inside is a quirk or not," said pitching coach Mark Wiley. "He was pitching (against the Twins) on seven days' rest because we had to set the rotation to get it ready for the postseason. So he was real strong, maybe too strong."

Whatever, Nagy was hammered for 10 hits and seven runs in 4 1/3 innings, and was succeeded by half the pitching staff - Poole, Plunk, Embree, Tavarez and Mesa. Embree also was roughed up for seven hits and six runs in two-thirds of an inning.

Despite the loss, Lofton stole his 48th base.

Belle, who also singled, homered in the sixth, when the Twins were leading, 7-1, and the game was all but lost. Alomar also hammered two solo homers, one in the third and the other in the eighth.

And then, just when it seemed that Belle could not get any hotter, he did the next night. He whacked two more homers, Nos. 48 and 49, in a 9-6 victory over the Twins, after which Hargrove said what all the Indians had to be thinking:

"If Albert Belle doesn't win the MVP after what he's done through tonight, it will be the biggest injustice in the history of the game. I was just pulling for him to reach 40. Now I hope he gets 50."

In his previous 10 games, eight of which were on the road, 12 of Belle's 16 hits were homers.


## HILL IS AMAZED BY BELLE

Though Belle again refused to talk to reporters after the game, Hill, who joined the team from St. Louis two months earlier, was amazed.

"The man is remarkable," said Hill. "He brings so much intensity to the plate. When he makes an out, he's really mad. I've never seen anybody like him. I mean you just don't find hitters like that."

With his 49 homers and 51 doubles, Belle became the eighth player in baseball history to reach 100 extra base hits in one season.

Stan Musial was the last to do it in 1948 when major league teams played 154 games. This one was only the Indians' 140th.

In addition to Musial, others who had 100 extra base hits in one season were Babe Ruth, Lou Gehrig, Chuck Klein, Hank Greenberg, Rogers Hornsby and Jimmie Foxx - all of whom are in the Hall of Fame.

Hill started and got credit for the victory, raising his record to 4-1 with the Tribe, but was wild, walking six batters, and was banished to the showers in the sixth when the Twins rallied for four runs, cutting their deficit to 5-4.

Belle's first homer was a solo shot in the fifth. His second was a two-run blow in the seventh when the Indians stretched their lead to 8-4.

Lofton also played a key role in the victory. He went 3-for-5 and stole his 49th base.

Mesa took over with one out in the ninth, after Shuey gave up a run on a couple of hits, and needed just five pitches to breeze to his 46th save.

Twenty-four hours later a heart-wrenching accident occurred in the Metrodome as the Indians were wrapping up their nine game trip and getting ready to return to Jacobs Field for the final three games of the regular season

Martinez, in his final tune-up prior to the start of the Division Series six days hence, hit Twins star Kirby Puckett in the face with a pitch in the first inning of what turned out to be a 12-4 victory - but a joyless one - for the Tribe.

"I lost one of my best friends in baseball," said Martinez. "I felt so bad that I almost took myself out of the game. But I'm a professional and it wasn't personal. I know Kirby knows I didn't mean to hit him."

The count was 1-and-2 and Puckett, obviously expecting a breaking pitch away, froze on Martinez's inside fast ball. It struck Puckett flush on the left side of his face and he fell to the ground as though he'd been shot.

Bleeding from his nose and mouth, Puckett was rushed to the hospital and treated for a broken upper left jaw bone.

Martinez said it was "the worst feeling I ever had in my life," when he hit Puckett. "We are good friends. My kids love Kirby. and so do I."

## RETALIATION AGAINST BELLE

Puckett was the second batter hit by a pitch in the first inning. Chuck Knoblauch, leading off for the Twins, was the first, and promptly stole second and third. Martinez retired the next batter and, after Puckett was hit, Knoblauch scored on a fielder's choice.

Then, when Belle led off the second inning, he was hit on the left shoulder by the first pitch from rookie right-hander Frankie Rodriguez that obviously was thrown in retaliation for what happened to Puckett.

It almost ignited a brawl as Belle shouted at Rodriguez and took a couple of menacing steps toward the mound before umpire Tim Tschida blocked his path.

Belle went to first base, but Wiley, the Indians pitching coach, continued to yell at Rodriguez and was ejected by Tschida, which brought Hargrove out of the dugout to argue with the umpire.

"I got very angry because I thought Rodriguez should have been kicked out of the game," said Hargrove. "It was clear that he threw at Albert intentionally. There are certain things you have to do in this game, and I understand that.

"But I thought Albert handled it well, and so did the Twins. They did what they thought they had to do, and that ended it."

Peace finally was restored and Tschida warned both teams that the next pitcher who threw at a batter also would be ejected out of the game. Nobody did and the Indians waltzed to a 12-4 victory, as Martinez pitched six innings on a yield of three runs and five hits for a final 12-5 record.

When asked if he was happy with his season - he went 8-0 in the first half and 4-5 after the All-Star break - Martinez replied, "Performance-wise I'm happy because we're in the playoffs.

"But I'm not happy because I'm not healthy. I'd like to be at least 90 percent for the playoffs, but I'm more like 70 or 75 percent."

After Belle was hit by Rodriguez's pitch, the Indians retaliated in their way as Murray singled, Thome doubled, and Ramirez and Pena singled for a 3-2 lead.

It held up until the third when the Twins tied the score on a two-run homer by Matt Lawton. But the rest of the way was easy for the Indians as Alvaro Espinoza and Murray homered in a five run seventh inning.

Murray's homer was his 20th of the season and 479th of his career.

Lofton also added to his personal statistics, stealing his 50th base, as the Indians recorded their 97th victory, keeping alive their hopes to reach the century mark in their final three games of the regular season at Jacobs Field.

## SORRENTO BREAKS OUT

Sorrento, who had been in and out of the lineup - mostly out - with a strained hamstring and then a pulled muscle in his rib cage, returned to action with a bang. He blasted two homers for a career high 24 with 76 RBI, and led the Indians to a 9-2 victory on September 29 in the first of those final three games against Kansas City.

"As long as I'm healthy, I know I can hit," said the oft-injured first baseman. "I'm stringing at-bats together and that helps. I'm getting healthy at the right time."

Sorrento, who also singled in four plate appearances, was outstanding in the field as well. He turned a shot off the bat of Johnny Damon into a 3-6-3 double play in the sixth inning, preserving a 1-1 tie.

Then Sorrento broke the deadlock with his first homer, leading the seventh. He homered again to highlight the Tribe's six run uprising in the eighth that turned a close game into a rout.

Murray also whacked a homer, his 21st and 480th of his career, as the Indians increased their lead over the Royals to a season-high 28 games.

Hargrove indicated that Sorrento's performance would result in more playing time for the first baseman who was benched when a southpaw opposed the Tribe. "Paul swung the bat with confidence ... he and we both needed that, just to prove he is healthy coming into the postseason," said the manager.

Also proving that he was healthy was Lofton, who moved ahead, 51-50, in his head-to-head battle with Goodwin for the stolen base championship of the AL.

Lofton, who singled in four trips, reached on a fielder's choice in the seventh and, obviously, intimidated catcher Brent Maynes into committing a passed ball. Then, after taking second on the miscue, Lofton stole third and trotted home when Maynes' throw was wild and wound up in left field.

Lofton's stolen base was his 19th since September 1, and 11th in nine games.

It also was the fourth straight year that Lofton swiped more than 50 bases. He led the AL with 66 in 1992, 70 in 1993, and 60 in the 1994 strike-shortened season of 1994.

"I really didn't think Kenny had a chance to repeat this year because of the injuries he had," said coach Dave Nelson. "But he's healthy now and is doing the thing he always was able to do since coming to Cleveland, and that's to worry catchers and steal bases in spurts."

Goodwin, who singled in four trips but didn't attempt to steal, said, "It would be nice to beat out Lofton for the stolen base championship, but I'd rather be in the playoffs as he and the Indians are."

Lofton didn't want to talk about his "race" with Goodwin. "I'm just glad I'm healthy and able to help the team," he said.

The beneficiary of the Indians' offensive outburst was Hershiser, whose record climbed to 16-6. The one earned run he allowed shrunk his ERA to 3.93.

"I had two goals in mind when the game started, and I was fortunate enough to reach both of them," he said. "I wanted to win because it would be my 150th career victory, and I also wanted to get my ERA down below 4.00, which I did.

"Winning 150 is a big personal achievement for me. It gives me 51 (victories) since my shoulder operation" in April 1990.

## BAERGA AND BELLE DELIVER AGAIN

The next day, September 30, it was Baerga's and Belle's turn - again - to spark the Indians to another overtime victory over Kansas City, this one, 3-2, giving them a 99-44 record with one game remaining in the regular season.

Lofton also stole another base to increase his lead to two, 52-50, over Goodwin who, in his only attempt, was thrown out by Pena.

Baerga drove in the winning run with a 10th inning single, and Belle clubbed his 50th homer in the seventh when the Tribe tied the score at 2-2.

It was the Indians' 48th come-from-behind victory, 27th in their last at-bat, 17 of them at Jacobs Field, and 13th (without a loss) in extra innings.

With his homer, Belle became the first player in major league history to hit 50 homers and 50 doubles - actually 52 - in the same season. His batting average was .316 with 126 RBI.

Belle's closest competitors to be elected MVP by the Baseball Writers Association of American - many members of which did not like Belle personally - were Mo Vaughn of Boston, AL batting champion Edgar Martinez of Seattle, and Mesa, who recorded a franchise record 46 saves in 48 opportunities.

When asked if he thought he would win the award, Belle, who seldom consented to interviews, replied, "With my statistics and the team's winning percentage, I think I have the advantage."

However, Belle also said his candidate would be Mesa.

"If Jose didn't establish himself as the best closer in the league this year, we wouldn't be where we are today. He is my MVP. He has given our team confidence going into the late innings. We know we can hand the ball to him and he'll keep the lead."

Hargrove's "personal opinion," he said, "Is that, if people don't vote for Albert, it's because they have their own personal agenda."

Belle's homer, a solo shot, was delivered in the sixth inning with two out and the Tribe trailing by one. It came on a 2-and-2 pitch from Melvin Brunch, who said, "Belle hit it like a missile. They lied when they said it went 405 feet. It had to go 450."

The "missile" shot landed deep on the plaza beyond the left field wall. It bounced against the security building that supports a walkway leading from the ballpark to the adjacent parking garage.

After rounding the bases Belle came out of the dugout twice for curtain calls as the crowd of 41,578 gave him an extended standing ovation. He responded to the cheers by pumping his fists into the air both times.

The homer was Belle's 36th since the All-Star break, 31st since August 1, and 17th in September.

Making Belle's achievement even more remarkable is the fact that Babe Ruth was the only other player in baseball history to hit that many homers in September.

"If someone had told me in spring training that I'd hit 50, I would have laughed," said Belle. "I felt like I was getting in a groove during the home run hitting contest at the All-Star game."

Belle also admitted that he felt more pressure at home than on the road "because there always are so many more people to deal with," and that the way he was treated on the road served to motivate him.

## BELLE'S REVENGE

"I'd like to thank the fans of Chicago especially," he said. "After I hit those home runs in Comiskey Park last week, everybody was yelling at (White Sox manager) Terry Bevington to have my bat checked. It was nice to get some revenge on them."

It was a reference to what happened on July 19, 1994 when then-White Sox manager Gene Lamont asked the umpires to examine Belle's bat. When they did, the bat was found to be corked. Belle was suspended for 10 days by AL President Dr. Bobby Brown, though the penalty was later reduced to seven games.

Clark started on the mound and pitched six strong innings in what was his final appearance of 1995. The victory was credited to Embree, who blanked the Royals on one hit in the ninth.

Clark was not retained on the 25-man postseason roster as the Indians chose to keep Ogea instead.

Another who didn't survive the cut was Winfield, bypassed in favor of Amaro.

In a nice gesture of respect for the 43-year old Winfield, Hargrove sent him to the plate as a pinch hitter - probably his final at-bat as a player - in the seventh inning. He was given a standing ovation by the capacity crowd, and twice stepped out of the batter's box and tipped his batting helmet in a return salute to the fans.

Then Winfield grounded out to second baseman Keith Lockhart.

Another who tipped his cap, this time toward Hargrove and the Indians, was the Royals' veteran infielder Gary Gaetti. When he stepped to the plate in the eighth inning he turned and looked into the Cleveland dugout, and tipped his helmet.

He said later, "100-44, that's quite a record. Hargrove kept the team focused, determined. Tipping my cap to him was the least I could do."

Also afterwards, Winfield said he was "shocked and disappointed" when informed that he was not included in the Tribe's postseason plans.

"I was never told directly that I would be on the playoff roster, but I was led to believe that I would," Winfield said in a news conference he called to express his disappointment.

With 3,110 hits, 465 homers and 1,833 RBI in his 23 year major league career, Winfield is a certain Hall of Famer. He was acquired from Minnesota in August 1994, but when the Players Association went on strike, the season was aborted before Winfield ever played a game for the Tribe.

## INDIANS INVEST $650,000 IN WINFIELD

Last winter, after becoming a free agent, Winfield was signed by the Indians to a one year, $650,000 contract. It was hoped he would be able to provide right-handed punch to a lineup that had trouble against left-handed pitchers, but it didn't happen that way.

Hargrove said the determining factor in the decision was Winfield's shoulder injury. "It affected Dave a lot when he batted. He could not extend his left arm properly. He had to choke his swing off. I don't think there has been a moment when (the strained rotator cuff) did not affect him."

Winfield disagreed. "If I felt I couldn't contribute, I would have had surgery long before now," he said, claiming the reason he didn't hit better was because he didn't get enough chances.

"The only time I felt I got a shot was right after the All-Star break for about four weeks. They told me I would play more down the stretch. I didn't.

I haven't had the opportunity to show what I can do. I would like to have had a few more at-bats before a judgment was made."

There was, however, another reason - an even more important reason than Winfield's shoulder injury. It was Amaro's versatility, his ability to play every outfield position, second base and even catch if necessary, plus serve as a pinch runner.

The next day, October 1, with 41,819 fans in Jacobs Field - the 52nd consecutive capacity crowd - the Indians ended the regular season with their 100th victory, routing Kansas City, 17-7. It was the fifth straight game they'd won.

It gave the Indians a final attendance of 2,842,725, largest in franchise history, an average of 39,482 for each of the 72 home games.

The Tribe took the suspense out of the final game early, scoring six runs on five hits in the first inning off Tom Gordon, who didn't retire anyone until Alomar, the ninth batter, flied out.

It boosted the Indians' lead over the runner-up Royals in the AL Central to 30 games. It was the largest margin by any championship team in major league history, bettering the Pittsburgh Pirates, who finished 27 1/2 games ahead of Brooklyn for the National League pennant in 1902.

As Mesa said, "If you win a division by six or seven games you might be considered lucky. But if you win by 30, it means one thing - you're very good."

It also raised the Indians' won-lost record at Jacobs field to 54-18, and if they fell short in anything, it was that they missed by .006 of finishing with an overall winning percentage of .700.

Nagy was the winning pitcher in that last regular season game, though it definitely wasn't one of his best performances. He gave up four runs on nine hits in just five innings, but prevailed for a 16-6 record, equaling Hershiser's numbers as the winningest pitchers on the staff.

## BILLY RIPKEN IS IMPRESSIVE

The Indians 17 runs were a season high and the most since May 4, 1991, when they beat Oakland, 20-6.

Sorrento hit his 25th homer and Billy Ripken, who spent the season at Buffalo, also homered, giving the Tribe 207 for the season. It helped establish Ripken as a prime candidate to make the club as a utility infielder in 1996.

Lofton stole two more bases, giving him 54 and his fourth consecutive championship, beating out Goodwin by four, and his 13 triples also led the league.

Belle, who tied Vaughn for the RBI crown with 126, received a congratulatory telephone call from Detroit first baseman Cecil Fielder, who was the last AL player to hit 50 homers (51 in 1990).

Individually, seven Tribe regular players batted .300 or better: Murray, .323; Belle, .317; Baerga, .314; Thome, .314; Lofton, .310; Ramirez, .308; and Alomar, .300.

As a team, the Indians led in virtually every major offensive and pitching category.

They were first with a .291 average, 840 runs, 1,461 hits, 2,407 total bases, 207 home runs, 803 RBI, 132 stolen bases.479 slugging average, and .361 on base percentage. Their 766 strikeouts were fewest, and 279 doubles were third most in the AL.

Tribe pitchers also dominated the statistics with the best team ERA of 3.83 (the only one under 4.00), 10 shutouts, and 50 saves. They also allowed the fewest runs, 607; earned runs, 554; and bases on balls, 445. They were second in hits allowed, 1,261; home runs, 135; and opponents batting average, .255; and third with 926 strikeouts.

Defensively, the Indians ranked fifth with a .982 fielding percentage after committing 101 errors, seventh most, and making 142 double plays, eighth most.

But, as Alomar correctly stated, "We can throw all of our numbers out the window. We have to approach every thing differently now. Every at-bat will be important, and so will every play in the field.

"We're going into a new season, and nothing that we've done matters anymore ... all that matters is what we *will* do."

Their opponent was to be the Boston Red Sox, who won the AL East and were seeking their first world championship since 1918. That best-of-five series would open in Cleveland on October 3, with the first two games at Jacobs Field.

In the other AL Division Series it would be Seattle against New York, with the first two games in the Kingdome, home of the Mariners. Seattle got there by staging a remarkable second half comeback to catch California and then beat the Angels in a one game playoff.

With the rejection of Clark and Winfield, the Tribe's 25-man postseason roster was finalized as follows:

## THE POSTSEASON ROSTER

Pitchers (11) - Paul Assenmacher, Alan Embree, Orel Hershiser, Ken Hill, Dennis Martinez, Jose Mesa, Charles Nagy, Chad Ogea, Eric Plunk, Jim Poole, and Julian Tavarez.

Catchers (2) - Sandy Alomar Jr. and Tony Pena.

Outfielders (5) - Ruben Amaro, Albert Belle, Wayne Kirby, Kenny Lofton, and Manny Ramirez.

Infielders (7) - Carlos Baerga, Alvaro Espinoza, Eddie Murray, Paul Sorrento, Jim Thome, and Omar Vizquel.

And with that, the Indians, with one dream realized, were ready to embark upon their quest for another, the franchise's third world championship and first in 47 years, since 1948.

Nobody was more impressed with their chances than Kansas City's manager Bob Boone. "There is no question the Indians are the dominant team in the American League - maybe in all of baseball," he said.

"We'll find out in the next three weeks."

Boone was right.

**Eddie Murray with his daughter, Jordan Alexandra, acknowledging the cheers of the crowd as he is honored by the Indians on July 7 after getting his 3,000th major league hit in Minnnesota eight days earlier.**

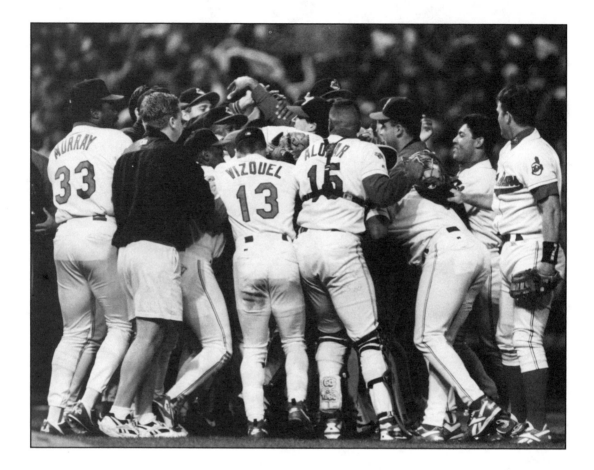

**Jose Mesa is mobbed by his happy teammates after he retires Baltimore's Jeff Huson on a pop foul caught by Jim Thome for the final out in the Indians' 3-2 victory over the Orioles that clinched the American League Central Division championship on September 8.**

**Tribe shortstop Omar Vizquel leaps over a sliding Shawn Green to turn a double play in a 3-0 victory over the Toronto Blue Jays on June 29.**

**Jim Thome is tagged out at the plate by Toronto catcher Sandy Martinez in the Tribe's 4-1 victory over the Blue Jays on August 29.**

**Manny Ramirez watches his home run fly into the right field stands for a grand slam off Chicago's Jason Bere as the Indians rout the White Sox, 13-3, on August 4.**

**Albert Belle is greeted at home plate by his Tribe teammates after hitting a ninth inning home run to beat the California Angels, 7-5, on July 18.**

**Boston's Mo Vaughn falls over catcher Jesse Levis after being called out as the Tribe beats the Red Sox, 6-5, on September 16.**

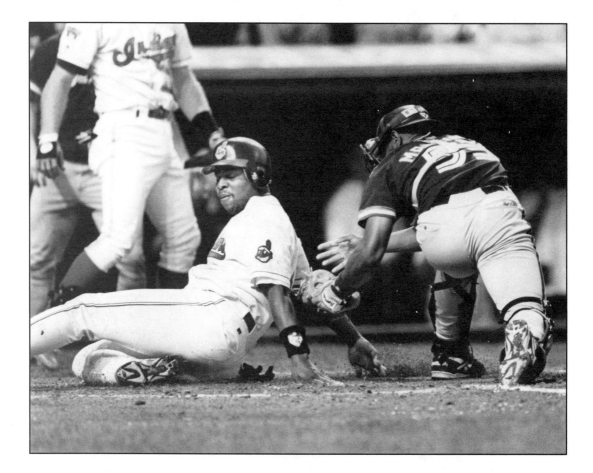

**Albert Belle slides across the plate, beating a tag by Toronto catcher Sandy Martinez, as the Indians beat the Blue Jays, 4-3, on August 28.**

**Carlos Baerga crashes into catcher Terry Steinbach and is tagged out in the Indians' 5-4 victory over Oakland on July 16.**

**Boston's Dwayne Hosey slides safely into home, upending Tribe catcher Jesse Levis, during the Indians' 6-5 victory over the Red Sox on September 16.**

**Carlos Baerga slides head first into home against Minnesota catcher Matt Walbeck as the Indians beat the Twins, 6-4, on August 3.**

**Tony Pena tags out Oakland's Terry Steinbach in the Indians' 5-4 victory over the Athletics on July 16.**

# 11

## The Division Series: Indians vs. Boston

The biggest problem the Indians had to resolve as they went into post season play for the first time in 41 years, against Boston in the Division Series, October 3 and 4 at Jacobs Field, was how to satisfy their fans who wanted to buy tickets.

They couldn't - at least not most of them.

With two weeks remaining in the regular season the Indians made about 20,000 tickets for the two games available by telephone. Fans had to call Ticketron at precisely 8 a.m. - not a minute sooner - to get their orders in.

It became a fiasco, crippling general telephone service by causing delayed dial tones, even blocked 9-1-1 calls, and interrupted pager and cellular phones, angering many callers, especially those trying to buy tickets.

Between 8 a.m. and 1 p.m. about 1.3 million calls were made, and nearly a third of them, approximately 437,000, according to Ameritech officials, never came close to getting through.

While fans were upset because they were shut out, it once again proved the newly-found popularity of the Indians, who used to be one of the weaker teams, one of the franchises that annually were splashed in red-ink.

But not anymore, thanks primarily to the rebuilding efforts of John Hart, Dan O'Dowd and Mike Hargrove - with Dick Jacobs' bankroll, of course - and the construction of Jacobs Field at the Gateway complex.

"I'm sorry there was a problem, but it's certainly nice to know that we are so popular," said Bob DiBiasio, vice president for public relations who well remembered, and suffered through so much of the bad times.

That was prior to the arrival of Jacobs in 1987, when he bought the franchise from the estate of the late F.J. (Steve) O'Neill and hired Hank Peters who, in turn, brought Hart and O'Dowd to Cleveland.

It also was Peters who promoted Hargrove to the Tribe coaching staff in 1990 from the minor leagues, where he'd managed Class AAA Colorado Springs. Then, on July 6, 1991, Hargrove replaced John McNamara as Tribe manager.

Despite the breakdown of the telephone system, Indians tickets for the Boston series were sold out in two hours - and because it did, a mail-in procedure for ordering tickets for the American League Championship Series and the World Series was implemented two weeks later.

Sacrificing speed for safety, the mail-order lottery didn't do much to help fans get tickets, but it did solve the telephone problem.

It was estimated that nearly two million requests for tickets were mailed, many of them in specially-prepared, eye-catching, uniquely-designed and oversize envelopes in the hope it would help them be selected by Tribe officials.

As for the action on the field, the Red Sox were the Indians' opponents after winning the AL East by seven games over New York, despite stumbling slightly down the stretch.

On September 1, Boston's record was 71-45, and led the Yankees by 14 lengths. In the final month, however, the Red Sox won only 15 games while losing 13, and might have blown the division title if the season had lasted a couple of weeks longer.

The Yankees, with their final 79-65 mark, qualified as the AL's wild card team, narrowly beating out California for that spot in the post season, as the Tribe paid close attention.

Had California or Seattle won the wild card, the Indians would have played one of them in the first round, whichever was the AL West champion.

The Angels and Mariners finished in a tie, each with 78-66 records. California swooned in the second half, losing 36 of 75 games, while Seattle, which was in fourth place at the All-Star break, went 44-31 to catch the Angels and won a one-game playoff, 9-1, on October 2.

Despite the Indians' success in their runaway to the AL Central title - but also probably because of some shoddy execution of fundamentals in the last couple of games of the season - Hargrove would not permit them to coast.

To the manager's credit, prior to the opening of the series against the Red Sox, he held several open date workouts in which the players practiced the things they'd learned in the minors and polished in spring training.

In fact, the day before the first game of the Division Series against Boston, Hargrove had pitchers fielding bunts, infielders covering bases and backing up throws, and outfielders hitting cutoff men while the catchers called out plays and took charge of all situations.

And a crowd of about 14,000 fans turned out to watch them.

"We're doing these things because they're important," said Hargrove. "I'm not saying I'm dissatisfied with what we've done so far, but there are some things we needed to be reminded about. I just want to make sure we continue to do things the right way."

As for the fans who flocked to Jacobs Field merely to see the practice session. Hargrove said, "I was shocked that so many people this early in the morning came down to watch guys go through a fairly boring workout.

"I was shocked, surprised ... and it gave me goose bumps."

Though the Indians insisted they had no preference as to which team they played in the first series, everybody knew they usually had trouble beating Roger Clemens, Boston's ace.

And, of course, it was Clemens who pitched the opener on October 3, against the Tribe's Dennis Martinez.

It was hard to determine which team - or which team's fans - was hungrier, as this was a match-up between two longtime losers.

Oh, sure, the Red Sox were seeking their ninth pennant, but had not won the World Series since 1918, failing three times since then.

Only the Chicago Cubs, who last won the World Series in 1908, and the Chicago White Sox, who prevailed in 1917, have lost more times than Boston.

As for the Indians, their last world championship team was 1948, placing them fourth on the losing list behind the Cubs, White Sox and Red Sox. The Tribe prevailed in head-to-head competition during the regular season, but only 7-6, and was 4-3 at Jacobs Field.

"It's going to come down to who is mentally tougher, us or Boston," said Jim Thome, "and which team can get its momentum going faster."

Clemens was 18-6 lifetime against the Indians, but as Carlos Baerga said, "Most of it was before we got good."

Baerga was right. Hampered by arm injuries, Clemens was 0-2 with an 8.25 ERA against the Tribe dating back to 1994.

"Everything is different now," said Baerga. "I don't care who is pitching against us, everytime we take the field we know we are capable of winning. Everybody in our lineup is hitting almost .300.  This year was unbelievable."

Orel Hershiser, who had played in more post season games than any of his teammates, said it this way:

"You can tell this city is ready. This has been baseball's Utopia this year. Everybody is looking at Cleveland for the formula to raise interest and build a team. What a thing for Cleveland to be looked up to instead of being looked down on as the Mistake by the Lake."

Martinez was 12-5 in 28 starts, but only 4-5 after the All-Star Game, and without a decision in three games against the Red Sox in 1995. The 40-year old grandfather was still nursing an aching right elbow and sore left knee, but wouldn't give in to the ailments.


## GAME ONE: Indians 5, Red Sox 4 (13 innings)

Tony Pena, who said he didn't see a take sign, clobbered a 3-and-0 pitch with two out in the 13th inning, for a home run that gave the Indians a 5-4 victory in the first game of the Division Series on October 4.

Pena, who usually is Martinez's personal catcher, didn't go behind the plate until the 10th inning, homered off Zane Smith into the left field bleachers.

The blow was struck at 2:08 a.m., sending home happy the fans who remained from a Jacobs Field record crowd of 44,218.

It was the 12th game the Indians had won with a homer in their last at-bat, 11 of them at home, raised their record in extra innings to 14-0, and was the longest post season game in terms of time - five hours, one minute - in history. It had been delayed twice by rain.

Pena, who called his game-winning homer "the most exciting moment of my career," claimed he didn't know if he was being flashed a take sign on the pitch he hit.

"I couldn't tell what it was," he quipped. "Ask Mike Hargrove."

Hargrove also smiled and replied, "It was amber."

Then, Hargrove admitted, "I gave Tony the take sign, but I gave it real late."

Third base coach Jeff Newman's only comment: "I'm glad Pena didn't see me."

It was the 107th career homer for Pena who was discarded by the Red Sox after hitting .181 in 1993.

"I don't feel like a hero," he said. "When something like this happens, you just have to enjoy the moment, because you never know if it's going to happen again. I just feel happy for being able to contribute."

Earlier, after Martinez was replaced in the seventh inning by Julian Tavarez with the Indians ahead, 3-2, the Red Sox tied it in the eighth, and went on top, 4-3, on Tim Naehring's solo homer in the 11th.

That set the stage for some histrionics by Albert Belle, who re-tied the game with a homer, after which Boston manager Kevin Kennedy asked plate umpire Tim Welke to confiscate and check his bat.

Kennedy was suggesting, of course, that the bat was corked, as was one of Belle's bats found to be last year.

It angered the Indians, and especially Belle. He shouted and gestured toward the Red Sox dugout, flexed his right arm, pointed to his biceps muscle and yelled, "Right there, right (expletive) there."

After the game, former AL President Dr. Bobby Brown, attending the game as a league representative, sawed off the end of Belle's bat - which didn't improve Belle's mood - and found nothing wrong.

Kennedy said he "just took a shot," contending that he'd received information from former Tribe players that "the Indians have a whole wood working place over there" in their equipment room.

"It's just a desperate effort to throw a monkey wrench into our season," said Belle.

Then, "I don't need to use corked bats. I've got muscles. What (Kennedy) did is kind of a slap in the face."

He also would have liked to have the bat back, said Belle, "But Bobby Brown split it into two pieces ... and he knows what he can do with those pieces."

Brown suspended Belle for 10 days last year when his bat was found to be corked, though the sentence later was reduced to seven games.

Belle's homer was his second big blow of the game. He doubled for two runs and scored another when the Tribe took a 3-2 lead against Clemens in the sixth.

It was Clemens' last inning for the Red Sox as he was followed by six relievers, including Rick Aguilera who surrendered Belle's homer.

Shortly after Belle's homer, Aguilera suffered a pulled hamstring that forced him out of the game and, as it turned out, the rest of the series.

Martinez allowed only two runs in his six inning stint, both of them coming in the third on Luis Alicea's one out single and John Valentin's two out homer.

The victory was credited to Ken Hill, the sixth reliever used by the Indians. Jose Mesa pitched the 10th and walked two batters without yielding a hit, Jim Poole took over in the 11th and was the victim of Naehring's homer in the 11th.

Hill came on in the 12th, bailing Poole out of an impending jam, and blanked the Red Sox in the 13th.

# GAME ONE BOX SCORE

## Indians 5, Red Sox 4 (13)

| Boston | AB | R | H | RBI | BB | SO | AVG |
|---|---|---|---|---|---|---|---|
| Hosey, rf | 5 | 1 | 0 | 0 | 1 | 1 | .000 |
| Jn Valentin, ss | 4 | 1 | 2 | 2 | 2 | 0 | .500 |
| M Vaughn, 1b | 6 | 0 | 0 | 0 | 0 | 3 | .000 |
| Canseco, dh | 6 | 0 | 0 | 0 | 0 | 1 | .000 |
| Greenwell,lf | 6 | 0 | 3 | 0 | 0 | 0 | .500 |
| Naehring, 3b | 5 | 1 | 2 | 1 | 0 | 1 | .400 |
| Tinsley, cf | 5 | 0 | 0 | 0 | 1 | 2 | .000 |
| Macfarlane, c | 3 | 0 | 0 | 0 | 0 | 1 | .000 |
| a-Stairs, ph | 1 | 0 | 0 | 0 | 0 | 1 | .000 |
| Haselman, c | 2 | 0 | 0 | 0 | 0 | 0 | .000 |
| Alicea, 2b | 5 | 1 | 4 | 1 | 0 | 0 | .800 |
| **Totals** | **48** | **4** | **11** | **4** | **4** | **10** | |

| Cleveland | AB | R | H | RBI | BB | SO | AVG |
|---|---|---|---|---|---|---|---|
| Lofton, cf | 5 | 0 | 1 | 0 | 0 | 2 | .200 |
| Vizquel, ss | 3 | 1 | 0 | 0 | 2 | 1 | .000 |
| Baerga, 2b | 5 | 1 | 2 | 0 | 0 | 1 | .400 |
| Belle, lf | 5 | 2 | 2 | 3 | 1 | 1 | .400 |
| Murray, dh | 6 | 0 | 1 | 1 | 0 | 0 | .167 |
| Thome, 3b | 6 | 0 | 1 | 0 | 0 | 3 | .167 |
| M Ramirez, rf | 6 | 0 | 0 | 0 | 0 | 1 | .000 |
| Sorrento, 1b | 5 | 0 | 1 | 0 | 0 | 2 | .200 |
| b-H Perry,ph | 1 | 0 | 0 | 0 | 0 | 0 | .000 |
| S Alomar, c | 4 | 0 | 1 | 0 | 0 | 0 | .250 |
| 1-Kirby, pr | 0 | 0 | 0 | 0 | 0 | 0 | ----- |
| Pena, c | 2 | 1 | 1 | 1 | 0 | 0 | .500 |
| **Totals** | **48** | **5** | **10** | **5** | **3** | **11** | |

| Boston | 002 | 000 | 010 | 010 | 0 | 4 | 11 | 2 |
|---|---|---|---|---|---|---|---|---|
| Cleveland | 000 | 003 | 000 | 010 | 1 | 5 | 10 | 2 |

Two outs when winning run scored.
**a:** struck out for Macfarlane in the 9th. **b:** flied out for Sorrento in the 13th. **1:** ran for Alomar in the 10th. **E:** Macfarlane (10), Alicea (1), Lofton (1), Sorrento (1). **LOB:** Boston 10, Cleveland 11. **2B:** Alicea (1), Belle(1). **HR:** Belle(1) off Aquilera; Pena (1) off Z Smith; Jn Valentin (1) off D Martinez; Naehring (1) off Poole; Alicea (1) off Tavarez. **RBI:** Jn Valentin 2 (2), Naehring (1), Alicea (1), Belle 3 (3), Murray (1), Pena (1). **SB:** Alicea (1), Vizquel (1), **CS:** Jn Valentin (1). **S:** Naehring, Vizquel

| Boston | IP | H | R | ER | BB | SO | NP | ERA |
|---|---|---|---|---|---|---|---|---|
| Clemens | 7 | 5 | 3 | 3 | 1 | 5 | 102 | 3.86 |
| Cormier | 1/3 | 0 | 0 | 0 | 1 | 1 | 11 | 0.00 |
| Belinda | 1/3 | 0 | 0 | 0 | 0 | 0 | 3 | 0.00 |
| Stanton | 2-1/3 | 1 | 0 | 0 | 0 | 4 | 32 | 0.00 |
| Aquilera | 2/3 | 3 | 1 | 1 | 0 | 1 | 23 | 13.50 |
| M Maddux | 2/3 | 0 | 0 | 0 | 1 | 0 | 12 | 0.00 |
| Z Smith L, 0-1 | 1-1/3 | 1 | 1 | 1 | 0 | 0 | 17 | 6.75 |

| Cleveland | IP | H | R | ER | BB | SO | NP | ERA |
|---|---|---|---|---|---|---|---|---|
| De Martinez | 6 | 5 | 2 | 2 | 0 | 2 | 85 | 3.00 |
| Tavarez | 1-1/3 | 2 | 1 | 1 | 0 | 2 | 20 | 6.75 |
| Assenmacher | 1/3 | 0 | 0 | 0 | 0 | 1 | 4 | 0.00 |
| Plunk | 1-1/3 | 1 | 0 | 0 | 1 | 1 | 24 | 0.00 |
| Mesa | 1 | 0 | 0 | 0 | 2 | 0 | 14 | 0.00 |
| Poole | 1-2/3 | 2 | 1 | 1 | 1 | 2 | 21 | 5.40 |
| K Hill W, 1-0 | 1-1/3 | 1 | 0 | 0 | 0 | 2 | 16 | 0.00 |

**HBP:** by M Maddux (Lofton). by Cormier (Baerga) **WP:** K Hill. **Umpires:** Welke, Hirschbeck, Brinkman, Roe, Denkinger, Morrison. **T:** 5:01. **A:** 44218

## GAME TWO: Indians 4, Red Sox 0

Hershiser and three relievers - Tavarez, Paul Assenmacher and Mesa - made it look easy, blanking the Red Sox, 4-0, on three hits in the second game of the series the next night, October 4, at Jacobs Field.

It was far from easy, however, and required some clutch pitching by Hershiser and those who followed him to the mound, as well as some clutch hitting by Gold Glove shortstop Omar Vizquel, who's better known for his defensive play.

Vizquel delivered a key hit, one of only four relinquished by Erik Hanson, when the Indians scored twice in the fifth inning. They added two more runs in the eighth on a home run by Eddie Murray.

"It was very important for us to go to Boston 2-0," said Vizquel. "If we were tied, 1-1, it would be tough to win two out of three games up there. Fenway Park is their ball park and they know how to play that green (left field) wall."

Hershiser, raising his career post season record to an unblemished 5-0 with a 1.52 earned run average, pitched 7 1/3 innings, and put down serious threats in the first two innings to keep the Red Sox off the scoreboard.

Belle and Paul Sorrento committed errors in the first, and Hershiser compounded the trouble with a wild pitch, but retired sluggers Mo Vaughn and Jose Canseco to squirm out of trouble.

Then, with two out in the second, the Red Sox loaded the bases on singles by Willie McGee and Mike Macfarlane, and a walk by Alicea, but Hershiser retired Dwayne Hosey to end that threat.

"I could have ruined the whole game right there," he said, correctly. "I was really wondering about my control. When I got out of the inning I told myself that I didn't want to get into another jam like that again."

And he didn't.

Hershiser went on to retire 16 of the next 17 batters in order, until Alicea walked as the lead batter in the eighth. Hosey forced him at second, and Tavarez stalked out of the bull pen to retire Valentin on a pop foul.

Then Assenmacher came on to strike out Vaughn, and Mesa pitched the ninth, needing only four pitches - *four!* - to end the game. Canseco grounded out, Mike Greenwell flied out, and Naehring popped out.

In the two games, Vaughn and Canseco, Boston's vaunted one-two punch, were a combined 0-for-20 with seven strikeouts - and it would get even worse.

"I don't think I've ever been around someone who is able to focus on what he's got to do, and then execute it as well as Hershiser," marveled Hargrove.

He could have said the same about the work of Tavarez, Assenmacher and Mesa.

The Indians needed strong pitching to overcome Hanson, who had control problems, walking four batters. Hanson was 3-0 in four starts against the Tribe in the regular season, with an overall record of 15-5.

Vizquel got his big hit, a double with one out in the fifth, driving in Sorrento and Lofton, both of whom had walked.

Another walk by Hanson, this one to Belle with one out in the eighth, preceded Murray's homer.

Then Mesa wrapped it up and the series moved to Boston for the third game on October 6, with the Red Sox backed against the wall.

It was the 12th consecutive post season game the Red Sox had lost, a new, and unenviable, major league record.

History also was on the side of the Indians.

Since the start of divisional play in 1969, 27 teams have held 2-0 leads in best-of-five and best-of-seven league championship series, and of them, 21 went on to win.

**Indians exult after Beating Boston, 4-0, in Game 2 of the American League Division Series.**

# GAME TWO BOX SCORE

## Indians 4, Red Sox 0

| Boston | AB | R | H | RBI | BB | SO | AVG |
|---|---|---|---|---|---|---|---|
| Hosey, rf | 4 | 0 | 0 | 0 | 0 | 0 | .000 |
| Jn Valentin, ss | 4 | 0 | 0 | 0 | 0 | 1 | .250 |
| M Vaughn, 1b | 4 | 0 | 0 | 0 | 0 | 2 | .000 |
| Canseco, dh | 4 | 0 | 0 | 0 | 0 | 1 | .000 |
| Greenwell,lf | 4 | 0 | 0 | 0 | 0 | 0 | .300 |
| Naehring, 3b | 4 | 0 | 0 | 0 | 0 | 0 | .222 |
| McGee, rf | 3 | 0 | 1 | 0 | 0 | 2 | .333 |
| Macfarlane, c | 2 | 0 | 2 | 0 | 0 | 1 | .333 |
| Alicea,, 2b | 1 | 0 | 0 | 0 | 2 | 1 | .667 |
| **Totals** | **31** | **0** | **3** | **0** | **2** | **8** | |

| Cleveland | AB | R | H | RBI | BB | SO | AVG |
|---|---|---|---|---|---|---|---|
| Lofton, cf | 3 | 1 | 0 | 0 | 1 | 0 | .125 |
| Vizquel,ss | 4 | 0 | 1 | 2 | 0 | 0 | .143 |
| Baerga, 2b | 4 | 0 | 0 | 0 | 0 | 0 | .222 |
| Belle, lf | 2 | 1 | 1 | 0 | 2 | 0 | .429 |
| Murray, dh | 4 | 1 | 2 | 2 | 0 | 1 | .300 |
| Thome, 3b | 4 | 0 | 0 | 0 | 0 | 3 | .100 |
| M Ramirez, rf | 4 | 0 | 0 | 0 | 0 | 1 | .000 |
| Kirby, rf | 0 | 0 | 0 | 0 | 0 | 0 | ----- |
| Sorrento, 1b | 1 | 1 | 0 | 0 | 1 | 0 | .167 |
| S Alomar, c | 2 | 0 | 0 | 0 | 0 | 0 | .167 |
| **Totals** | **28** | **4** | **4** | **4** | **4** | **5** | |

| | | | | | | | |
|---|---|---|---|---|---|---|---|
| **Boston** | 000 | 000 | 000 | | 0 | 3 | 1 |
| **Cleveland** | 000 | 020 | 02x | | 4 | 4 | 2 |

**E:** Jn Valentin (1), Belle (1), Sorrento (2). **LOB:** Boston 6, Cleveland 6. **2B:** Vizquel (1). **1B:** Murray (1). **HR:** Murray (1) of Hanson. **RBI:** Vizquel 2 (2), Murray 2 (3). **SB:** Hosey (1). **S:** S Alomar

| Boston | IP | H | R | ER | BB | SO | NP | ERA |
|---|---|---|---|---|---|---|---|---|
| Hanson L, 0-1 | 8 | 4 | 4 | 4 | 4 | 5 | 115 | 4.50 |

| Cleveland | IP | H | R | ER | BB | SO | NP | ERA |
|---|---|---|---|---|---|---|---|---|
| Hershiser W, 1-0 | 7-1/3 | 3 | 0 | 0 | 2 | 7 | 92 | 0.00 |
| Tavarez | 1/3 | 0 | 0 | 0 | 0 | 0 | 7 | 5.40 |
| Assnmacher | 1/3 | 0 | 0 | 0 | 0 | 1 | 4 | 0.00 |
| Mesa | 1 | 0 | 0 | 0 | 0 | 0 | 4 | 0.00 |

**WP:** Hershiser. **PB:** Macfarlane. **Umpires:** Hirschbeck, Brinkman, Roe, Denkinger, Morrison, Welke. **T:** 2:33. **A:** 44,264

## GAME THREE: Indians 8, Red Sox 2

Three outstanding fielding plays, two by Vizquel, the other by Sorrento, were keys to the Indians' 8-2 victory that swept the Division Series against Boston at Fenway Park on October 7.

It propelled the Indians into the AL Championship Series, and a shot at the World Series for the first time since 1954.

But it wasn't just the Indians' strong defense that won this one, it also was Thome's hitting and some decent, if unspectacular pitching by Charles Nagy.

Thome, 2-for-10 in the first two games, smashed a two-run homer off a Tim Wakefield knuckleball in the second inning, and the Indians were off and running.

"The Red Sox were the team that scared us the most because of Fenway," said Thome, who was only 2-for-13 in the first two games.

"The home run was big, extra big because I was struggling. I think my first postseason is a learning experience, and the bottom line is to win and get big hits in big situations.

"I kept telling myself to be patient and keep fighting."

Still, those two runs provided by Thome would not have vaulted the Indians into a lead if not for the first of Vizquel's Gold Glove wizardry in the first inning. It saved Nagy considerable embarrassment, and possibly even kept him in the game.

Shaky at the onset, Nagy walked Valentin with one out and Canseco with two down. Greenwell slapped a shot up the middle that would have gone into center field and scored at least one run.

It didn't because the ball glanced off Nagy's leg, and it wasn't even a hit because Vizquel lunged to his left, speared the ball and flipped it to Baerga for a force at second that ended the inning.

"It was a tough play," conceded Vizquel. "I thought I was going to have to dive for the ball, In your mind that's a big play because you put the other team under pressure to try to score. But the ball bounced off (Nagy) and made it easy for me."

An inning later Vizquel made another play that, while it came with the bases bare, helped to maintain the two-run lead provided by Thome and again kept Nagy out of trouble.

Reggie Jefferson led the second with a wicked shot to the shortstop side of second base. Vizquel somehow reached the ball, fielded it cleanly and his throw caught Jefferson by plenty at first base.

"Don't ask me how I do it ... I can't answer that," said Vizquel. "I just look at the ball and concentrate on getting it."

The Indians were handed a third run in the third when Wakefield lost command of his knuckleball after Baerga singled with two out. Then Belle, Murray and Thome walked in succession, forcing in Baerga.

It was in the fourth inning that Sorrento, who grew up in Boston cheering for the Red Sox, made a big play that saved Nagy who was struggling and on the verge of blowing up.

With one out, Jefferson, Naehring and Alicea singled, loading the bases. Macfarlane lofted a sacrifice fly that scored Jefferson, and Hosey shot a grounder toward right field close to the line.

If it had gone through, two runs would have scored, Hosey probably would have reached second as the potential go-ahead run, and Nagy would have been sent to the showers.

Instead, Sorrento made a diving stop behind first base, scrambled to his knees and flipped the ball to Nagy covering first for the out that ended the inning and preserved the Tribe's two run margin - and kept Nagy in the game.

"It was a huge play," acknowledged Kennedy. "(Sorrento) made a great play. We knew he's had a sore leg, and to make a play like that, you've got to give him credit."

Hargrove called it "the play of the game."

After that it was easy for Nagy and the Indians as they erupted for five runs on five hits and a walk in the sixth, knocking out Wakefield.

They coasted thereafter as Nagy pitched through the seventh, Tavarez worked the eighth, and Assenmacher retired the Red Sox in order in the ninth.

"My heart is beating like a rabbit right now," said an excited and elated Nagy, who won 16 and lost six with a 4.55 ERA during the regular season. "I wanted to be sure to be in the dugout to see the final out.

"I've been around this team for a long time. I've seen a lot of players come and go in this organization, so it was great to see this happen for the city of Cleveland and this team."

The victory gave the Indians the pennant - but there was no wild celebration after the game.

"The division championship erased 41 years, and we celebrated appropriately then," said Hart. "This is just another step toward the World Series."

It was that indeed. A very impressive step, as Tribe pitchers held Boston's heavy hitters - Vaughn and Canseco - hitless in a combined 27 at-bats. Vaughn was 0-for-14 with seven strikeouts, and Canseco 0-for-13 with two strikeouts.

The Red Sox, whose team batting average during the season was .280, third best in the AL, with 754 RBI and 175 homers, batted .184 in the Division Series.

The Indians didn't hit much better, .219, to be exact. Thome, despite triggering the uprising that led to the victory in the third and deciding game, was just 2-for-13 in the series, as was Kenny Lofton, and Manny Ramirez went hitless in 12 at-bats.

Vizquel, the littlest Indian of them all, also batted only .167 with two hits in 12 plate appearances, but led the team with four RBI.

Tavarez was another who didn't produce as well as he had during the regular season, allowing two runs in 2 2/3 innings after yielding just 23 earned runs in 85 innings prior to the post season.

But, as Hershiser said, "The longer we go into this thing, the more you'll see those players start producing."

And, as Hart reassured Tribe fans, "It was important to have the good old war horses around, like Murray, Pena, Hershiser, Assenmacher and

Martinez. Our veterans stepped up when some of our younger players were a little nervous."

There was no doubting that Kennedy was impressed. "Losing the first game took its toll," he said. "Then Orel (Hershiser) came out and threw a beauty and we never got our offense untracked."

Then, referring to the Tribe's pitchers, who compiled a 1.74 ERA, Kennedy said, "It all starts with (the Indians) pitching. I respect their lineup an awful lot, and I think we pitched well to them.

"I'm a big believer in pitching, and I think that's the key to their club, and to the possibility of them winning it all," added the first year manager of the vanquished Red Sox, who now have lost 13 consecutive post season games.

"To jump out on them the way we did was very important," said Hargrove. "You come in here (to Fenway Park) with their fans, and it's very difficult to beat them."

As for the Indians, it was on to the best-of-seven American League Championship Series - but first, a return to Cleveland to await the outcome of the other Division Series between Seattle and New York.

And when they arrived at Hopkins International Airport at 3 a.m. on October 7, lo and behold, there were more than 3,000 fans waiting to greet them, to express their admiration for what the Indians already had accomplished, and their anticipation of more to come.

**Bring on the Mariners! Indians and Seattle players are introduced prior to the start of the American League Championship Series**

# GAME THREE BOX SCORE

## Indians 8, Red Sox 2

| Cleveland | AB | R | H | RBI | BB | SO | AVG |
|---|---|---|---|---|---|---|---|
| Lofton, cf | 5 | 0 | 1 | 0 | 0 | 1 | .154 |
| Vizquel, ss | 5 | 1 | 1 | 2 | 0 | 1 | .167 |
| Baerga, 2b | 5 | 1 | 2 | 1 | 0 | 0 | .286 |
| Belle, lf | 4 | 0 | 0 | 0 | 1 | 2 | .273 |
| Murray, dh | 3 | 2 | 2 | 0 | 2 | 0 | .385 |
| Thome, 3b | 3 | 1 | 1 | 3 | 1 | 0 | .154 |
| Espinoza, 3b | 1 | 0 | 0 | 0 | 0 | 0 | .000 |
| M Ramirez, rf | 2 | 1 | 0 | 0 | 1 | 0 | .000 |
| Kirby, rf | 1 | 0 | 1 | 0 | 0 | 0 | 1.000 |
| Sorrento, 1b | 4 | 1 | 2 | 1 | 1 | 1 | .300 |
| S Alomar, c | 5 | 1 | 1 | 1 | 0 | 1 | .182 |
| Pena, c | 0 | 0 | 0 | 0 | 0 | 0 | .500 |
| **Totals** | **38** | **8** | **11** | **8** | **6** | **6** | |

| Boston | AB | R | H | RBI | BB | SO | AVG |
|---|---|---|---|---|---|---|---|
| Hosey, cf | 3 | 0 | 0 | 0 | 1 | 2 | .000 |
| a-McGee, ph-cf | 1 | 0 | 0 | 1 | 0 | 0 | .250 |
| Jn Valentin, ss | 4 | 0 | 1 | 0 | 1 | 0 | .250 |
| M Vaughn, 1b | 4 | 0 | 0 | 0 | 1 | 2 | .000 |
| Canseco, rf | 3 | 0 | 0 | 0 | 2 | 0 | .000 |
| Greenwell, lf | 5 | 0 | 0 | 0 | 0 | 1 | .200 |
| Jefferson, dh | 4 | 1 | 1 | 0 | 0 | 1 | .250 |
| Naehring, 3b | 4 | 1 | 2 | 0 | 0 | 0 | .306 |
| Alicea, 2b | 4 | 0 | 2 | 0 | 0 | 1 | .600 |
| Macfarlane, c | 3 | 0 | 1 | 1 | 0 | 1 | .333 |
| **Totals** | **35** | **2** | **7** | **2** | **5** | **8** | |

| | | | | | | | | |
|---|---|---|---|---|---|---|---|---|
| Cleveland | 021 | 005 | 000 | | 8 | 11 | 2 | |
| Boston | 000 | 100 | 010 | | 2 | 7 | 1 | |

**a:** grounded into fielder's choice for Hosey in the 8th
**E:** Lofton (2), Baerga (1), Macfarlane (2). **LOB:** Cleveland 10, Boston 12.
**2B:** Baerga (1), S Alomar (1), Jn Valentin (1). **HR:** Thome (1) off Wakefield.
**RBI:** Vizquel 2 (4), Baerga (1), Thome 3 (3), Sorrento (1), S Alomar (1),
McGee (1), Macfarlane (1). **SF:** Macfarlane

| Cleveland | IP | H | R | ER | BB | SO | NP | ERA |
|---|---|---|---|---|---|---|---|---|
| Nagy W, 1-0 | 7 | 4 | 1 | 1 | 5 | 6 | 114 | 1.29 |
| Tavarez | 1 | 3 | 1 | 1 | 0 | 1 | 23 | 6.75 |
| Assenmacher | 1 | 0 | 0 | 0 | 0 | 1 | 14 | 0.00 |

| Boston | IP | H | R | ER | BB | SO | NP | ERA |
|---|---|---|---|---|---|---|---|---|
| Wakefield L, 0-1 | 5-1/3 | 5 | 7 | 7 | 5 | 4 | 113 | 11.81 |
| Cormier | 1/3 | 2 | 1 | 1 | 0 | 1 | 16 | 13.50 |
| M Maddux | 2-1/3 | 2 | 0 | 0 | 0 | 1 | 34 | 0.00 |
| Hudson | 1 | 2 | 0 | 0 | 1 | 0 | 20 | 0.00 |

**HBP:** by Wakefield (M Ramirez). **WP:** Hudson. **PB:** Macfarlane.
**UMPIRES:** Mckean, McCoy, Garcia, Joyce, Reilly, Scott. **T:** 3:18, **A:** 34,211

# DIVISION SERIES COMPOSITE BOX

### (Indians win, 3-0)

## BATTING
## BOSTON RED SOX

| NAME | AB | R | H | 2B | 3B | HR | RBI | AVG |
|------|----|----|----|----|----|----|-----|-----|
| Alicea, 2b | 10 | 1 | 6 | 1 | 0 | 1 | 1 | .600 |
| Macfarlane, c | 9 | 0 | 3 | 0 | 0 | 0 | 1 | .333 |
| McGee, rf-ph | 4 | 0 | 1 | 0 | 0 | 0 | 1 | .333 |
| Naehring, 3b | 13 | 2 | 4 | 0 | 0 | 1 | 1 | .308 |
| Jn Valentine, ss | 12 | 1 | 3 | 1 | 0 | 1 | 2 | .250 |
| Jefferson, dh | 4 | 1 | 1 | 0 | 0 | 0 | 0 | .250 |
| Greenwell, lf | 15 | 0 | 3 | 0 | 0 | 0 | 0 | .200 |
| Canseco, dh | 13 | 0 | 0 | 0 | 0 | 0 | 0 | .000 |
| Hosey, rf | 12 | 1 | 0 | 0 | 0 | 0 | 0 | .000 |
| Haselman, c | 2 | 0 | 0 | 0 | 0 | 0 | 0 | .000 |
| Stairs, ph | 1 | 0 | 0 | 0 | 0 | 0 | 0 | .000 |
| Tinsley, ph | 5 | 0 | 0 | 0 | 0 | 0 | 0 | .000 |
| M Vaughn | 14 | 0 | 0 | 0 | 0 | 0 | 0 | .000 |
| **Totals** | **114** | **6** | **21** | **2** | **0** | **0** | **6** | **.184** |

## CLEVELAND INDIANS

| NAME | AB | R | H | 2B | 3B | HR | RBI | AVG |
|------|----|----|----|----|----|----|-----|-----|
| Kirby, pr-rf | 1 | 0 | 1 | 0 | 0 | 0 | 0 | 1.000 |
| Pena, c | 2 | 1 | 1 | 0 | 0 | 1 | 1 | .500 |
| Murray, dh | 13 | 3 | 5 | 0 | 1 | 1 | 3 | .385 |
| Sorrento, 1b | 10 | 2 | 3 | 0 | 0 | 0 | 1 | .300 |
| Baerga, 2b | 14 | 2 | 4 | 1 | 0 | 0 | 1 | .286 |
| Belle, lb | 11 | 3 | 3 | 1 | 0 | 1 | 3 | .273 |
| S Alomar, c | 11 | 1 | 2 | 1 | 0 | 0 | 1 | .182 |
| Vizquel, ss | 12 | 2 | 2 | 1 | 0 | 0 | 4 | .167 |
| Lofton, cf | 13 | 1 | 2 | 0 | 0 | 0 | 0 | .154 |
| Thome, 3b | 13 | 1 | 2 | 0 | 0 | 1 | 3 | .154 |
| H. Perry, 1b | 1 | 0 | 0 | 0 | 0 | 0 | 0 | .000 |
| M Ramirez, rf | 12 | 1 | 0 | 0 | 0 | 0 | 0 | .000 |
| Espinoza, 3b | 1 | 0 | 0 | 0 | 0 | 0 | 0 | .000 |
| **Totals** | **114** | **17** | **25** | **4** | **1** | **4** | **17** | **.219** |

## PITCHING
## BOSTON RED SOX

| PITCHING | G | IP | H | R | ER | BB | SO | ERA |
|----------|----|----|----|----|----|----|----|-----|
| Belinda | 1 | 1/3 | 0 | 0 | 0 | 0 | 0 | 0.00 |
| M Maddux | 2 | 3 | 2 | 0 | 0 | 1 | 1 | 0.00 |
| Hudson | 1 | 1 | 2 | 0 | 0 | 1 | 0 | 0.00 |
| Stanton | 1 | 2-1/3 | 1 | 0 | 0 | 0 | 4 | 0.00 |
| Clemens | 1 | 7 | 5 | 3 | 3 | 1 | 5 | 3.86 |
| Hanson, 0-1 | 1 | 8 | 4 | 4 | 4 | 4 | 5 | 4.50 |
| Z Smith, 01 | 1 | 1-1/3 | 1 | 1 | 1 | 0 | 0 | 6.75 |
| Wakefield, 0-1 | 1 | 5-1/3 | 5 | 7 | 7 | 5 | 4 | 11.81 |
| Cormier | 2 | 2/3 | 2 | 1 | 1 | 1 | 2 | 13.49 |
| Aquilera | 1 | 2/3 | 3 | 1 | 1 | 0 | 1 | 13.50 |
| **TOTALS** | **3** | **29-2/3** | **25** | **17** | **17** | **13** | **22** | **5.16** |

## CLEVELAND INDIANS

| PITCHING | G | IP | H | R | ER | BB | SO | ERA |
|----------|----|----|----|----|----|----|----|-----|
| Assenmacher | 3 | 1-2/3 | 0 | 0 | 0 | 0 | 3 | 0.00 |
| Hershiser, 1-0 | 1 | 7-1/3 | 3 | 0 | 0 | 2 | 7 | 0.00 |
| K Hill, 1-0 | 1 | 1-1/3 | 1 | 0 | 0 | 0 | 2 | 0.00 |
| Mesa | 2 | 2 | 0 | 0 | 0 | 2 | 0 | 0.00 |
| Plunk | 1 | 1-1/3 | 1 | 0 | 0 | 1 | 1 | 0.00 |
| Nagy, 1-0 | 1 | 7 | 4 | 1 | 1 | 5 | 6 | 0.78 |
| De Martinez | 1 | 6 | 5 | 2 | 2 | 0 | 2 | 3.00 |
| Poole | 1 | 1-2/3 | 2 | 1 | 1 | 1 | 2 | 5.40 |
| Tavarez | 3 | 2-2/3 | 5 | 2 | 2 | 0 | 3 | 6.75 |
| **TOTALS** | **3** | **31** | **21** | **6** | **6** | **11** | **26** | **1.74** |

## SCORE BY INNINGS

| | | |
|---|---|---|
| Boston | 002 100 020 010 0 --- | 6 |
| Cleveland | 021 028 020 010 1 --- | 17 |

**E:** Lofton (2), Baerga (1), Macfarlane (2) **DP:** Bos 0, CLE 1, **LOB:** Bos 28, CLE 27. **SB:** Alicea, Hosey, Vizquel. **CS:** Valentin. **S:** S Alomar, Naehring, Vizquel. **SF:** Macfarlane **IBB:** off M Maddux (Belle); off Poole (Jn Valentin); off Plunk (Tinsley); off Hanson (Belle). **HBP:** by M Maddux (Lofton); by Cormier (Baerga); By Hansen (Sorrento); by Wakefield (M Ramirez). **WP** Hershiser, Hudson. **PB:** Macfarlane 2. **UMPIRES:** (Game 1&2) Welke, Hirschbeck, Brinkman, Roe, Denkinger, Morrison. (Game 3) McKean, McCoy, Garcia, Joyce, Reilly, Scott. **T** Game 1: 5:01 Game 2: 2:33, Game 3: 3:18 **ATT:** Game 1 at Cleveland 44,218, Game 2 at Cleveland 44,264, Game 3 at Boston 34,211

# 12

## AL Championship Series: Indians vs. Seattle

After sweeping the Red Sox in their best-of-five American League Division Series, the Indians returned to Cleveland for three days of rest and relaxation while awaiting the winner of the other Division Series between Seattle and New York.

Because of their dislike for the Kingdome where the Indians' record was only 6-19 since 1991, most of the players were hoping the Yankees would prevail, as it seemed they would. New York won the first two games, 9-6 and 7-5 in 15 innings, at Yankee Stadium.

But the Mariners fought back to take the next three - 7-4, 11-8 and 6-5 in 11 innings. The Indians re-packed their bags and headed for Seattle for the best-of-seven AL Championship Series beginning October 10. The first two games would be played in the hated Kingdome.

When the Mariners beat the Yankees, it was their second impressive comeback in two months. They caught California down the stretch in the regular season, then knocked off the Angels, 9-1, in a one game playoff for the AL West championship. It was Seattle's first title since entering the league as an expansion team in 1977.

The collapse of the Angels was the fourth worst in baseball's modern era. They'd held a 13 game lead over Seattle on August 2, but lost 36 of their final 75 games, while the Mariners were winning 44 of 75.

The only teams that blew bigger leads in major league baseball history:

The New York Giants had a 15 game lead over Boston in 1914, but were overtaken by the Braves, who won the National League pennant by 10 1/2 games.

The Boston Red Sox led New York by 14 games on July 19, 1978, but the Yankees finished strong to win the AL East Division title by 2 1/2 games over both Boston and Baltimore.

And Brooklyn was ahead of New York by 13 1/2 lengths on August 11, 1951, but the Giants came back to beat the Dodgers by one game.

If the Yankees had prevailed over the Mariners in their Division Series, the Indians would have had the home field advantage, with the first two games (and sixth and seventh if necessary) played at Jacobs Field.

Still, by facing the Mariners, it seemed that the Indians were getting a break. Randy Johnson, arguably the best pitcher in the AL, pitched three innings in relief two days earlier, saving Seattle's third and deciding victory over the Yankees.

As it turned out, they didn't.

### GAME ONE: Seattle 3, Indians 2

Rookie Bob Wolcott, who was activated only a few hours before the series opener, did almost everything right after a shaky start. He was the winning pitcher as the Mariners beat the Tribe, 3-2.

Obviously nervous at the onset, Wolcott walked the first three batters he faced on 13 pitches - Kenny Lofton, Omar Vizquel and Carlos Baerga - and it seemed a rout was in the making.

Seattle manager Lou Piniella rushed to the mound and told Wolcott, "'We don't care if you get beat, 11-0, just relax, throw strikes and give us five or six innings.' We needed at least that much because our starters were burned out," said Piniella.

His words of wisdom helped - but so did the next two Indians.

Albert Belle, the fourth batter, swung at and fouled off the first pitch he saw. Then, after the count went to 1-and-2, Belle struck out.

Eddie Murray followed and also swung at, and fouled out on the first pitch from Wolcott.

Jim Thome, the third batter, grounded out and the Indians were blanked.

It proved to be a portent of things to come later that night, in front of a roaring, raucous crowd of 57,065 fans in the Kingdome.

Manager Mike Hargrove knew the Indians were in trouble when they let Wolcott off the hook. "That probably was the tale of the game right there," he said. "It set the tone."

Dennis Martinez, facing the Mariners for the first time in 1995 and with a 9-3 career record against them, had an easy first inning. Ken Griffey Jr. walked and was thrown out stealing, but Martinez ran into trouble in the second.

"El Presidente," as he has been nicknamed, retired the first two batters, but walked Jay Buhner and Mike Blowers blasted a home run over the center field fence.

The Indians fought back for a run in the third - but should have scored more - when Carlos Baerga led with a single and Belle walked. After Murray lined out, Thome lashed a single to get Baerga home, and Manny Ramirez did the same, loading the bases.

But the rally ended as Paul Sorrento grounded into a double play.

Neither team threatened again until the seventh, when Belle tied the score with a one-out, 440 foot solo home run over the center field fence.

But the Mariners, with their fans screaming and waving "Refuse to Lose" placards, came right back in their half of the inning and kayoed Martinez.

Tino Martinez was retired by Dennis Martinez, but Buhner doubled, went to third as Blowers reached on a throwing error by Thome, and scored on another double by Luis Sojo, breaking the deadlock.

It also finished Martinez in favor of Julian Tavarez, who got Dan Wilson on a grounder back to the mound, and struck out Vince Coleman, leaving Blowers stranded on third and Sojo on second.

However, the Mariners' run proved to be enough, despite another threat by the Indians that rekindled hope, but ended without reaching fruition.

Jeff Nelson took over for Wolcott to start the eighth and set down the first two batters before Sandy Alomar beat out an infield single. That brought Norm Charlton to the mound and Lofton greeted him with a single.

But, with the potential tying run at second, Charlton induced Vizquel to foul out, and the Tribe went down in order in the ninth as Baerga and Belle fanned, and Murray grounded out.

"We had our chances, but we didn't capitalize on them," said Hargrove, referring to the 12 runners the Indians stranded on base. "We've got to do better if we hope to keep this thing going."

As for Martinez's pitching, Hargrove said, "Dennis was outstanding ... he just made one bad pitch, the one that Sojo hit for a double."

Alomar, again behind the plate, though Martinez's "personal" catcher during the regular season was Tony Pena, said Sojo's double was off a sinker that didn't sink, as was the pitch that Blowers hit for a home run.

"Otherwise, Dennis threw very well. He was hitting his spots all night," said Alomar.

The loss left Martinez with a 4-6 record (and six no decisions) since going 8-0 in the first half of the season.

Of the Indians' failure to score against Wolcott in the first inning, Alomar said, "We were kind of shocked. Usually we come through when we're presented opportunities like that.

"Unfortunately, we swung at too many first pitches when the guy (Wolcott) was a little wild."

Hargrove called it "a matter of us being too impatient," especially in the first inning.

Piniella offered lavish - but also somewhat unusual - praise of Sojo, the Mariners shortstop who replaced Felix Fermin (traded to Seattle for Vizquel in 1994). "Sojo did a heckuva job ... he takes his hacks," said Piniella.

"Sometimes he's not pretty, but he's productive. What I mean is that sometimes Sojo swings at left field and the ball goes to right."

Coleman, the veteran outfielder who played for the St. Louis Cardinals in the 1987 World Series, talked about the Mariners being under-rated.

"We are a team that a lot of teams thought they could beat," he said. "But I'm telling you, don't just look at us today, look at us this week, this last month. If the game's not over, this team isn't done," he said.

Since the beginning of September, and including the Division Series against the Yankees, the Mariners had 15 come-from-behind victories in the span of 34 games.

They beat New York in Game 4 when Edgar Martinez broke a 6-6 tie with a grand slam in the eighth inning.

And they won the deciding fifth game when the same Martinez smacked a two-run double off Jack McDowell, wiping out a 5-4 deficit, in the bottom of the 11th.

"I guess we are getting used to this," said Martinez, who was the AL batting champion with a .356 average, repeating the title he'd previously won in 1992 when he hit .343. He batted .571 (12-for-21) with two homers and 10 RBI in the series against New York.

**Kenny Lofton steals third base in the Indians' 5-2, 11 inning loss to Seattle in the third game of the ALCS**

# GAME ONE BOX SCORE

## Mariners 3, Indians 2

| Cleveland | AB | R | H | RBI | BB | SO | AVG |
|---|---|---|---|---|---|---|---|
| Lofton, cf | 3 | 0 | 3 | 0 | 2 | 0 | 1.000 |
| Vizquel, ss | 4 | 0 | 0 | 0 | 1 | 0 | .000 |
| Baerga, 2b | 4 | 1 | 1 | 0 | 1 | 1 | .250 |
| Belle, lf | 4 | 1 | 1 | 1 | 1 | 2 | .250 |
| Murray, dh | 5 | 0 | 0 | 0 | 0 | 1 | .000 |
| Thome, 3b | 4 | 0 | 2 | 1 | 0 | 0 | .500 |
| M Ramirez, rf | 4 | 0 | 1 | 0 | 0 | 0 | .250 |
| Sorrento, 1b | 4 | 0 | 1 | 0 | 0 | 1 | .250 |
| S Alomar, c | 4 | 0 | 1 | 0 | 0 | 0 | .250 |
| Amaro | 0 | 0 | 0 | 0 | 0 | 0 | ---- |
| Pena, c | 0 | 0 | 0 | 0 | 0 | 0 | ---- |
| **Totals** | **36** | **2** | **10** | **2** | **5** | **5** | |

| Seattle | AB | R | H | RBI | BB | SO | AVG |
|---|---|---|---|---|---|---|---|
| Coleman, lf | 4 | 0 | 0 | 0 | 0 | 2 | .000 |
| Cora, 2b | 4 | 0 | 2 | 0 | 0 | 0 | .500 |
| Griffey Jr, cf | 3 | 0 | 2 | 0 | 1 | 1 | .667 |
| E. Martinez, dh | 3 | 0 | 0 | 0 | 1 | 0 | .000 |
| T. Martinez, 1b | 3 | 0 | 0 | 0 | 1 | 0 | .000 |
| Buhner, rf | 3 | 2 | 1 | 0 | 1 | 2 | .333 |
| Blowers, 3b | 4 | 1 | 1 | 2 | 0 | 0 | .250 |
| Sojo, ss | 3 | 0 | 1 | 1 | 0 | 0 | .333 |
| D Wilson, c | 3 | 0 | 0 | 0 | 0 | 1 | .000 |
| **Totals** | **30** | **3** | **7** | **3** | **4** | **6** | |

| | | | |
|---|---|---|---|
| **Cleveland** | 001 | 000 | 100--2 10 1 |
| **Seattle** | 020 | 000 | 10x--3  7 0 |

**1:** Ran for Alomar in the 8th. **E:** Thome. **LOB:** Cleveland 12, Seattle 7. **2B:** Sorrento, Cora, Griffey Jr, Buhner, Sojo. **3B:** Lofton. **HR:** Blowers off D Martinez, Belle off Wolcott. **CS:** Griffey Jr. **GIDP:** Sorrento, E Martinez. **DP:** Cleveland 1 (Vizquel, Baerga and Sorrento); Seattle 1 (Sojo and T Martinez).

| Indians | IP | H | R | ER | BB | SO | NP | ERA |
|---|---|---|---|---|---|---|---|---|
| D Martinez L, 0-1 | 6-1/3 | 6 | 3 | 3 | 2 | 4 | 100 | 4.26 |
| Tavarez | 1 | 1 | 0 | 0 | 1 | 1 | 20 | 0.00 |
| Assenmacher | 0 | 0 | 0 | 0 | 1 | 0 | 5 | --- |
| Plunk | 2/3 | 0 | 0 | 0 | 0 | 1 | 6 | 0.00 |

| Seattle | IP | H | R | ER | BB | SO | NP | ERA |
|---|---|---|---|---|---|---|---|---|
| Wolcott W, 1-0 | 7 | 8 | 2 | 2 | 5 | 2 | 102 | 2.57 |
| J Nelson | 2/3 | 1 | 0 | 0 | 0 | 1 | 12 | 0.00 |
| Charlton S, 1 | 1-1/3 | 1 | 0 | 0 | 0 | 2 | 15 | 0.00 |

Assenmacher faced one batter in the 8th. **IBB:** off Tavarez (E Martinez)
**UMPIRES:** Phillips, Cousins, Reed, Ford, McClelland, Coble. **T:** 3:07. **A:** 57,065

**GAME TWO: Indians 5, Seattle 2**

Manny Ramirez, the Indians' precocious right fielder who blossomed into one of the AL's most productive hitters in 1995, but whose bat had been dozing through most of the post season, came alive in the second game of the ALCS against the Mariners.

After going 0-for-12 against the Red Sox, and 1-for-4 in Game 1 against the Mariners, Ramirez was the Indians' hitting star in a 5-2 victory that evened the series at 1-1 on October 11 in the Kingdome.

Orel Hershiser did, too, in the first of two must-win games he pitched for the Tribe, this one against his former Los Angeles Dodgers teammate Tim Belcher.

Scattering four hits through eight innings, Hershiser raised his career post season record to 6-0 with a 1.47 ERA in 73 1/3 innings.

"As far as we were concerned, this was a game we absolutely had to win," confirmed Hargrove, knowing full well that Johnson would be ready to start Game 3 at Jacobs Field two days later. "We certainly didn't want to be down, 0-2, facing Johnson."

"This win was huge," said Hershiser, "from an emotional point of view as well as physically, coming as it did after the first game. We didn't feel we got beat in that game. We felt we gave it away, and it was important to come back the way we did to win this one."

The comeback was triggered - as well as powered - by Ramirez, who went 4-for-4 with two homers, and a share of credit also belonged to Vizquel, whose fielding continued to border on the sensational.

It was Ramirez's single off Belcher leading the fifth that started the Indians' comeback, after they'd been blanked on two hits by Belcher until then.

Belcher retired the next two batters, but Lofton singled and Vizquel walked, loading the bases, and Baerga singled for a 2-0 lead.

Ramirez solo homered with two out in the sixth, after which Sorrento singled, and Alomar tripled for another run and a 4-0 cushion for Hershiser.

Griffey led off the bottom of the sixth with a homer, but that was the only blemish on Hershiser's record.

After Ramirez started the eighth with his second homer of the game, and though Griffey got another hit, a single in the Mariners' half of the eighth, no damage was done and Mesa took over in the ninth.

It was not one of Mesa's best performances, as Blowers homered with one out and Alex Diaz singled with two down before Doug Strange grounded out ending the game.

Vizquel, as he has done most of the two seasons he's worn a Cleveland uniform, made two big plays on behalf of Hershiser, the first in the fourth inning, robbing Buhner of a hit, the other in the seventh on a ball hit by Sojo.

"He is a magician with a glove," Hershiser said of Vizquel, who played five seasons for the Mariners before the Indians acquired him.

Coach Buddy Bell, who was an excellent fielding third baseman himself, also was impressed. "We may have been in this position without him, but it certainly wouldn't have been easy," said Bell. "Omar really understands this game ... he is one of the smartest guys in the game."

On the play he made to rob Buhner, Vizquel dived to his right to make a back handed catch of the ball headed through the hole toward left field.

Vizquel also went into the hole to retire Sojo three innings later, this time with a bare handed grab and throw that caught the runner by half-a-step.

"It's instinct," said Vizquel, accepting congratulations in the clubhouse after the game. "You don't plan those kind of things, they just happen instinctively.

"It was really important that we won this game. We're trying to play good defensively because we have not been scoring too many runs. I think this will get us going. Anyway, I hope it will."

Hargrove pointed out another element of the victory, in addition to Hershiser's pitching, Vizquel's fielding and Ramirez's hitting.

"To me, the biggest hit of the game was Sandy Alomar's triple (in the sixth inning)," said the manager. It came in the wake of Ramirez's first homer and followed a single by Sorrento.

"Our advance scouts told us that this place (the Kingdome) is wild and crazy. They said if we get a chance to tack on runs, we should do it whenever we can."

The run that Alomar tacked on with his triple gave the Tribe a 4-0 lead and definitely hushed the 58,144 fans in the Kingdome.

The din and clamor did not bother Hershiser, he said. "I like the noise. I like the fans screaming the way they were doing. I just make believe they are yelling for me ... but I also try to quiet them down.

Among those paying tribute to Hershiser was Belcher. He said "the uniform" is the only difference between Hershiser now and when he pitched for the Dodgers in 1988, before he suffered a career-threatening shoulder injury that required extensive surgery.

"Orel was awesome against a tough lineup," said Belcher. "It was a must-win situation for him, and he came up big."

Charlton, the Mariners' ace reliever, also saw a lot of Hershiser in the NL, and also was greatly impressed by the veteran right-hander.

"He might have thrown the ball a little harder when he was with the Dodgers, but now he has better location," said Charlton. "What it proves is that velocity is not everything."

Ditto for Edgar Martinez, who was 0-for-6 in the first two games. "(Hershiser) had command of all his pitches, and he kept them all down," said the two-time NL batting champion. "He was throwing sliders and breaking pitches for strikes when he got behind in the count.

"Hershiser pitched a helluva game."

Despite Hershiser's ability to imagine the Kingdome fans were cheering for him, the Indians to a man were eager to get out of Seattle.

As Ramirez said, "It's great to be going back to Cleveland with the series tied. Even though we have to face Randy Johnson (in Game 3), we feel a lot more comfortable at home."

And away from those "Refuse to Lose" signs that were everywhere in the Kingdome.

# GAME TWO BOX SCORE

## Indians 5, Mariners 2

| Cleveland | AB | R | H | RBI | BB | SO | AVG |
|---|---|---|---|---|---|---|---|
| Lofton, cf | 4 | 1 | 1 | 0 | 1 | 1 | .571 |
| Vizquel, ss | 3 | 0 | 0 | 0 | 2 | 0 | .000 |
| Baerga, 2b | 5 | 0 | 2 | 2 | 0 | 0 | .333 |
| Belle, lf | 3 | 0 | 1 | 0 | 2 | 0 | .286 |
| Murray, dh | 5 | 0 | 2 | 0 | 0 | 0 | .200 |
| Thome, 3b | 4 | 0 | 0 | 0 | 0 | 1 | .250 |
| Espinoza, 3b | 1 | 0 | 0 | 0 | 0 | 0 | .000 |
| M Ramirez, rf | 4 | 2 | 4 | 2 | 0 | 0 | .625 |
| Kirby, rf | 0 | 0 | 0 | 0 | 0 | 0 | ---- |
| Sorrento, 1b | 4 | 2 | 1 | 0 | 0 | 0 | .250 |
| S Alomar, c | 4 | 0 | 1 | 1 | 0 | 1 | .250 |
| **Totals** | **37** | **5** | **12** | **5** | **5** | **3** | |

| Seattle | AB | R | H | RBI | BB | SO | AVG |
|---|---|---|---|---|---|---|---|
| Coleman, lf | 4 | 0 | 1 | 0 | 0 | 3 | .125 |
| Cora, 2b | 3 | 0 | 0 | 0 | 0 | 0 | .286 |
| Griffey Jr, cf | 4 | 1 | 2 | 1 | 0 | 0 | .571 |
| E. Martinez, dh | 3 | 0 | 0 | 0 | 1 | 0 | .000 |
| T. Martinez, 1b | 4 | 0 | 0 | 0 | 0 | 2 | .000 |
| Buhner, rf | 4 | 1 | 1 | 1 | 0 | 1 | .286 |
| Blowers, 3b | 4 | 0 | 1 | 0 | 0 | 1 | .250 |
| Sojo, ss | 3 | 0 | 0 | 0 | 0 | 0 | .167 |
| a-A Diaz, ph | 1 | 0 | 1 | 0 | 0 | 0 | 1.000 |
| D Wilson, c | 3 | 0 | 0 | 0 | 0 | 0 | .000 |
| b-Strange, ph | 1 | 0 | 0 | 0 | 0 | 0 | .000 |
| **Totals** | **34** | **2** | **6** | **2** | **1** | **7** | |

| | | | |
|---|---|---|---|
| **Cleveland** | 000 | 022 | 010--5　12　0 |
| **Seattle** | 000 | 001 | 001--2　6　1 |

**a:** singled for Sojo in the 9th. **b:** grounded out for Wilson in the ninth.
**E:** Sojo. **LOB:** Cleveland 10, Seattle 7. **3B:** S Alomar. **HR:** Griffey Jr. off
Hershiser; Buhner off Mesa; M Ramirez(2) off Belcher, Ayala. **SB:** Vizquel,
Coleman. **GIDP:** Thome, Sorrento. **DP:** Seattle 2 (T Martinez, Sojo, and
T Martinez), (Ayala, Cora, Sojo and T Martinez)

| Indians | IP | H | R | ER | BB | SO | NP | ERA |
|---|---|---|---|---|---|---|---|---|
| Hershiser W, 1-0 | 8 | 4 | 1 | 1 | 1 | 7 | 107 | 1.12 |
| Mesa | 1 | 2 | 1 | 1 | 0 | 0 | 14 | 9.00 |

| Seattle | IP | H | R | ER | BB | SO | NP | ERA |
|---|---|---|---|---|---|---|---|---|
| Belcher L, 1-0 | 5-2/3 | 9 | 4 | 4 | 2 | 1 | 100 | 6.35 |
| Ayala | 2-2/3 | 2 | 1 | 1 | 3 | 2 | 51 | 3.38 |
| Risley | 2/3 | 1 | 0 | 0 | 0 | 0 | 11 | 0.00 |

**HBP:** by Hershiser (Cora). **WP:** Hershiser. **UMPIRES:** Cousins, Reed,
Ford, McClelland, Coble, Phillips. **T:** 3:14. **A:** 58,144

GAME THREE: Seattle 5, Indians 2 (11 innings)

While it was Johnson - a.k.a. the "Big Unit" - who was most feared by the Indians and their fans when the ALCS returned to Jacobs Field on October 13, after the game it was Buhner they resented.

Johnson pitched as well as ever, though he left after eight innings, but it was Buhner who wreaked the damage and beat the Tribe, 5-2, with two homers in Game 3 to the dismay of 43,643 fans.

Buhner's first homer was a solo shot off Charles Nagy into the left field bleachers in the second inning, and his second was a three-run blast off fourth reliever Eric Plunk with two out in the 11th.

Charlton, the hard-throwing southpaw who was picked up by the Mariners at mid season, pitched three hitless innings in relief of Johnson to earn credit for the victory.

It was the Indians' first extra inning loss, after going 14-0 during the regular season.

For Buhner, his second homer was redemption.

"I came out of this thing smelling like a rose," said the right fielder who hit six homers against the Tribe earlier in the season. "I was upset with myself, and very frustrated after screwing up the way I did in the eighth.

"And I'd be lying if I said I didn't go up to hit thinking that somehow, some way I had to make up for it."

In the eighth, with one out and the Mariners ahead, 2-1, Buhner missed a deep fly ball by Alvaro Espinoza for a two base error. Lofton followed with a single to drive in the tying run, and it stayed that way until Buhner redeemed himself.

Joey Cora opened the inning with a single and Tavarez, who had taken over for Mesa in the 10th, was in turn replaced by Paul Assenmacher. He retired Griffey, and Hargrove then turned to Plunk to face Edgar Martinez. The strategy worked well as Martinez fouled to Herbert Perry for the second out.

When Plunk fell behind in the count, 3-and-1, and Cora stole second, the Indians chose to intentionally walk left-handed hitting Tino Martinez, which brought Buhner to the plate.

Plunk's second pitch, after a called strike to Buhner, wound up in the right field seats for a three-run homer. "I just tried to get a pitch and juice it," said Buhner. He "juiced it" quite well.

"I don't usually get down on myself," said Buhner. "But to do something that stupid, that late in the game and with Randy in such a groove, it kind of got to me.

"I have to go back to high school when I let a ball hit me right between the eyes to remember a play like the one I just did.

"This is a very humbling game. You go from hero to goat, or goat to hero in a hurry. I thought I'd really screwed it up."

Buhner did ... but he also quickly unscrewed it.

"Obviously, looking back, it wasn't a good pitch," said Plunk. "But it was a fast ball and I can handle that a little better than a hanging breaking ball."

The Indians, who previously had won 28 games in their last at-bat this year, couldn't do it this time.

Charlton put them down one-two-three, and the Indians were down in the series, two games to one.

An inning after Buhner's first homer, the Mariners took a 2-0 lead on a pair of errors. It happened with two out as Griffey singled, stole second, went to third on Alomar's throwing error, and scored on another error by Espinoza, playing third in place of the left-handed hitting Thome.

The Indians got a run back in the fourth on Lofton's leadoff triple and Vizquel's sacrifice fly, and four innings later, Buhner allowed the trying run to score, setting the stage for his 11th inning redemption.

Though the loss was charged to Tavarez, it was Nagy who lamented, "To beat Randy Johnson you pretty much have to pitch a shutout."

The remark was in response to Johnson, who said, "Charles Nagy did a great job. He pretty much matched me across the board."

That Nagy did, allowing five hits, one earned run and striking out six and walking two in eight innings. Johnson gave up four hits, one earned run, struck out six and walked none.

Of Buhner's homer, Nagy said, "I made a bad pitch. I hung it, he turned on it. He's a tough batter and he came up big."

Piniella bristled when asked if he was pleased because the victory guaranteed that the ALCS would return to Seattle for a sixth game, assuming the Indians would win the next one, or even two.

"Hell no," he snapped. "We're looking for more than that. When you're up, two games to one, you're not thinking about going back to Seattle down, three games to two. You're looking to win it in five games right here, which we can do."

Hargrove was disappointed, of course, but not discouraged.

At least not overtly. "We've got a very resilient club," he said. "They come to play every day. They'll be back tomorrow."

**Carlos Baerga scores with a head first slide in the Indians' 7-0 victory over Seattle in the fourth game of the ALCS**

# GAME THREE BOX SCORE

## Mariners 5, Indians 2

| Seattle | AB | R | H | RBI | BB | SO | AVG |
|---|---|---|---|---|---|---|---|
| Coleman, lf | 5 | 0 | 0 | 0 | 0 | 0 | .077 |
| Widger, c | 0 | 0 | 0 | 0 | 0 | 0 | ----- |
| Cora, 2b | 4 | 1 | 1 | 0 | 0 | 0 | .273 |
| Fermin, 2b | 0 | 0 | 0 | 0 | 0 | 0 | ----- |
| Griffey Jr, cf | 5 | 1 | 2 | 0 | 0 | 1 | .500 |
| E. Martinez, dh | 5 | 0 | 0 | 0 | 0 | 1 | .000 |
| T. Martinez, 1b | 4 | 1 | 1 | 0 | 1 | 1 | .091 |
| Buhner, rf | 5 | 2 | 2 | 4 | 0 | 1 | .333 |
| Blowers, 3b | 3 | 0 | 1 | 0 | 0 | 0 | .273 |
| a-A Diaz, ph- lf | 2 | 0 | 0 | 0 | 0 | 1 | .333 |
| Sojo, ss | 4 | 0 | 2 | 0 | 0 | 0 | .300 |
| D Wilson, c | 3 | 0 | 0 | 0 | 0 | 2 | .000 |
| b-Strange, ph-3b | 1 | 0 | 0 | 0 | 0 | 0 | .000 |
| **Totals** | **41** | **5** | **9** | **4** | **1** | **7** | |

| Cleveland | AB | R | H | RBI | BB | SO | AVG |
|---|---|---|---|---|---|---|---|
| Lofton, cf | 5 | 1 | 2 | 1 | 0 | 2 | .500 |
| Vizquel, ss | 4 | 0 | 0 | 1 | 0 | 0 | .000 |
| Baerga, 2b | 5 | 0 | 1 | 0 | 0 | 1 | .286 |
| Belle, lf | 4 | 0 | 0 | 0 | 0 | 0 | .182 |
| Murray, dh | 4 | 0 | 0 | 0 | 0 | 1 | .143 |
| 2-Amaro,pr-dh | 1 | 0 | 0 | 0 | 0 | 0 | .000 |
| M Ramirez, rf | 3 | 0 | 0 | 0 | 1 | 2 | .455 |
| H Perry, 1b | 3 | 0 | 0 | 0 | 1 | 1 | .000 |
| S Alomar, c | 3 | 0 | 0 | 0 | 1 | 0 | .182 |
| Espinoza, 3b | 3 | 0 | 1 | 0 | 0 | 1 | .250 |
| 1-Kirby, pr | 0 | 1 | 0 | 0 | 0 | 0 | ----- |
| Thome, 3b | 1 | 0 | 0 | 0 | 0 | 0 | .222 |
| **Totals** | **36** | **2** | **4** | **2** | **3** | **8** | |

| | | | | | | |
|---|---|---|---|---|---|---|
| Seattle | 011 | 000 | 000 | 03--5 | 9 | 1 |
| Cleveland | 000 | 100 | 010 | 00--2 | 4 | 2 |

**a:** grounded out for Blowers in the 9th. **b:** flied out for Wilson in the 10th.
**1:** ran for Espinoza in the 8th. **2:** ran for Murray in the 9th
**E:** Buhner, S Alomar, Espinoza. **LOB:** Seattle 5, Cleveland 6. **3B:** Lofton .
**HR:** Buhner 2 off Nagy, Plunk. **SB:** Cora, Griffey Jr, Lofton, **CS:** E.
Martinez, H Perry. **SF:** Vizquel. **DP:** Cleveland 1 (Mesa and H Perry)

| Seattle | IP | H | R | ER | BB | SO | NP | ERA |
|---|---|---|---|---|---|---|---|---|
| R Johnson | 8 | 4 | 2 | 1 | 2 | 6 | 100 | 1.12 |
| Charlton W, 1-0 | 3 | 0 | 0 | 0 | 1 | 2 | 35 | 0.00 |

| Cleveland | IP | H | R | ER | BB | SO | NP | ERA |
|---|---|---|---|---|---|---|---|---|
| Nagy | 8 | 5 | 2 | 1 | 0 | 6 | 111 | 1.12 |
| Mesa | 1 | 1 | 0 | 0 | 0 | 0 | 12 | 4.50 |
| Tavarez L, 0-1 | 1 | 2 | 1 | 1 | 0 | 0 | 15 | 4.50 |
| Assenmacher | 1/3 | 0 | 0 | 0 | 0 | 0 | 2 | 0.00 |
| Plunk | 2/3 | 1 | 2 | 2 | 1 | 1 | 10 | 13.50 |

**IBB:** off Plunk (T Martinez). **HBP:** by Charlton (Belle), by Nagy (Cora).
**UMPIRES:** Reed, Ford, McClelland, Coble, Phillips, Cousins. **T:** 3:18 **A:**
43,643

### GAME FOUR: Indians 7, Seattle 0

The Indians were back - and *came* all the way back - the next day behind Ken Hill, though they did so without two of their best players, Belle and Alomar.

Though Hill had not started a game in 17 days, he never pitched better since his acquisition from St. Louis 11 weeks earlier, and the Indians beat the Mariners, 7-0, in front of 43,686 fans at Jacobs Field on October 14.

Belle was on the sidelines with a badly bruised, sprained and swollen right ankle, and Alomar was unable to play because of a pinched nerve in his neck.

As Belle entered the clubhouse on crutches, Hargrove said, "When I saw that, I thought they'd need a stretcher for me."

But the Tribe's "alternate" power source, Murray and Thome, each homered off Andy Benes, and this one was wrapped up in a hurry, as early as the third inning, in fact.

Murray drilled his homer in the first inning, after Lofton led with a single, stole second and went to third on Wilson's throwing error. Vizquel walked and, when Baerga grounded out, Lofton scored.

Then Murray took Benes deep - 430 feet deep into the right-center field seats. It was his first homer of the ALCS and only his third hit in 15 at-bats against the Mariners.

Another run came home in the second when Pena singled and, with some daring base running, went all the way to third - reaching it with a head first slide - on a routine ground out by Wayne Kirby. Then he scored on Lofton's sacrifice fly.

"Anytime you take a risk like that, you have to tell yourself you're going to be able to do it," said Pena, the 38-year old back-up catcher. "I was positive about it. If I had any doubts, I would have stayed at second base.

"Something like that can bring the team's spirits up," which very well could have been what happened to the Indians.

Hitting instructor Charlie Manuel also had a theory. "Getting three runs right away was very big," he said. "It helped get our minds off the loss (the night before). It turned the corner for us."

Thome homered in the third, after Baerga opened with a single, and Hill had a six run lead, more than enough the way he was pitching.

The Mariners got to him for only five hits through seven innings, Jim Poole fired a hitless eighth, and Chad Ogea and Alan Embree combined to extend the shutout through the ninth.

"Kenny gave us our money's worth in the division series," said General Manager John Hart. "Now we're getting some more bang for our buck."

"We were in a situation where we needed a win," said Hill. "I made the pitches when I had to. They (the Indians) gave me a three run lead and I relaxed."

It was only the third time the Mariners were held without a run in 1995, which surprised Piniella.

"The story of this game was how well Hill pitched," he said. "Frankly,

I felt pretty good going in (to the game) because our guys, with the exception of Edgar (Martinez), are swinging the bats well.

"And I've also got to admit that anytime you get a guy (Belle) who hit 50 home runs out of the other team's lineup, you feel fortunate."

Not only did Hill not need Belle's big bat in the lineup, he wasn't even aware until later that Belle wasn't able to play.

"First I saw Sandy (Alomar) in the trainer's room with something on his neck," said Hill. "Then I found out that Albert came into the locker room on crutches.

"But we have a bench that is dependable and capable of doing good things."

Well said - and well done.

Hill allowed only five hits and was in serious trouble just once, in the fourth inning when Tino Martinez led off with a single and Buhner followed with a double.

Then, with runners on second and third and nobody out, and Tavarez heating up in the Tribe bullpen, Hill struck out Blowers and Sojo, and got Wilson to ground out.

It tied the series again at two games apiece, but suddenly it was the Indians' turn to deal with a pitching problem: Martinez needed another day's rest because of his sore elbow and left knee. It meant that Hershiser would have to go back to the mound with one day's less rest.

"I feel fine," he said. "I'll take the ball if it's given to me. You don't want to say no. You want them to give you the ball."

Which is the reason Hershiser long ago was nicknamed "Bulldog."

**Sandy Alomar's throw is on the mark, but Seattle's Vince Coleman slides under Jim Thome's tag and steals third base in Game 5 of the ALCS, won by the Indians, 3-2.**

# GAME FOUR BOX SCORE

## Indians 7, Mariners 0

| Seattle | AB | R | H | RBI | BB | SO | AVG |
|---|---|---|---|---|---|---|---|
| Coleman, lf | 3 | 0 | 0 | 0 | 1 | 0 | .063 |
| Cora, 2b | 4 | 0 | 0 | 0 | 0 | 0 | .200 |
| Griffey Jr, cf | 3 | 0 | 0 | 0 | 1 | 1 | .400 |
| E. Martinez, dh | 4 | 0 | 1 | 0 | 0 | 1 | .067 |
| T. Martinez, 1b | 4 | 0 | 1 | 0 | 0 | 2 | .133 |
| Buhner, rf | 3 | 0 | 3 | 0 | 1 | 0 | .467 |
| Blowers, 3b | 4 | 0 | 0 | 0 | 0 | 3 | .200 |
| Sojo, ss | 3 | 0 | 1 | 0 | 0 | 1 | .308 |
| a-Amaral, ph | 1 | 0 | 0 | 0 | 0 | 1 | .000 |
| D Wilson, c | 2 | 0 | 0 | 0 | 0 | 0 | .000 |
| Widger, c | 1 | 0 | 0 | 0 | 0 | 1 | .000 |
| b-Strange, ph | 0 | 0 | 0 | 0 | 0 | 0 | .000 |
| c-A Rodriguez, ph | 1 | 0 | 0 | 0 | 0 | 1 | .000 |
| **Totals** | **33** | **0** | **6** | **0** | **3** | **11** | |

| Cleveland | AB | R | H | RBI | BB | SO | AVG |
|---|---|---|---|---|---|---|---|
| Lofton, cf | 3 | 1 | 1 | 1 | 1 | 0 | .467 |
| Vizquel, ss | 4 | 1 | 1 | 1 | 1 | 2 | .067 |
| Baerga, 2b | 4 | 1 | 2 | 1 | 0 | 0 | .333 |
| Murray, dh | 3 | 1 | 1 | 2 | 1 | 1 | .176 |
| Thome, 3b | 3 | 1 | 1 | 2 | 1 | 1 | .250 |
| M Ramirez, rf | 3 | 0 | 1 | 0 | 1 | 1 | .429 |
| Sorrento, 1b | 3 | 0 | 0 | 0 | 1 | 1 | .182 |
| Pena, c | 3 | 1 | 1 | 0 | 1 | 0 | .333 |
| Kirby, lf | 4 | 1 | 1 | 0 | 0 | 0 | .250 |
| **Totals** | **30** | **7** | **9** | **7** | **7** | **6** | |

| | | | | | |
|---|---|---|---|---|---|
| **Seattle** | 000 | 000 | 000--0 | 6 | 1 |
| **Cleveland** | 312 | 001 | 00x--7 | 9 | 0 |

**a:** struck out for Sojo in the 9th. **b:** announced for Widger in the 9th. **c:** struck out for Strange in the 9th
**E:** D Wison. **LOB:** Seattle 9, Cleveland 7. **2B:** Buhner, Vizquel **HR:** Murray off Benes, Thome off Benes. **SB:** Coleman, Griffey jr, Lofton, Kirby.**SF:** Lofton. **GIDP:** Sorrento, Kirby. **DP:** Seattle 2 (J Nelson, Sojo and T Martinez), (J Nelson, Sojo and T Martinez)

| Seattle | IP | H | R | ER | BB | SO | NP | ERA |
|---|---|---|---|---|---|---|---|---|
| Benes L, 0-1 | 2-1/3 | 6 | 6 | 6 | 2 | 3 | 70 | 23.14 |
| B Wells | 3 | 2 | 1 | 1 | 2 | 2 | 55 | 3.00 |
| Ayala | 1 | 1 | 0 | 0 | 0 | 1 | 17 | 2.45 |
| J Nelson | 1-1/3 | 0 | 0 | 0 | 2 | 0 | 23 | 0.00 |
| Risley | 1/3 | 0 | 0 | 0 | 1 | 0 | 11 | 0.00 |

| Cleveland | IP | H | R | ER | BB | SO | NP | ERA |
|---|---|---|---|---|---|---|---|---|
| K Hill W, 1-0 | 7 | 5 | 0 | 0 | 3 | 6 | 121 | 0.00 |
| Poole | 1 | 0 | 0 | 0 | 0 | 2 | 12 | 0.00 |
| Ogea | 2/3 | 1 | 0 | 0 | 0 | 2 | 15 | 0.00 |
| Embree | 1/3 | 0 | 0 | 0 | 0 | 1 | 5 | 0.00 |

**WP:** Ogea. **UMPIRES:** Ford, McClelland, Coble, Phillips, Cousins, Reed.
**T:** 3:30 **A:** 43,686

**GAME FIVE: Indians 3, Seattle 2**

The last time Orel Hershiser pitched on three days rest was on July 19, 1993, when he was with the Dodgers. That day he fired a complete game victory over the New York Mets.

And, on October 15, 1995, Hershiser beat the Mariners, 3-2.

This one wasn't a complete game; the "Bulldog" pitched six strong innings, holding the Mariners to two runs, one earned, and five hits before turning the job over to the Tribe's bull pen, which came through splendidly again.

Tavarez pitched successfully to one batter in the seventh, Assenmacher was outstanding in retiring two Mariners in the seventh and one in the eighth, Plunk closed out the eighth without giving up a hit (though he walked two), and Mesa hurled a perfect ninth - though Edgar Martinez threw a scare into the 43,607 fans at Jacobs Field before locking up the victory.

Edgar Martinez, who hit well in the Mariners' five game victory over New York in the Division Series, had only one hit in 15 at-bats in the first four games against the Indians.

And after Lofton went back - back, back, 'way back - to the center field wall to haul down Martinez's long fly for the final out of Game 5, the AL batting champion was 1-for-20 in the ALCS.

"I was very glad Lofton caught it," said Mesa. "I didn't think it would go out of the park because of the wind, and the ball was hit too low. But he really worked me hard, so we were glad to get him."

But it didn't happen until after a nearly five minute duel between the league's most consistent hitter and best relief pitcher. Mesa got ahead of Martinez, 1-and-2, then a foul, a ball, and three more fouls, one of them carrying into the seats just outside fair territory in right field.

"I hit that pitch good and I thought it was going to be fair," said Martinez. "But the wind took it too far to the right."

Another ball from Mesa raised the count to 3-and-2, and Martinez lashed the next pitch to center.

"We thought it was going to get out (of the park)," said Mariners outfielder Alex Diaz. "Everybody started jumping in the dugout like, 'He got it! He got it! But that wind was blowing across the field so hard, the ball just died."

So did the Mariners as soon as Lofton reached up and caught the ball in front of the wall.

The Indians again broke on top early, scoring a run in the first against Chris Bosio when, with one out, Vizquel reached on an error, went to second on Baerga's single, waited as Belle struck out, stole third and scored on a single by Murray.

A walk, stolen base and Griffey's two-out double tied the score in the third, and the Mariners went ahead, 2-1, in the fifth when Joey Cora beat out an infield single, and came around on a pair of errors by Belle on a ball hit by Griffey with two out.

But Thome came through with a two run homer in the sixth to regain the lead, and the Indians bull pen held it. The homer was Thome's second of the ALCS, and followed a one-out double by Murray.

"That's one of the best feelings I've ever had," said the 25-year old Thome, playing only his second full season in the major leagues. "By far, that's the biggest hit of my career."

It undoubtedly was.

But though the box score shows that it was Thome's home run that won for the Indians, those who saw the game in person or on television give much of the credit for the victory to Assenmacher, and Hargrove as well.

It was Assenmacher who eased the Indians out of a horrendous jam in the seventh inning, when the Mariners had the potential tying and go-ahead runs on third and first and one out, after Sorrento committed two errors.

That's when Hargrove gave the ball to Assenmacher with the left-handed hitting Griffey coming to the plate. The count went to 2-and-2 and Assenmacher fanned Griffey with his next pitch, a letter-high fast ball.

Then, based on by-the-book strategy, with the right-handed Buhner up next, Hargrove was expected to bring Plunk or Mesa into the game.

He didn't - and Assenmacher justified Hargrove's confidence by striking out Buhner, too.

Hargrove said Assenmacher's instructions were to "more or less pitch around Buhner" because if he walked, left-handed hitting Tino Martinez was due to bat next.

"Once I got two strikes on (Buhner), I felt I wanted to be a little more aggressive and go after him," said Assenmacher, "I threw him a curve ball higher than I wanted to get it, but he just swung over the top of it."

It was a remarkable performance by Assenmacher, and an equally remarkable show of faith by Hargrove.

Hargrove was reluctant to elaborate upon the reason he stuck with Assenmacher, and didn't call upon Plunk to pitch to Buhner.

The last time he did, in the 11th inning of Game 3, Buhner smashed a three-run, game-winning home run off Plunk.

"Obviously, we didn't get the results we were looking for the last time," Hargrove said,

But there was still more that the Indians had to do to win the game and take a 3-2 lead in the series.

In the eighth, after Plunk was summoned from the bull pen with one out, he walked the first batter he faced, Coleman, who promptly stole second.

Then, pitching carefully - *too carefully* - to Diaz, Plunk also walked him, putting the Indians in serious jeopardy with the potential tying and go-ahead runs on first and second, still with only one out.

But Visquel stepped to the front and saved the day with his Gold Glove and remarkable instincts.

Sojo, a notorious bad-ball hitter, stepped in and, after a nine pitch, one-on-one battle with Plunk, lashed a line drive toward center that seemed sure to score at least one run.

But it didn't, as Vizquel lunged to his left and leaped high, snaring the ball in the webbing of his glove for the second out of the inning. Then he tagged Diaz going into second base, and stepped on the base for good measure.

It was a double play that ended the inning, and would have been a triple play had the Indians needed three outs.

All of which set the stage for the ninth inning and Mesa's successful duel with Edgar Martinez.

"It shows the character of that team (the Indians)," correctly stated Bosio. "They commit four errors, two in one inning and we get nothing out of it."

And with that it was back to the Kingdome for the Indians, who needed one more victory to get back to the World Series for the first time in 41 years, and the Mariners two to win their first-ever AL pennant.

"We're going back into the mouth of the lion," said Hargrove. "I know we only need one win out of the next two games, but Seattle is a very good ball club, which has proved its resiliency over the last two months."

Wilson, the Mariners' scrappy catcher, acknowledged Hargrove's remarks, and made a statement of his own.

"We're not afraid of what we're up against," said Wilson. "We came back (from an 0-2 deficit) against New York and, with Randy Johnson going in Game 6, we can come back from this, too.

If nothing else, Johnson's numbers were enough to hearten Wilson. The Mariners were 30-3 when he pitched in 1995. He was 31-5 since May 15, 1994. And left-handed batters were hitting .127 against him.

No wonder Wilson said, "You can put it in the books that this series will go seven games."

**The Indians congratulate each other after beating Seattle in the fifth game of the ALCS, 3-2, taking a three-games-to-two lead.**

# GAME FIVE BOX SCORE

## Indians 3, Mariners 2

| Seattle | AB | R | H | RBI | BB | SO | AVG |
|---|---|---|---|---|---|---|---|
| Cora, 2b | 4 | 2 | 1 | 0 | 1 | 0 | .211 |
| E. Martinez, dh | 5 | 0 | 0 | 0 | 0 | 2 | .050 |
| Griffey Jr, cf | 3 | 0 | 1 | 1 | 1 | 1 | .389 |
| Buhner, rf | 4 | 0 | 0 | 0 | 0 | 3 | .368 |
| T. Martinez, 1b | 4 | 0 | 1 | 0 | 0 | 1 | .158 |
| Strange, 3b | 2 | 0 | 0 | 0 | 0 | 2 | .000 |
| a-Coleman, ph | 0 | 0 | 0 | 0 | 1 | 0 | .063 |
| Blowers, 3b | 0 | 0 | 0 | 0 | 0 | 0 | .200 |
| A Diaz, lf | 3 | 0 | 2 | 0 | 1 | 0 | .500 |
| Sojo, ss | 4 | 0 | 0 | 0 | 0 | 0 | .235 |
| D Wilson, c | 3 | 0 | 0 | 0 | 0 | 1 | .000 |
| b-Amaral, ph | 1 | 0 | 0 | 0 | 0 | 0 | .000 |
| **Totals** | **33** | **2** | **5** | **1** | **4** | **10** | |

| Cleveland | AB | R | H | RBI | BB | SO | AVG |
|---|---|---|---|---|---|---|---|
| Lofton, cf | 5 | 0 | 2 | 0 | 0 | 1 | .450 |
| Vizquel, ss | 4 | 1 | 1 | 0 | 1 | 0 | .105 |
| Baerga, 2b | 3 | 0 | 1 | 0 | 1 | 0 | .333 |
| Belle, lf | 3 | 0 | 0 | 0 | 0 | 2 | .143 |
| Kirby, lf | 0 | 0 | 0 | 0 | 0 | 0 | .250 |
| Murray, dh | 3 | 1 | 3 | 1 | 1 | 0 | .300 |
| Thome, 3b | 3 | 1 | 1 | 2 | 1 | 1 | .267 |
| Espinoza, 3b | 0 | 0 | 0 | 0 | 0 | 0 | .250 |
| M Ramirez, rf | 4 | 0 | 0 | 0 | 0 | 1 | .333 |
| Sorrento, 1b | 2 | 0 | 0 | 0 | 1 | 1 | .154 |
| H Perry, 1b | 1 | 0 | 0 | 0 | 0 | 1 | .000 |
| S Alomar, c | 4 | 0 | 2 | 0 | 0 | 0 | .267 |
| Pena, c | 0 | 0 | 0 | 0 | 0 | 0 | .333 |
| **Totals** | **32** | **3** | **10** | **3** | **5** | **7** | |

| | | | | | |
|---|---|---|---|---|---|
| Seattle | 001 | 010 | 000--2 | 5 | 2 |
| Cleveland | 100 | 002 | 00x--3 | 10 | 4 |

**a:** walked for Strange in the 8th. **b:** grounded out for Wilson in the 9th.
**E:** Griffey Jr, T Martinez, Belle 2, Sorrento 2. **LOB:** Seattle 9, Cleveland 11
**2B:** Griffey Jr, A Diaz, Murray, S Alomar. **HR:** Thome off Bosio. **SB:** Cora, Coleman 2,Vizquel, Lofton 2. **S:** Strange, Kirby. **GIDP:** M Ramirez. **DP:** Seattle 2 (Cora and Sojo), (Sojo, Cora and T Martinez), Cleveland 1 (Vizquel)

| Seattle | IP | H | R | ER | BB | SO | NP | ERA |
|---|---|---|---|---|---|---|---|---|
| Bosio L, 0-1 | 5-1/3 | 7 | 3 | 2 | 2 | 3 | 79 | 3.38 |
| J Nelson | 1 | 2 | 0 | 0 | 3 | 2 | 36 | 0.00 |
| Risley | 1-2/3 | 1 | 0 | 0 | 0 | 2 | 33 | 0.00 |

| Cleveland | IP | H | R | ER | BB | SO | NP | ERA |
|---|---|---|---|---|---|---|---|---|
| Hershiser W, 2-0 | 6 | 5 | 2 | 1 | 2 | 8 | 93 | 1.29 |
| Tavarez | 1/3 | 0 | 0 | 0 | 0 | 0 | 7 | 3.86 |
| Assenmacher | 1 | 0 | 0 | 0 | 0 | 2 | 13 | 0.00 |
| Plunk | 2/3 | 0 | 0 | 0 | 2 | 0 | 19 | 9.00 |
| Mesa S, 1 | 1 | 0 | 0 | 0 | 0 | 0 | 14 | 3.00 |

**IBB:** off J Nelson (Murray). **UMPIRES:** McClelland, Coble, Cousins, Reed, Ford, **T:** 3:37 **A:** 43,607

## GAME SIX: Indians 4, Seattle 0

Despite Wilson's brave words, and Johnson's ability to throw baseballs at close to 100 miles per hour, the 1995 ALCS did not go seven games.

Only six.

And the Indians were on their way to Atlanta and a return to the World Series for the first time since they were ignominiously swept by the New York Giants in 1954 in what still ranks as the greatest embarrassment in Cleveland sports history.

Never mind what might happen in the World Series, the Indians by finally winning the franchise's fourth pennant exorcised the ghosts of Chico Salmon and Richie Scheinblum and Leon Wagner and, yes, even Rocky Colavito.

In beating the Mariners, 4-0, in front of 58,489 suddenly subdued fans in the Kingdome, Dennis Martinez out-pitched - and out-gutted - Johnson, while Lofton put on a display of dash and verve the likes of which have not been seen in a long time.

Except by Cleveland fans the last four years.

When it was over, when the Indians had finally prevailed, Hargrove said he had "to pinch myself to be sure I wasn't dreaming."

Hargrove also praised Martinez and his personal catcher, Tony Pena, who was behind the plate because, the manager said, Alomar had a recurrence of the neck injury that forced him out of Game 4.

"Dennis and Tony impressed the hell out of me. They're two veterans who were given a good plan and they stuck to that plan," said the manager.

"Dennis Martinez wanted this game, and then he went out and showed why he's one of the best pitchers in baseball," said Baerga after the crafty, 40-year old right-hander allowed only four hits through seven innings. He left out of sheer exhaustion with a 1-0 lead.

Then Tavarez and Mesa extended the shutout, pitching hitless ball in the eighth and ninth innings, while their teammates - especially Lofton - were providing a more comfortable cushion.

"After all I've been through in my career, this was the game I was looking for," said Martinez, a recovering alcoholic who finally recorded his first post season victory.

"Finally I did something we can all remember. The people of Cleveland have been waiting for this for such a long time."

Not to be overlooked either, in the distribution of credits, were several more outstanding contributions again by Vizquel, whose near-flawless glove and remarkable instincts pulled Martinez through a couple of serious impending crises.

It was the second shutout of the series for the Indians whose starters were 4-1 with a 1.29 ERA, and the combined staff set an ALCS record with a 1.64 ERA.

The Mariners, the sixth-best hitting team in the AL with a .275 average, were held to a .184 average in the series, and Edgar Martinez, who won his second batting title with a .356 mark, went 2-for-23 (.087) in the six games against the Tribe.

The Indians, whose season average of .290 was best in the league, hit for a cumulative .275 against Seattle.

The defensive magic of Vizquel also was particularly significant in the third, fifth and eighth innings, with plays that a less gifted shortstop would not have been able to make.

In the third, after Sojo led off with a double, the only extra base hit allowed by Martinez, Vizquel made a splendid bare handed pickup of a sharp bouncing ball by Wilson and threw him out at first, holding Sojo at second.

Sojo reached third when Perry made a nice play behind first to retire Coleman, and Baerga threw out Cora.

Vizquel did it again in the fifth, after the Indians had taken a 1-0 lead in their top of the inning, when Espinoza reached with one out on a two base error by Cora and Lofton singled.

Blowers opened Seattle's half of the fifth with a single, but didn't last long as Vizquel turned Sojo's grounder into a double play, and then bare handed Wilson's bounder again and threw him out.

Then in the eighth, Vizquel made a diving stop to retire Diaz leading off the inning, and Tavarez went on to get the next two without trouble.

Though Hershiser, who won two games in the ALCS, was named the Most Valuable Player, many thought - with good reason - the award should have gone to Lofton.

Even Hershiser, while pleased to be the winner, said he would not have complained had it gone to the Indians center fielder, the triggerman of their offense.

"It's unbelievable ... I don't have any words to describe how I feel," he said. "This whole team is the MVP, and certainly Kenny (Lofton) deserved the honor, too." It earned for Hershiser a $50,000 bonus.

Lofton set an ALCS record by hitting .458, on 11-for-24, in the series, with four runs, three RBI, and stole five bases without being caught.

Not only did Lofton produce the first run in the deciding game, he also scored the run that seemed to break the spirit of Johnson and the Mariners in the eighth.

It began with Pena's double, after which Lofton used his blazing speed to beat out a bunt single, sending pinch runner Ruben Amaro to third.

Then, with Vizquel at the plate, Lofton stole second, and a few moments later Wilson, the Mariners catcher, committed a passed ball as Johnson pitched to Vizquel.

Amaro scored easily from third and, amazingly, so did Lofton from second. All the red-faced Wilson and the startled and angry Johnson could do was talk to themselves.

"I wasn't going to try and score at first," said Lofton. "I was just bluffing (by rounding third). But Wilson kind of took his time getting to the ball, so I just came home." He slid in easily for a 3-0 margin.

"There's not a player in either league that has the talent Kenny does," said Hart, who made the deal to acquire Lofton from the Houston Astros in exchange for catcher Ed Taubensee and pitcher Willie Blair in December 1991. "Obviously, he's the offensive catalyst. He is special."

After Lofton slid across the plate moments behind Amaro, Vizquel lined out, but Baerga followed with a home run over the center field wall.

For all practical purposes this game was over. Charlton came on to replace the vanquished Johnson, but it didn't matter.

It was too late for the Mariners, and the Indians had a date with the Braves in Atlanta-Fulton County Stadium four days hence, on October 21.

But just to make sure, Tavarez, with help from Vizquel, shut down the Mariners in the eighth, and Mesa - of course! - did the same in the ninth.

Griffey grounded out, Edgar Martinez struck out for the fifth time, leaving him with only two hits in 23 at-bats in the series, Tino Martinez walked, and Espinoza threw out Buhner.

The drought officially ended at 11:03 p.m., and a few minutes later the champagne flowed freely again.

A Cleveland team had finally won something that no other team from the city had been able to do since the Browns were champions of the National Football League in 1964. That was 31 years ago!

And again Hargrove, while expressing relief, said he could hardly believe it.

But it was true, and it was on to Atlanta for phase four of the Indians dream season.

**Kenny Lofton reaches third base as Seattle third baseman Mike Blowers awaits a throw that never comes in the Indians' 3-2 victory over the Mariners in Game 5 of the ALCS.**

# GAME SIX BOX SCORE

## Indians 4, Mariners 0

| Cleveland | AB | R | H | RBI | BB | SO | AVG |
|---|---|---|---|---|---|---|---|
| Lofton, cf | 4 | 1 | 2 | 1 | 0 | 2 | .458 |
| Vizquel, ss | 4 | 0 | 0 | 0 | 0 | 0 | .087 |
| Baerga, 2b | 4 | 1 | 3 | 1 | 0 | 1 | .400 |
| Belle, lf | 4 | 0 | 2 | 0 | 0 | 1 | .222 |
| Murray, dh | 4 | 0 | 0 | 0 | 0 | 0 | .250 |
| M Ramirez, rf | 3 | 0 | 0 | 0 | 0 | 1 | .288 |
| Kirby, lf | 1 | 0 | 0 | 0 | 0 | 0 | .200 |
| H Perry, 1b | 4 | 0 | 0 | 0 | 0 | 1 | .000 |
| Espinoza, 3b | 4 | 1 | 0 | 0 | 0 | 2 | .125 |
| Pena, c | 3 | 0 | 1 | 0 | 0 | 0 | .333 |
| 1-Amaro, pr | 0 | 1 | 0 | 0 | 0 | 0 | .000 |
| S Alomar, c | 0 | 0 | 0 | 0 | 0 | 0 | .267 |
| **Totals** | **35** | **4** | **8** | **2** | **0** | **8** | |

| Seattle | AB | R | H | RBI | BB | SO | AVG |
|---|---|---|---|---|---|---|---|
| Coleman, lf | 4 | 0 | 1 | 0 | 0 | 1 | .100 |
| Widger, c | 0 | 0 | 0 | 0 | 0 | 0 | .000 |
| Cora, 2b | 4 | 0 | 0 | 0 | 0 | 0 | .174 |
| Griffey Jr, cf | 3 | 0 | 0 | 0 | 1 | 0 | .333 |
| E. Martinez, dh | 3 | 0 | 1 | 0 | 0 | 1 | .087 |
| T. Martinez, 1b | 3 | 0 | 0 | 0 | 1 | 1 | .136 |
| Buhner, rf | 4 | 0 | 0 | 0 | 0 | 1 | .304 |
| Blowers, 3b | 3 | 0 | 1 | 0 | 0 | 0 | .222 |
| Sojo, ss | 3 | 0 | 1 | 0 | 0 | 1 | .250 |
| Fermin, ss | 0 | 0 | 0 | 0 | 0 | 0 | ----- |
| D Wilson, c | 2 | 0 | 0 | 0 | 0 | 0 | .000 |
| a-A Diaz, ph-lf | 1 | 0 | 0 | 0 | 0 | 0 | .429 |
| **Totals** | **30** | **0** | **4** | **0** | **2** | **5** | |

| | | | | | | |
|---|---|---|---|---|---|---|
| Cleveland | 000 | 010 | 030--4 | 8 | 0 | |
| Seattle | 000 | 000 | 000--0 | 4 | 1 | |

a: grounded out for wilson in the 9th. 1: ran for Pena in the 8th.
E: Cora. LOB: Seattle 6, Cleveland 4. 2B: Belle, Pena, Sojo. HR: Baerga off R Johnson. SB: Coleman, Lofton. GIDP: Sojo. DP: Cleveland 1 (Vizquel, Baerga, H Perry)

| Cleveland | IP | H | R | ER | BB | SO | NP | ERA |
|---|---|---|---|---|---|---|---|---|
| D Martinez W,1-1 | 7 | 4 | 0 | 0 | 1 | 3 | 90 | 2.03 |
| Tavarez | 1 | 0 | 0 | 0 | 0 | 1 | 10 | 2.70 |
| Mesa | 1 | 0 | 0 | 0 | 1 | 1 | 12 | 2.25 |

| Seattle | IP | H | R | ER | BB | SO | NP | ERA |
|---|---|---|---|---|---|---|---|---|
| R Johnson L, 0-1 | 7-1/3 | 8 | 4 | 3 | 0 | 7 | 108 | 2.35 |
| Charlton | 1-2/3 | 0 | 0 | 0 | 0 | 1 | 20 | 0.00 |

HBP: by De Martinez (E Martinez). PB: D Wilson. UMPIRES: Coble, Kaiser, Cousins, Reed, Ford, McClelland. T: 2:54. A: 58,489

# American League Championship Series Composite Box

### (Indians win, 4-2)

## BATTING

### CLEVELAND INDIANS

| BATTING | G | AB | R | H | 2B | 3B | HR | RBI | BB | SO | AVG | SB | CS | E |
|---|---|---|---|---|---|---|---|---|---|---|---|---|---|---|
| Lofton, cf | 6 | 24 | 4 | 11 | 0 | 2 | 0 | 3 | 4 | 6 | .458 | 5 | 0 | 0 |
| Baerga, 2b | 6 | 25 | 3 | 10 | 0 | 0 | 1 | 4 | 2 | 3 | .400 | 0 | 0 | 0 |
| Pena, c | 4 | 6 | 1 | 2 | 1 | 0 | 0 | 0 | 1 | 0 | .333 | 0 | 0 | 0 |
| Ramirez, rf | 6 | 21 | 2 | 6 | 0 | 0 | 2 | 2 | 2 | 5 | .286 | 0 | 0 | 0 |
| Alomar, c | 5 | 15 | 0 | 4 | 1 | 1 | 0 | 1 | 1 | 1 | .267 | 0 | 0 | 1 |
| Thome, 3b | 5 | 15 | 2 | 4 | 0 | 0 | 2 | 5 | 2 | 3 | .267 | 0 | 0 | 1 |
| Murray, dh | 6 | 24 | 2 | 6 | 1 | 0 | 1 | 3 | 2 | 3 | .250 | 0 | 0 | 0 |
| Belle, lf | 5 | 18 | 1 | 4 | 1 | 0 | 1 | 1 | 3 | 5 | .222 | 0 | 0 | 2 |
| Kirby, rf - lf | 5 | 5 | 2 | 1 | 0 | 0 | 0 | 0 | 0 | 0 | .200 | 1 | 0 | 0 |
| Sorrento, 1b | 4 | 13 | 2 | 2 | 1 | 0 | 0 | 0 | 2 | 3 | .154 | 0 | 0 | 2 |
| Espinoza, 3b | 4 | 8 | 1 | 1 | 0 | 0 | 0 | 0 | 0 | 3 | .125 | 0 | 0 | 1 |
| Vizquel, ss | 6 | 23 | 2 | 2 | 1 | 0 | 0 | 2 | 5 | 2 | .087 | 3 | 0 | 0 |
| Perry, 1b | 3 | 8 | 0 | 0 | 0 | 0 | 0 | 0 | 1 | 3 | .000 | 0 | 1 | 0 |
| Amaro, pr | 3 | 1 | 1 | 0 | 0 | 0 | 0 | 0 | 0 | 0 | .000 | 0 | 0 | 0 |
| Totals | 6 | 206 | 23 | 53 | 6 | 3 | | 73 | 21 | 25 | 37 | .257 | 9 | 1 | 7 |

### SEATTLE MARINERS

| BATTING | G | AB | R | H | 2B | 3B | HR | RBI | BB | SO | AVG | SB | CS | E |
|---|---|---|---|---|---|---|---|---|---|---|---|---|---|---|
| Diaz, ph-lf | 4 | 7 | 0 | 3 | 1 | 0 | 0 | 0 | 1 | 1 | .429 | 0 | 0 | 0 |
| Griffey Jr, cf | 6 | 21 | 2 | 7 | 2 | 0 | 1 | 2 | 4 | 4 | .333 | 2 | 1 | 1 |
| Buhner, rf | 6 | 23 | 5 | 7 | 2 | 0 | 3 | 5 | 2 | 8 | .304 | 0 | 0 | 1 |
| Sojo, ss | 6 | 20 | 2 | 5 | 2 | 0 | 0 | 1 | 0 | 2 | .250 | 0 | 0 | 1 |
| Cora, 2b | 6 | 23 | 2 | 4 | 1 | 0 | 0 | 0 | 1 | 0 | .174 | 2 | 0 | 1 |
| Blowers, 3b | 6 | 18 | 1 | 4 | 0 | 0 | 1 | 2 | 0 | 4 | .222 | 0 | 0 | 0 |
| T.Martinez,1b | 6 | 22 | 0 | 3 | 0 | 0 | 0 | 0 | 3 | 7 | .136 | 0 | 0 | 1 |
| Coleman, lf | 6 | 20 | 0 | 2 | 0 | 0 | 0 | 0 | 2 | 6 | .100 | 4 | 0 | 0 |
| E.Martinez,dh | 6 | 23 | 0 | 2 | 0 | 0 | 0 | 0 | 2 | 5 | .087 | 1 | 1 | 0 |
| Wilson, c | 6 | 16 | 0 | 0 | 0 | 0 | 0 | 0 | 0 | 4 | .000 | 0 | 0 | 1 |
| Strange,ph-3b | 4 | 4 | 0 | 0 | 0 | 0 | 0 | 0 | 0 | 2 | .000 | 0 | 0 | 0 |
| Amaral, ph | 2 | 2 | 0 | 0 | 0 | 0 | 0 | 0 | 0 | 1 | .000 | 0 | 0 | 0 |
| Rodriguez, ph | 1 | 1 | 0 | 0 | 0 | 0 | 0 | 0 | 0 | 1 | .000 | 0 | 0 | 0 |
| Widger, c | 3 | 1 | 0 | 0 | 0 | 0 | 0 | 0 | 0 | 0 | .000 | 0 | 0 | 0 |
| Fermin, 2b | 1 | 0 | 0 | 0 | 0 | 0 | 0 | 0 | 0 | 0 | ----- | 0 | 0 | 0 |
| TOTALS | 6 | 201 | 12 | 37 | 8 | 0 | 5 | 10 | 15 | 46 | .184 | 9 | 2 | 6 |

## PITCHING

### CLEVELAND INDIANS

| PITCHING | G | CG | IP | H | R | BB | SO | HB | WP | W | L | SV | ER | ERA |
|---|---|---|---|---|---|---|---|---|---|---|---|---|---|---|
| Hill | 1 | 0 | 7 | 5 | 0 | 3 | 6 | 0 | 1 | 1 | 0 | 0 | 0 | 0.00 |
| Assenmacher | 3 | 0 | 1-1/3 | 0 | 0 | 1 | 2 | 0 | 0 | 0 | 0 | 0 | 0 | 0.00 |
| Poole | 1 | 0 | 1 | 0 | 0 | 0 | 2 | 0 | 0 | 0 | 0 | 0 | 0 | 0.00 |
| Ogea | 1 | 0 | 2/3 | 1 | 0 | 0 | 2 | 0 | 1 | 0 | 0 | 0 | 0 | 0.00 |
| Embree | 1 | 0 | 1/3 | 0 | 0 | 0 | 1 | 0 | 0 | 0 | 0 | 0 | 0 | 0.00 |
| Nagy | 1 | 0 | 8 | 5 | 2 | 0 | 6 | 1 | 0 | 0 | 0 | 0 | 1 | 1.12 |
| Hershiser | 2 | 0 | 14 | 9 | 3 | 3 | 15 | 1 | 1 | 2 | 0 | 0 | 2 | 1.29 |
| D Martinez | 2 | 0 | 13-1/3 | 10 | 3 | 3 | 7 | 1 | 0 | 1 | 1 | 0 | 3 | 2.03 |
| Mesa | 4 | 0 | 4 | 3 | 1 | 1 | 1 | 0 | 0 | 0 | 0 | 1 | 1 | 2.25 |
| Tavarez | 4 | 0 | 3-1/3 | 3 | 1 | 1 | 2 | 0 | 0 | 0 | 1 | 0 | 1 | 2.70 |
| Plunk | 3 | 0 | 2 | 1 | 2 | 3 | 2 | 0 | 0 | 0 | 0 | 0 | 2 | 9.00 |
| TOTALS | 6 | 0 | 55 | 37 | 12 | 15 | 46 | 3 | 2 | 4 | 2 | 1 | 10 | 1.64 |

### SEATTLE MARINERS

| PITCHING | G | CG | IP | H | R | BB | SO | HB | WP | W | L | SV | ER | ERA |
|---|---|---|---|---|---|---|---|---|---|---|---|---|---|---|
| Charlton | 3 | 0 | 6 | 1 | 0 | 1 | 5 | 1 | 1 | 1 | 0 | 1 | 0 | 0.00 |
| Nelson | 3 | 0 | 3 | 3 | 0 | 5 | 3 | 0 | 0 | 0 | 0 | 0 | 0 | 0.00 |
| Risley | 3 | 0 | 2-2/3 | 2 | 0 | 1 | 2 | 0 | 0 | 0 | 0 | 0 | 0 | 0.00 |
| Johnson | 2 | 0 | 15-1/3 | 12 | 6 | 2 | 13 | 0 | 0 | 0 | 1 | 0 | 4 | 2.35 |
| Ayala | 2 | 0 | 3-2/3 | 3 | 1 | 3 | 3 | 0 | 0 | 0 | 0 | 0 | 1 | 2.45 |
| Wolcott | 1 | 0 | 7 | 8 | 2 | 5 | 2 | 0 | 0 | 1 | 0 | 0 | 2 | 2.57 |
| Wells | 1 | 0 | 3 | 2 | 1 | 2 | 2 | 0 | 0 | 0 | 0 | 0 | 1 | 3.00 |
| Bosio | 1 | 0 | 5-1/3 | 7 | 3 | 2 | 3 | 0 | 0 | 0 | 1 | 0 | 2 | 3.38 |
| Belcher | 1 | 0 | 5-2/3 | 9 | 4 | 2 | 3 | 0 | 0 | 0 | 1 | 0 | 4 | 6.35 |
| Benes | 1 | 0 | 2-1/3 | 6 | 6 | 2 | 3 | 0 | 0 | 0 | 1 | 0 | 6 | 23.14 |
| TOTALS | 6 | 0 | 54 | 53 | 23 | 25 | 37 | 1 | 1 | 2 | 4 | 1 | 20 | 3.33 |

## SCORE BY INNINGS

| | | | | | | |
|---|---|---|---|---|---|---|
| Cleveland | 413 | 135 | 150 | 00 | --23 |
| Seattle | 032 | 011 | 101 | 03 | --12 |

**DP:** Cle 4, Sea 7. **LOB:** Cle 50, Sea 43. **S:** Strange, Kirby. **SF:** Vizquel, Lofton. Assenmacher faced 1 batter in 8th (Game 1), Tavarez faced 1 batter in 11th (Game 3). **IBB:** off Tavarez (E Martinez);off Hershiser (E Martinez): off Plunk (T Martinez); off Nelson (Murray).

**HBP:** by Hershiser (Cora);by Nagy (Cora);by Charlton (Belle);by D Martinez (E Martinez). **PB:** Wilson.
**UMPIRES:** Phillips, Cousins, Reed, Ford, McClelland, Cobie **T:** Game 1 at Seattle, 3:07. Game 2 at Seattle, 3:14. Game 3 at Clevleand, 3:18. Game 4 at Cleveland, 3:30. Game 5 at Cleveland, 3:37. Game 6 at Seattle,2:54
**A:** Game 1 at Seattle, 57,065. Game 2 at Seattle, 59,166. Game 3 at Clevleand, 43,643. Game 4 at Cleveland, 43,686. Game 5 at Cleveland, 43,607. Game 6 at Seattle,58,489.

**Jim Thome is welcomed back to the dugout after his home run helps the Indians beat Seattle, 7-0, in Game 4 of the ALCS.**

**Jim Thome, who won the Indians "Good Guy" award presented  by the Cleveland chapter of the Baseball Writers Association, waves to his parents in the stands after hitting a home run in the fourth game of the ALCS**

**Pinch runner Wayne Kirby, who scored the tying run in the eighth inning, is greeted by his teammates, though the Indians went on to lose Game 3 of the ALCS to Seattle, 5-2, in 11 innings.**

**Jose Mesa gets ready to deliver the final pitch in the Indians' 3-2 victory over Seattle in Game 5 of the ALCS.**

**Carlos Baerga greets Jim Thome at the plate as the Indians beat Seattle, 3-2, in the fifth game of the ALCS.**

**Alvaro Espinoza, a pinch runner for Carlos Baerga, scores the winning run in the Indians' 7-6, 11 -inning victory over Atlanta in Game 3 of the World Series.**

**Omar Vizquel slides into third base, beating Chipper Jones' tag as the Indians beat Atlanta, 3-2, in 11 innings in the third game of the World Series.**

**Albert Belle watches the ball as it flies into the stands for a home run in the sixth inning of the Indians' 5-2 loss to Atlanta in Game 4 of the World Series.**

**A jubilant Albert Belle is congratulated by coach Jeff Newman as he rounds third base after hitting a home run in Game 4 of the World Series.**

**Eddie Murray is greeted by his happy teammates after hitting a single to score pinch runner Alvaro Espinoza in the 11th inning to beat Atlanta, 7-6, in the third game of the World Series.**

**Atlanta catcher Javy Lopez leaps into the arms of relief pitcher Mark Wohlers after the final out of Game 6, in which the Braves beat the Indians, 1-0, to win the World Series.**

# 13

## The World Series:
## Indians vs. Atlanta

Considering the build-up, the hype that preceded the 91st World Series, it appeared the meeting between the Atlanta Braves and Indians would be a mismatch.

The Braves, ballyhooed by owner Ted Turner as "America's Team," had the greatest pitching staff in the history of baseball (some were claiming), and last but not least, were "the team of the '90s" because they'd won the National League pennant in 1991 and 1992.

They were in the World Series for the third time in four seasons (the classic was cancelled in 1994 because of the players strikes') after winning the NL East with a 90-54 record (best in the league); beating Colorado, 5-4, 7-4 and 10-4, after losing Game 3, 7-5 in 10 innings in the Division Series; and sweeping Cincinnati, 2-1, 6-2 in 10 innings, 5-2, and 6-0, in the NLCS.

The Braves also finished the regular season strong after meandering for a couple of months early. They won 71 of their last 108 games, moving from six games behind to prevail by 21 over the New York Mets and Philadelphia Phillies.

On the other side of Atlanta-Fulton County Stadium for the opener on October 21, were the (previously) bedraggled and lowly Indians, one of the game's all-time biggest losers who, until 1994, hadn't had a winning season since 1986, finished under .500 in 11 of 12 years, lost a franchise record 105 games in 1991 (when they wound up 34 games out of first place), and before the major leagues realigned into four team divisions in 1994, managed to finish as high as fourth only twice in 17 years.

What's more, the Indians hadn't reached baseball's Promised Land - the World Championship - since 1948, and the last time they even got close to it was 41 years ago, only to be swept in the 1954 World Series by the New York Giants.

Atlanta also had a decided edge in individual experience. Ten of its players participated in a combined 71 World Series games, most of it accumulated when the Braves lost to Minnesota in seven games four years earlier, and in six games when they were beaten by Toronto in 1992.

Only six members of the Indians had played in the World Series for a combined 28 games, all with other teams, of course.

In at least one respect the teams were close; both led their leagues in dramatic finishes. The Tribe won 27 games in its last at-bat, and Atlanta 25 during the regular season.

"We're here because we're the best team in the American League, and we're going to try to prove that we're the best team in baseball," said Manager Mike Hargrove on the eve of the World Series.

"Do we have to win to validate our season? No. Do we want to win? Absolutely.

"But, whatever happens, I want to make one thing very clear," added Hargrove. "That is, we're not intimidated by the Braves."

And then the Indians proved Hargrove's contention, even though they lost the opener.

### GAME ONE: Atlanta 3, Indians 2

The experts always said that "great pitching stops great hitters," and they proved to be correct in the opener of the World Series in front of a roaring crowd of 51,876 tomahawk-chopping fans in Atlanta.

Greg Maddux, the greatest pitcher in the game in 1995 when he went 19-2 with a 1.63 earned run average and won his fourth consecutive NL Cy Young Award, stopped the Indians cold, allowing two hits in a 3-2 Braves victory.

Maddux got 19 of the 27 outs on grounders, and only two outs were fly balls to the outfield. Two Indians popped out to the infield, and four struck out.

Hargrove called it "about as well a pitched game as I've ever seen," after Maddux effectively changed speeds with excellent location. "We've been shut down before, but that was a masterful job of pitching."

Both of the Indians' runs were unearned, the first in the first inning when Kenny Lofton opened the game by reaching on an error by Rafael Belliard and stealing second as Omar Vizquel struck out.

With Carlos Baerga at the plate, Lofton also swiped third, and scored as Baerga grounded to Belliard.

Lofton became the first AL player to steal two bases in one inning of a World Series game since a fellow named Babe Ruth did it in 1921.

The Indians didn't get their first hit until the fifth when Jim Thome blooped a single to left with one out, but died on base. Their other hit, also an opposite field single, didn't come until the ninth when Lofton got it with one out.

He stole second and, even though the Braves were ahead, 3-1, at that point, Lofton continued to third when Vizquel grounded into the second out. A good throw to third by Fred McGriff would have nailed Lofton for the game-ending third out.

Instead, the ball got away from third baseman Chipper Jones, enabling Lofton to score. But it was only the Tribe's second run and when Baerga subsequently fouled out, Maddux and the Braves had a 1-0 lead in the series.

It was the 16th two-hitter in World Series history.

Orel Hershiser, unbeaten in six post season games, including four with the Los Angeles Dodgers in 1986 and 1988, was almost as effective as Maddux through six innings, allowing only three hits, one of them McGriff's solo homer in the second.

When Hershiser walked McGriff and David Justice leading the seventh, he took himself out of the game, and the Braves scored twice without a hit after Paul Assenmacher and Julian Tavarez came aboard.

"Orel caught (pitching coach) Mark Wiley by surprise," said Hargrove, explaining the move from Hershiser to Assenmacher. "Mark was going to the mound to let Orel catch a break, and he (Hershiser) took himself out of the game.

"At first I thought he'd hurt himself, but that wasn't it. He just felt he didn't have it anymore."

Assenmacher faced pinch hitter Mike Devereaux and walked him, loading the bases. Tavarez entered at that point and the tie-breaking run scored as Luis Polonia grounded to Vizquel.

It would have been - *should have been* - a double play, but wasn't because Vizquel lost control of the ball as he crossed second base. Actually, the Indians got a break when umpire Bruce Froemming ruled that Vizquel held the ball long enough, forcing Devereaux at second.

At any rate, McGriff scored and, a few minutes later, so did Justice on Belliard's squeeze bunt for a 3-1 lead before Maddux was retired, ending the inning.

"All of a sudden it was just gone, and I felt I wasn't the right man for the job," said a crestfallen Hershiser later. "Every pitch I threw was high and outside. I tried to make adjustments, but nothing was working."

As for Maddux's mastery, Vizquel probably explained it best: "You try to hit a line drive, you hit a ground ball. I tried to bunt, I bunted foul.

"I don't think there's another pitcher, David Cone maybe, who keeps the ball down like that."

Maddux accepted the praise modestly. "That's just the way I pitch," he said. "I don't try to overpower anybody, because I know I can't. I just try to hit my spots, throw off their timing and let them hit the ball so that my fielders can pick it up.

"To my way of thinking, that's what pitching is all about."

Which would indicate that the Indians would find Mr. Maddux just as difficult the next time they see him.

# GAME ONE BOX SCORE

## Braves 3, Indians 2

| Cleveland | AB | R | H | RBI | BB | SO | AVG |
|---|---|---|---|---|---|---|---|
| Lofton, cf | 4 | 2 | 1 | 0 | 0 | 0 | .250 |
| Vizquel, ss | 4 | 0 | 0 | 0 | 0 | 1 | .000 |
| Baerga, 2b | 4 | 0 | 0 | 1 | 0 | 1 | .000 |
| Belle, lf | 3 | 0 | 0 | 0 | 0 | 0 | .000 |
| Murray, dh | 3 | 0 | 0 | 0 | 0 | 0 | .000 |
| Tavarez, p | 0 | 0 | 0 | 0 | 0 | 0 | ----- |
| Embree, p | 0 | 0 | 0 | 0 | 0 | 0 | ----- |
| Thome, 3b | 3 | 0 | 1 | 0 | 0 | 0 | .333 |
| Ramirez, rf | 3 | 0 | 0 | 0 | 0 | 2 | .000 |
| Alomar, c | 3 | 0 | 0 | 0 | 0 | 0 | .000 |
| Hershiser, p | 2 | 0 | 0 | 0 | 0 | 0 | .000 |
| Assenmacher, p | 0 | 0 | 0 | 0 | 0 | 0 | ----- |
| Sorrento, 1b | 1 | 0 | 0 | 0 | 0 | 0 | .000 |
| **Totals** | **30** | **2** | **2** | **1** | **0** | **4** | |

| Atlanta | AB | R | H | RBI | BB | SO | AVG |
|---|---|---|---|---|---|---|---|
| Grissom, cf | 4 | 0 | 1 | 0 | 0 | 1 | .250 |
| Lemke, 2b | 3 | 0 | 1 | 0 | 1 | 1 | .333 |
| Jones, 3b | 4 | 0 | 0 | 0 | 0 | 2 | .000 |
| McGriff, 1b | 3 | 2 | 1 | 1 | 1 | 1 | .333 |
| Justice, rf | 1 | 1 | 0 | 0 | 2 | 0 | .000 |
| Klesko, lf | 2 | 0 | 0 | 0 | 0 | 2 | .000 |
| a- Devereaux, ph-lf | 0 | 0 | 0 | 0 | 1 | 0 | ---- |
| O'Brien, c | 2 | 0 | 0 | 0 | 0 | 1 | .000 |
| b-Polonia, ph | 1 | 0 | 0 | 1 | 0 | 0 | .000 |
| Lopez, c | 0 | 0 | 0 | 0 | 0 | 0 | ---- |
| Belliard, ss | 2 | 0 | 0 | 1 | 0 | 0 | .000 |
| Maddux, p | 3 | 0 | 0 | 0 | 0 | 1 | .000 |
| **Totals** | **25** | **3** | **3** | **3** | **5** | **9** | |

| | | | | | |
|---|---|---|---|---|---|
| **Cleveland** | 100 | 000 | 001--2 | 2 | 0 |
| **Atlanta** | 010 | 000 | 20x--3 | 3 | 2 |

**a:** walked for Klesko in the 7th. **b:** grounded into fielders choice for O'Brien in the 7th **E:** McGriff, Belliard. **LOB:** Cleveland 1, Atlanta 4. **HR:** McGriff off Hershiser. **SB:** Lofton 2. **S:** Belliard. **DP:** Cleveland 1 (Vizquel and Baerga ).

| Cleveland | IP | H | R | ER | BB | SO | NP | ERA |
|---|---|---|---|---|---|---|---|---|
| Hershiser L, 0-1 | 6 | 3 | 3 | 3 | 3 | 7 | 101 | 4.50 |
| Assenmacher | 0 | 0 | 0 | 0 | 1 | 0 | 5 | --- |
| Tavarez | 1-1/3 | 0 | 0 | 0 | 1 | 0 | 15 | 0.00 |
| Embree | 2/3 | 0 | 0 | 0 | 0 | 2 | 8 | 0.00 |

| Atlanta | IP | H | R | ER | BB | SO | NP | ERA |
|---|---|---|---|---|---|---|---|---|
| Maddux W, 1-0 | 9 | 2 | 2 | 0 | 0 | 4 | 95 | 0.00 |

Hershiser faced 2 batters in the 7th, Assenmacher faced one batter in the 7th.
**UMPIRES:** Wendelstedt, McKean, Froemming, Hirschbeck, Pulli, Brinkman
**T:** 2:37. **A:** 51,876

**GAME TWO: Atlanta 4, Indians 3**

It didn't get any better for the Indians the next day as left-hander Tom Glavine and three relievers were almost as difficult as Maddux and Atlanta prevailed, 4-3, on Javy Lopez's two-run homer in the eighth inning.

It wiped out a 2-2 tie and, after the Indians fought back to cut their deficit to one run, a base running blunder by Manny Ramirez in the eighth inning all but sealed the verdict.

Suddenly, with the Indians down, two games to none, the terrible specter of their being swept by the Giants in the 1954 World Series presented itself in the minds of some, though not Hargrove's - at least not that he'd admit.

"We're not going to get swept ... that's the least of my worries," he said.

But still, there had to be concern about the sudden silencing of the Tribe's bats, which had produced a club record 207 home runs and led the AL with a .291 batting average.

If nothing else, the 2-0 advantage by the Braves certainly stacked the odds in their favor. Forty-three teams had taken similar leads in previous World Series, and 32 of them went on to win the world championship.

The New York Mets were the last team to defy the odds, rallying to beat Boston in seven games in 1987.

"This is as big a test as we've faced in a long time," correctly stated Hargrove after Dennis Martinez made his first World Series start since 1979 and allowed all of the Braves runs on eight hits in 5 2/3 innings.

Martinez's personal catcher, Tony Pena was behind the plate with him again. In Martinez's first two post season starts, Alomar caught him. Martinez pitched well in both of them, but went 0-1.

But Pena caught Martinez's third game against Seattle when Alomar was sidelined with a pinched nerve in his neck.

"At this point in their careers, Sandy is a better catcher than Tony," said Hargrove. "But I did notice a real improvement in Dennis (when Pena caught him in the deciding game of the ALCS). And we want to maximize our chances of winning any way we can."

Pena said, "This is a psychological game. There are times when a pitcher just feels better with one person than another."

Alomar said, "I'm not going to worry about it now. I haven't worried about it all year."

The crowning blow, that which ruined Martinez's otherwise credible performance, was Lopez's homer to straightaway center field. It came with one out after Justice singled and reached second when Belle misplayed the ball for an error, and went to third on a ground out.

The score was 2-2 at the time and, with light-hitting Belliard and Glavine the next two scheduled batters, Hargrove was asked if he considered intentionally walking Lopez to set up a potential double play.

"I felt Martinez could get (Lopez) out," said the manager, who pulled the infield in, hoping to cut down the go-ahead run at the plate.

Martinez got two quick strikes on Lopez, who fouled off two pitches, then lined the next over the center field fence.

"My game plan was to pitch around Lopez and get to Belliard," said Martinez. "But when I got ahead of him, 0-and-2, the plan changed. I started thinking strikeout."

Until then it was anybody's game. The Indians broke on top, 2-0, when Belle led the second inning with a single and Murray followed with his third post season homer, and first of the World Series.

The Braves retaliated with two in the third. The uprising began when Marquis Grissom was hit by a pitch and Mark Lemke singled. Grissom went to third on Martinez's wild pickoff attempt at second base, and scored on a sacrifice fly by Jones. Lemke moved to second as McGriff grounded out, and scored the second run of the inning on another single by Justice.

There was no quit in the Indians, but the trouble was a base running blunder by Ramirez, the likes of which he'd committed on other occasions earlier in the season.

This time, in the eighth inning after second reliever Alejandro Pena had taken the mound, Ramirez looped a broken bat single into center field with one out.

Two pitches later, with Ramirez representing the potential tying run and eager to get a good break off first base, Lopez took a high pitch from Pena to Thome and fired to first base, picking off the Tribe runner.

"That's a play that should not happen," said General Manager John Hart. "It should never happen ... it especially should not happen, the circumstances being what they were. Not in the eighth inning of a one run game."

And then, to add to the frustration, after the count on Thome went to 3-and-2, he walked, though reliever Mark Wohlers came on to retire pinch hitter Paul Sorrento, ending the inning.

"We set up the play when (Ramirez) singled in the fourth inning," said Lopez, who preferred to talk more about the pickoff than his game-winning homer.

"McGriff told me that Ramirez was taking a very big lead and that, if he got on again, we should try to get him.

"So, after he singled (in the eighth), McGriff gave me the sign. I called for a fast ball up and in. I figured (Thome) would swing at it, but he didn't. I was ready to throw the ball as soon as I got it."

Lopez did, and he got Ramirez.

Ramirez didn't want to talk about the play - "No questions," he said. "I don't have anything to say." But first base coach Dave Nelson did.

"It was a helluva throw from Lopez," said Nelson. "Manny just sat out there and didn't push back in time. I had warned him to be alert ... he was just a little late."

Hargrove didn't criticize Ramirez, at least not publicly. "He just got out too far and didn't get back," said the manager. "It's in our scouting report that Lopez likes to throw. Manny's aware of it. We're aware of it."

The Indians made one last effort to stay alive as Vizquel singled with two out in the ninth and daringly stole second. But he got no further as Baerga popped out to end the game.

It was the Indians' second consecutive loss by one run after they'd gone 28-14 in one run games during the season.

"We're just not coming through in clutch situations," said hitting coach Charlie Manuel. He was right.

In that second game loss to Glavine and the Braves relief corps:

\* Thome took a called third strike from Glavine with two on and two out in the fourth;

\* Baerga flied out on a Glavine pitch with two on in the fifth.

\* Belle fouled out against Pena with two on in the seventh.

\* Sorrento flied out against Wohlers with one on in the eighth.

It put the Indians in another "must-win" situation upon their return to Jacobs Field where their two-year record was a glossy 93-35, including 54-18 during the regular season in 1995, and 4-1 through the Division Series and AL Championship Series.

**With signs in the stands promoting him as the American League's Most Valuable Player, Albert Belle jogs to left field during the fifth game of the World Series.**

# GAME TWO BOX SCORE

## Braves 4, Indians 3

| Cleveland | AB | R | H | RBI | BB | SO | AVG |
|---|---|---|---|---|---|---|---|
| Lofton, cf | 5 | 1 | 1 | 0 | 0 | 0 | .222 |
| Vizquel, ss | 4 | 0 | 1 | 0 | 1 | 0 | .125 |
| Baerga, 2b | 4 | 0 | 0 | 0 | 1 | 0 | .000 |
| Belle, lf | 3 | 1 | 1 | 0 | 1 | 1 | .167 |
| Murray, dh | 3 | 1 | 1 | 2 | 1 | 0 | .167 |
| Ramirez, rf | 4 | 0 | 2 | 0 | 0 | 1 | .286 |
| Thome, 3b | 3 | 0 | 0 | 0 | 1 | 1 | .167 |
| Pena, c | 3 | 0 | 0 | 0 | 0 | 0 | .000 |
| c-Sorrento, 1b | 1 | 0 | 0 | 0 | 0 | 0 | .000 |
| Alomar, c | 0 | 0 | 0 | 0 | 0 | 0 | .000 |
| Martinez, p | 2 | 0 | 0 | 0 | 0 | 0 | .000 |
| Embree, p | 0 | 0 | 0 | 0 | 0 | 0 | ----- |
| b-Kirby, ph | 1 | 0 | 0 | 0 | 0 | 1 | .000 |
| Poole, p | 0 | 0 | 0 | 0 | 0 | 0 | ----- |
| Tavarez, p | 0 | 0 | 0 | 0 | 0 | 0 | ----- |
| d-Amaro | 1 | 0 | 0 | 0 | 0 | 1 | .000 |
| **Totals** | **34** | **3** | **6** | **2** | **5** | **5** | |

| Atlanta | AB | R | H | RBI | BB | SO | AVG |
|---|---|---|---|---|---|---|---|
| Grissom, cf | 3 | 1 | 1 | 0 | 0 | 0 | .286 |
| Lemke, 2b | 3 | 1 | 1 | 0 | 1 | 0 | .333 |
| Jones, 3b | 3 | 0 | 2 | 1 | 0 | 0 | .286 |
| McGriff, 1b | 4 | 0 | 0 | 0 | 0 | 0 | .143 |
| Justice, rf | 3 | 1 | 2 | 1 | 1 | 0 | .500 |
| Wohlers, p | 0 | 0 | 0 | 0 | 0 | 0 | ----- |
| Klesko, lf | 3 | 0 | 0 | 0 | 0 | 1 | .000 |
| Devereaux, lf-rf | 1 | 0 | 0 | 0 | 0 | 0 | .000 |
| Lopez, c | 3 | 1 | 1 | 2 | 0 | 0 | .333 |
| Belliard, ss | 4 | 0 | 0 | 0 | 0 | 1 | .000 |
| Glavine, p | 1 | 0 | 0 | 0 | 1 | 1 | .000 |
| a-Smith, ph | 1 | 0 | 1 | 0 | 0 | 0 | 1.000 |
| McMichael, p | 0 | 0 | 0 | 0 | 0 | 0 | ----- |
| Pena, p | 0 | 0 | 0 | 0 | 0 | 0 | ----- |
| Polonia, lf | 0 | 0 | 0 | 0 | 0 | 0 | .000 |
| **Totals** | **29** | **4** | **8** | **4** | **3** | **3** | |

| | | | | | | |
|---|---|---|---|---|---|---|
| Cleveland | 020 | 000 | 100--3 | 6 | 2 | |
| Atlanta | 002 | 002 | 00x--4 | 8 | 2 | |

**a:** singled for Glavine in the 6th. **b:** struck out for Embree in the 7th. **c:** flied out for Pena in the 8th. **d:** struck out for Tavarez in the 9th.
**E:** Belle, Martinez, Jones, Devereaux. **LOB:** Cleveland 9, Atlanta 7. **2B:** Jones. **HR:** Lopez off Martinez, Murray off Glavine **SB:** Vizquel, Lofton 2. **SF:** Jones **GIDP:** McGriff, Belliard. **DP:** Cleveland 2 (Baerga, Vizquel and Murray), (Vizquel, Baerga and Murray)

| Cleveland | IP | H | R | ER | BB | SO | NP | ERA |
|---|---|---|---|---|---|---|---|---|
| Martinez L, 0-1 | 5-2/3 | 8 | 4 | 4 | 3 | 3 | 98 | 6.35 |
| Embree | 1/3 | 0 | 0 | 0 | 0 | 0 | 3 | 0.00 |
| Poole | 1 | 0 | 0 | 0 | 0 | 0 | 14 | 0.00 |
| Tavarez | 1 | 0 | 0 | 0 | 0 | 0 | 7 | 0.00 |

| Atlanta | IP | H | R | ER | BB | SO | NP | ERA |
|---|---|---|---|---|---|---|---|---|
| Glavine W, 1-0 | 6 | 3 | 2 | 2 | 3 | 3 | 99 | 3.00 |
| McMichael | 2/3 | 1 | 1 | 0 | 1 | 1 | 19 | 0.00 |
| Pena | 1 | 1 | 0 | 0 | 1 | 0 | 16 | 0.00 |
| Wohlers S, 1 | 1-1/3 | 1 | 0 | 0 | 0 | 1 | 17 | 0.00 |

**HBP:** by Martinez (Grissom), by Tavarez (Lopez). **WP:** Glavine McMichaels.
**UMPIRES:** McKean, Froemming, Hirschbeck, Pulli, Brinkman, Wendelstedt.
**T:** 3:17. **A:** 51,877

## GAME THREE: Indians 7, Atlanta 6 (11 innings)

If the Indians didn't already know it, they were reminded often by the media of the difficult task they faced upon returning to Cleveland for the city's first World Series game since October 2, 1954.

They were down, 0-2, to the Atlanta Braves, and only four of 27 teams that previously lost the first two games in the World Series were able to come back to win the championship - and the 1954 Tribe was not one of them.

Furthermore, *no* team had ever come back from an 0-3 deficit.

But the Indians spoke confidently, buoyed by the fact that they would be playing in front of a friendly crowd - Jacobs Field was sold out for the 58th consecutive game - and also because, being in an American League park, the designated hitter rule would be back in effect.

"We're well aware of the situation because you guys keep reminding us," said Charles Nagy, who was assigned the task of halting the Indians' skid against the Braves on October 24.

"But whatever happened in the past was then. This is now. And just because we're down, 0-2, doesn't mean I've got to throw the ball harder. I can't do anything more than I normally do. I'm going to pitch the way the game dictates.

"When you're in something like this, you throw everything but the kitchen sink. The name of the game is to get the hitters out."

Thome, too, was upbeat. "We need to break loose and play like we did much of the season," he said. "We've done a terrific job of winning big games when we needed to, and there's no reason we can't do it now.

"Besides, it seems that just about every time we play here weird things happen. We just seem to be able to find ways to win here."

Vizquel, however, was more candid in his assessment of the situation. "We are in trouble," he said. "We have to win two of the next three games. No one is panicking, though, No one is frustrated. We just have to go out and do it."

Then Nagy made a valiant effort toward reversing the trend against the Braves. Though he wasn't around at the end, the Tribe prevailed, 7-6, in 11 innings, to the delight of 43,584 fans who jammed Jacobs Field.

The Indians won it on Murray's single after Baerga led off with a double and Belle was intentionally walked by Pena.

But it probably never should have reached that point and, on the other hand, wouldn't have, but for a widely second-guessed decision by Hargrove, and then an outstanding defensive play by rookie first baseman Herbert Perry.

Murray's hit ended the longest game in terms of time - four hours, nine minutes - in World Series history, although to Hargrove it probably seemed like an eternity.

The Indians blew leads of 4-1 and 5-3, and went into the bottom of the eighth trailing, 6-5, after the Braves rallied against an obviously tiring

Nagy, and capitalized on an error by Baerga to continue an assault against two relievers.

Instead of immediately going to the bull pen at the start of the eighth, as he'd done most of the season, Hargrove elected to stick with Nagy.

"Charlie had thrown only 81 pitches, which is a very low pitch count for him, and he'd handled Grissom and Polonia the whole game," Hargrove justified his decision.

But Nagy also had allowed solo homers by McGriff in the sixth and Ryan Klesko in the seventh, when the Tribe's 4-1 lead shrunk to 4-2 and then 4-3.

The Indians got a little breathing room in the bottom of the seventh when Lofton walked with one out, moved up as Vizquel grounded out, stole third and dashed home when Baerga beat out an infield hit.

Hargrove still didn't call for relief after Grissom led the eighth with the seventh hit off Nagy, a double to left. When Luis Polonia followed with another hit, a single that scored Grissom, cutting the Indians' lead to 5-4, Assenmacher was summoned.

Polonia promptly stole second, and Jones worked Assenmacher for a walk. Both runners moved up on McGriff's long fly, and with first base open and one out, it was expected that Hargrove would order Justice intentionally walked.

But he didn't, and Justice grounded to Baerga who booted the ball for an error, allowing Polonia to score the tying run.

When Devereaux was announced as a pinch hitter, Hargrove replaced Assenmacher with Tavarez, who was greeted with a single, getting Jones home with the go-ahead run.

The inning finally ended when Lopez grounded into a double play, but the Braves had regained the lead and the Indians' hopes of avoiding an 0-3 deficit in the series had taken a severe downward turn.

"I hated to think about it, but I was worried, sure I was," Alomar admitted later, after his double featured a rally that re-tied the game in the bottom of the eighth.

Ramirez started it when he walked with one out, Sorrento singled and Alomar lashed a double past first base, just inside the foul line, on the first pitch from Wohlers, who'd replaced third reliever Greg McMichael.

The uprising continued as Lofton was intentionally walked, reaching base for the fifth consecutive time, putting runners at first and third with one out. But Vizquel struck out on a checked-swing and Baerga grounded out.

Mesa took over in the ninth and preserved the deadlock, but couldn't have done it without the help of Perry, who had just entered the game for defensive purposes - one of Hargrove's best decisions of the night.

After Lemke led off with a single, was sacrificed to second, and Polonia walked with two out, Jones smashed one of Mesa's fast balls toward right field. It appeared to be a sure hit, probably a double that would have scored both runners.

"When he hit it, and the *way* he hit it, I thought it was through for sure, we all did," said Atlanta manager Bobby Cox.

But Perry lunged to his left, speared the ball on its first bounce, and trotted to first for the third out, ending the inning.

"It was a helluva play by the kid. It probably saved the game," added Cox.

Hargrove agreed, calling it "the play of the game."

Pitching three innings, his longest stint of the year, Mesa gave up leadoff hits to McGriff and Lemke in each the 10th and 11th, but avoided further trouble.

Wohlers did the same in the ninth and 10th, but Alejandro Pena couldn't stop the Indians in the 11th, and they were back in contention, instead of having their backs to the wall.

"It was a huge win for us," said a much relieved Hargrove. "I don't think there's a team in (World Series) history that has come back from being down 3-0, so this was big."

When Alomar was asked if he thought Hargrove stuck with Nagy too long, the catcher replied, "I was hoping nobody was going to ask me that question," leaving it unanswered, though there was no doubt about his opinion.

Murray, who was 0-for-5 before his game-winning hit, had nothing to say - at least not verbally.

He told the media in a written statement, "It was a fast ball middle-in. I was looking for a fast ball in that situation.

"It was good to get this one over with. We worked pretty hard. It should have been over a lot sooner.

"This one would have been hard to swallow, but we stopped them a few times. This was a great win. It's nice to get this little World Series jinx over with and get on with the series."

The latter remark was a reference to the fact that the Indians had not won a World Series game in Cleveland since October 8, 1948, when Gene Bearden hurled a five-hitter to beat the Braves, then representing Boston, 2-0.

And, while Alomar didn't want to expound upon his opinion of Hargrove's strategy, he talked about a pre-game meeting held by the Indians that he said inspired the team.

"It was called by Kenny Lofton, and we told each other, if we lose, we're going to go down fighting," he said.

# GAME THREE BOX SCORE

## Indians 7, Braves 6 (11)

| Atlanta | AB | R | H | RBI | BB | SO | AVG |
|---|---|---|---|---|---|---|---|
| Grissom, cf | 6 | 1 | 2 | 0 | 0 | 2 | .308 |
| Polonia, lf | 4 | 1 | 1 | 1 | 1 | 1 | .200 |
| Jones, 3b | 3 | 2 | 1 | 0 | 2 | 0 | .300 |
| McGriff, 1b | 5 | 1 | 3 | 2 | 0 | 1 | .333 |
| Justice, rf | 5 | 0 | 0 | 1 | 0 | 0 | .222 |
| Klesko, dh | 3 | 1 | 2 | 1 | 0 | 0 | .250 |
| b-Devereaux, ph-dh | 2 | 0 | 1 | 1 | 0 | 1 | .333 |
| Lopez, c | 5 | 0 | 0 | 0 | 0 | 0 | .125 |
| Lemke, 2b | 5 | 0 | 2 | 0 | 0 | 0 | .364 |
| Belliard, ss | 2 | 0 | 0 | 0 | 0 | 1 | .000 |
| a-Smith, ph | 1 | 0 | 0 | 0 | 0 | 0 | .500 |
| Mordecai, ss | 1 | 0 | 0 | 0 | 0 | 1 | .000 |
| **Totals** | 42 | 6 | 12 | 6 | 3 | 7 | |

| Cleveland | AB | R | H | RBI | BB | SO | AVG |
|---|---|---|---|---|---|---|---|
| Lofton, cf | 3 | 3 | 3 | 0 | 3 | 0 | .417 |
| Vizquel, ss | 6 | 2 | 2 | 1 | 0 | 1 | .214 |
| Baerga, 2b | 6 | 0 | 3 | 3 | 0 | 0 | .214 |
| 2-Espinoza, pr | 0 | 1 | 0 | 0 | 0 | 0 | ----- |
| Belle, lf | 4 | 0 | 1 | 1 | 2 | 0 | .200 |
| Murray, dh | 6 | 0 | 1 | 1 | 0 | 3 | .167 |
| Thome, 3b | 4 | 0 | 0 | 0 | 1 | 1 | .100 |
| Ramirez, rf | 2 | 1 | 0 | 0 | 3 | 0 | .222 |
| Sorrento, 1b | 4 | 0 | 1 | 0 | 0 | 3 | .167 |
| 1-Kirby, pr | 0 | 0 | 0 | 0 | 0 | 0 | .000 |
| Perry, 1b | 1 | 0 | 0 | 0 | 0 | 1 | .000 |
| Alomar, c | 5 | 0 | 1 | 1 | 0 | 1 | .125 |
| **Totals** | 41 | 7 | 12 | 7 | 9 | 10 | |

| | | | | | | | |
|---|---|---|---|---|---|---|---|
| Atlanta | 100 | 001 | 130 | 00--6 | 12 | 1 | |
| Cleveland | 202 | 000 | 110 | 01--7 | 12 | 2 | |

**a:** grounded out for Belliard in the 7th. **b:** singled for Klesko in the 8th.
**1:** ran for Sorrento in the 7th. **2:** ran for Baerga in the 11th
**E:** Belliard, Baerga, Sorrento. **LOB:** Atlanta 7, Cleveland 12. **2b:** Grissom, Jones, Alomar, Baerga, Lofton. **3B:** Vizquel. **HR:** McGriff off Nagy, Klesko off Nagy. **SB:** Polonia, McGriff, Ramirez, Lofton, **CS:** Grissom, Lofton. **S:** Mordecai.**GIDP:**Grissom, Lopez, Ramirez **DP:** Cleveland 2 (Baerga, Vizquel and Sorrento), (Baerga, Vizquel and Perry). Atlanta 1 (Lemke and McGriff)

| Atlanta | IP | H | R | ER | BB | SO | NP | ERA |
|---|---|---|---|---|---|---|---|---|
| Smoltz | 2-1/3 | 6 | 4 | 4 | 2 | 4 | 56 | 15.43 |
| Clontz | 2-1/3 | 1 | 0 | 0 | 0 | 1 | 32 | 0.00 |
| Mercker | 2 | 1 | 1 | 1 | 2 | 2 | 34 | 4.50 |
| McMichael | 2/3 | 1 | 1 | 1 | 1 | 1 | 17 | 6.75 |
| Wohlers | 2-2/3 | 1 | 0 | 0 | 3 | 2 | 32 | 0.00 |
| Pena L, 0-1 | 0 | 2 | 1 | 1 | 1 | 0 | 10 | 9.00 |

| Cleveland | IP | H | R | ER | BB | SO | NP | ERA |
|---|---|---|---|---|---|---|---|---|
| Nagy | 7 | 8 | 5 | 5 | 1 | 4 | 86 | 6.43 |
| Assenmacher | 1/3 | 0 | 1 | 1 | 1 | 0 | 10 | 27.00 |
| Tavarez | 2/3 | 1 | 0 | 0 | 0 | 0 | 3 | 0.00 |
| Mesa W, 1-0 | 3 | 3 | 0 | 0 | 1 | 3 | 51 | 0.00 |

Nagy faced two batters in the 8th.
Pena faced three batters in the 11th
**UMPIRES:** Froemming, Hirschbeck, Pulli, Brinkman, Wendelstedt, McKean
**T:** 4:09. **A:** 43,584

## GAME FOUR: Atlanta 5, Indians 2

The home field advantage wasn't enough to help the Indians, and this time they did "go down fighting," 5-2, as the Braves stepped to within one game of winning their first world championship since 1957 when they were located in Milwaukee.

And, in view of what was to come next, the Indians' chances of engineering another comeback looked even less promising. Greg Maddux, who held them to two hits in Game 1, was waiting in the wings to pitch Game 5 the next night, which Atlanta hoped would be the clincher.

"I've faced more pleasing prospects," acknowledged Hargrove. "But I've also got to remind you there are 26 clubs sitting at home that would like to have the chance to still be playing, the chance that we still have.

"We'll show up, and I'm sure we'll play hard."

In 1985 the Kansas City Royals rallied from a three-games-to-one deficit to capture the World Series. But they were the last to do so, and only the sixth of 39 teams in baseball history to be down 3-1 and come back to win three straight.

In the first four games of this series Braves pitchers stopped the Tribe cold as only Lofton (5-for-17) was hitting with any degree of consistency. The Indians' batting average, which was a robust .291 during the regular season, was a puny .190 (on 26-for-137), and had scored only 14 runs.

"It's hard to beat anybody when you only get four or five hits," said Hargrove.

The Indians were held to six hits by Steve Avery and three relievers, and though two were home runs by Belle and Ramirez, both were solo shots. Belle's was delivered in the sixth, tying the score, 1-1, and Ramirez's led the ninth.

Ken Hill, the former National Leaguer, started for the Indians and pitched well into the seventh, though Klesko homered with the bases bare an inning earlier.

In the seventh, after Belle tied the game, Hill walked Grissom with one out, and he scored on a double by Polonia.

"Except for the ball that Klesko hit, I made pretty good pitches until the seventh," said Hill.

"I don't know what happened then. I thought I was still throwing well enough, but after I struck out the first guy (Belliard), I fell behind on Grissom, and then, with the next guy (Polonia), I got the ball up, a fast ball that I left over the plate and he hit it hard."

Quickly this time, Hargrove made a pitching change, bringing Assenmacher in to intentionally walk Jones. It was an attempt to set up a double play, but didn't work as Assenmacher's first pitch to McGriff got away from Alomar for a passed ball allowing the runners to move up.

Assenmacher reached back and struck out McGriff, and thought he also had fired a called third strike past Justice.

"I thought he got (Justice), and so did Paul," said pitching coach Mark Wiley.

But umpire John Hirschbeck didn't. He said Assenmacher's pitch was out of the strike zone for ball one.

Justice swung at Assenmacher's next offering, a slider down and away, and stroked it on a line to center for a single. It scored Polonia and Jones, giving Atlanta a 4-1 lead.

Justice's hit was the first off Assenmacher in nine post season appearances.

The Braves added another run in the ninth on doubles by McGriff and Lopez off Alan Embree, that helped surmount the Indians' last gasp after Ramirez's ninth inning homer of Wohlers.

Sorrento, pinch hitting for Perry, followed with a double, but Pedro Borbon came out of the bull pen and retired the next three. Thome was called out on strikes, Alomar went down swinging, and Lofton, who had reached base six consecutive times in Game 3, lined out to complete an 0-for-5 night, and end the game.

"We hit some balls hard in the first two innings, but then (Avery) started throwing his change-up, and we couldn't get the good part of the bat on the ball after that," said Hargrove.

Dennis Martinez, who remembered that his Baltimore Orioles blew a three-games-to-one lead to Pittsburgh in the 1979 World Series, tried to express optimism.

"Anything can happen," he said. "We just have to bounce back the way the Pirates bounced back on us (the Orioles). We can do it. We have to keep our head up and remember what we did all year."

The latter was a reference to the Indians' 51 comeback victories to date, 29 of them in their last at-bat.

While the Indians' clubhouse was understandably grim, the Braves were gleeful, but restrained in their enthusiasm.

"No matter what happens (in Game 6), we'll be in great shape," said Jones, the rookie third baseman who played an integral role in the Braves success.

"We'll either be world champions, or have a 3-2 lead going back to the 'Chop Shop,'" the nickname given to the Atlanta-Fulton County Stadium.

# GAME FOUR BOX SCORE

## Braves 5, Indians 2

| Atlanta | AB | R | H | RBI | BB | SO | AVG |
|---|---|---|---|---|---|---|---|
| Grissom, cf | 4 | 1 | 3 | 0 | 1 | 0 | .412 |
| Polonia, lf | 4 | 1 | 2 | 1 | 0 | 0 | .333 |
| Devereaux, lf | 0 | 0 | 0 | 0 | 1 | 0 | .333 |
| Jones, 3b | 4 | 1 | 0 | 0 | 1 | 0 | .214 |
| McGriff, 1b | 3 | 1 | 1 | 0 | 2 | 1 | .333 |
| Justice, rf | 5 | 0 | 1 | 2 | 0 | 0 | .214 |
| Klesko, dh | 3 | 1 | 1 | 1 | 1 | 1 | .273 |
| b-Mordecai, ph-dh | 1 | 0 | 0 | 0 | 0 | 0 | .000 |
| Lopez, c | 5 | 0 | 2 | 1 | 0 | 1 | .231 |
| Lemke, 2b | 5 | 0 | 1 | 0 | 0 | 0 | .313 |
| Belliard, ss | 3 | 0 | 0 | 0 | 0 | 1 | .000 |
| **Totals** | **37** | **5** | **11** | **5** | **6** | **4** | |

| Cleveland | AB | R | H | RBI | BB | SO | AVG |
|---|---|---|---|---|---|---|---|
| Lofton, cf | 5 | 0 | 0 | 0 | 0 | 1 | .294 |
| Vizquel, ss | 3 | 0 | 0 | 0 | 1 | 0 | .176 |
| Baerga, 2b | 4 | 0 | 1 | 0 | 0 | 0 | .222 |
| Belle, lf | 3 | 1 | 1 | 1 | 1 | 1 | .231 |
| Murray, dh | 2 | 0 | 0 | 0 | 2 | 0 | .143 |
| Ramirez, rf | 3 | 1 | 1 | 1 | 1 | 0 | .250 |
| Perry, 1b | 3 | 0 | 0 | 0 | 0 | 1 | .000 |
| c-Sorrento, ph | 1 | 0 | 1 | 0 | 0 | 0 | .286 |
| Espinoza, 3b | 2 | 0 | 1 | 0 | 0 | 0 | .500 |
| a-Thome, ph 3b | 2 | 0 | 1 | 0 | 0 | 1 | .167 |
| Alomar, c | 4 | 0 | 0 | 0 | 0 | 1 | .083 |
| **Totals** | **32** | **2** | **6** | **2** | **5** | **5** | |

| | | | | | |
|---|---|---|---|---|---|
| Atlanta | 000 | 001 | 301--5 | 11 | 1 |
| Cleveland | 000 | 001 | 001--2 | 6 | 0 |

**a:** doubled for Espinoza in the 7th. **b:** lined out for Klesko in the 9th. **c:** doubled for Perry in the 9th.

**E:**Lemke. **LOB:** Atlanta 12, Cleveland 8. **2B:** Polonia, McGriff, Lopez 2, Sorrento, Thome. **HR:** Belle off Avery, Ramirez off Wohlers, Klesko off Hill. **SB:** Grissom 2. **CS:** Espinoza. **S:** Belliard. **GIDP:**Baerga. **DP:** Atlanta 1 (Jones, Lemke and McGriff)

| Atlanta | IP | H | R | ER | BB | SO | NP | ERA |
|---|---|---|---|---|---|---|---|---|
| Avery W, 1-0 | 6 | 3 | 1 | 1 | 5 | 3 | 109 | 1.50 |
| McMichael | 2 | 1 | 0 | 0 | 0 | 0 | 15 | 2.70 |
| Wohlers | 0 | 2 | 1 | 1 | 0 | 0 | 10 | 2.25 |
| Borbon S, 1 | 1 | 0 | 0 | 0 | 0 | 2 | 11 | 0.00 |

| Cleveland | IP | H | R | ER | BB | SO | NP | ERA |
|---|---|---|---|---|---|---|---|---|
| Hill L, 0-1 | 6-1/3 | 6 | 3 | 3 | 4 | 1 | 94 | 4.26 |
| Assenmacher | 2/3 | 1 | 1 | 0 | 1 | 2 | 12 | 9.00 |
| Tavarez | 2/3 | 2 | 0 | 0 | 1 | 1 | 18 | 0.00 |
| Embree | 1-1/3 | 2 | 1 | 1 | 0 | 0 | 24 | 3.86 |

Wohlers faced 2 batters in the 9th. **PB:** Alomar. **Balk:** Avery. **UMPIRES:** Hirschbeck, Pulli, Brinkman, Wendelstedt, McKean, Froemming. **T:** 3:14 **A:** 43,578

## GAME FIVE: Indians 5, Atlanta 4

"We're still in a hole, a deep hole," acknowledged Mike Hargrove after the "Bulldog," Orel Hershiser and Jose Mesa beat the Braves, 5-4, on October 26, sending the World Series back to Atlanta for Game 6.

But the depth of the hole notwithstanding, the Indians were still alive, and if they're breathing, they still had a chance, as 13 American League teams would quickly attest.

Facing extinction at the hands of the best pitcher in the National League, Greg Maddux, the Indians scored twice in the first inning when Belle smashed his second homer of the series, fourth of the post season and 54th of the year into the Braves bull pen in right field.

It came with two outs and followed a base on balls to Vizquel.

The two run homer fired up the crowd of 43,595 fans in Jacobs Field - and Maddux's next pitch fired up the Tribe.

Maddux, whose control was usually excellent, unleashed a fast ball up and close to Murray, who fell to the ground to avoid being hit by the pitch.

When he got up, there was fire in Murray's eyes. He shouted at Maddux and took a couple of menacing steps toward the mound before umpire Frank Pulli jumped out from behind the plate and blocked Murray's path.

Both dugouts emptied and players from the two bull pens ran in from the outfield, though the skirmish never escalated beyond the point of shouting and glaring.

Murray and Braves catcher Charlie O'Brien got into each other's face with some harsh words, but order was quickly restored and there were no further incidents.

Maddux claimed he didn't throw at Murray. "I was just trying to come in on him," he said. "I threw him a cutter inside, and he didn't like it. I was surprised by his reaction. I really have a lot of respect for Eddie Murray. He's great for baseball. He never shows up opposing teams. It's unfortunate.

"I don't think I go looking for trouble. I had just given up a home run which might have made it look bad. But I never take it out on anyone after I give up a home run."

In the opinion of some, Murray's angry reaction and threat to charge the mound might have served as a wake up call for the Indians - which very well might have been Murray's objective.

"Everybody wanted a piece of (Maddux) after that," said Vizquel.

Lofton said, "In a sense, it might have been on purpose. Maddux hadn't thrown a ball like that all year. No doubt, it got the guys fired up."

And as Wayne Kirby commented, "Eddie's one of those guys, you know, he's quiet. But, like they say, don't wake up a sleeping dog.

"I think it got us psyched. Maybe we needed it. We haven't had it all year. Maybe we needed it to regroup and get our cockiness back."

Maybe they did. Whatever, the Indians responded well.

So did Hershiser, who pitched eight strong innings and left what seemed to be a comfortable, 5-2, lead in the hands of Mesa.

But this one wasn't locked up until Mesa uncharacteristically staggered in the ninth inning as the Braves scored twice, cutting their deficit to one.

Jones led off with a drive to right field that Kirby caught on the warning track. Then McGriff lined a double just inside the right field foul line. Justice grounded out, but Klesko drilled an 0-and-2 pitch into the right field stands.

No longer were the Indians coasting. Suddenly trouble was brewing, and it was time for Mesa to bear down, which he did.

He caught Lemke looking at a third strike, ending the game.

Mesa shrugged off the suggestion that, perhaps with all the pitching he'd done this year - 62 appearances in the regular season, two in the Division Series, four in the ALCS, and two in the World Series for a total of 70 in the Indians' 158 games to date - his arm was weary.

"No, no, no," he insisted. "Klesko hit a good pitch. You pitch different with a three-run lead. You go after them. After that (Klesko's homer) I threw more sinkers, trying for ground outs."

Actually, there was nothing comfortable about this game for the Indians until they scored twice in the sixth.

They broke a 2-2 tie when Baerga doubled with one out, Belle was intentionally walked (for the 12th time in the post season), Murray flied deep to right for the second out, Thome singled for one run and Ramirez also singled for another.

Two innings later Thome blasted a 3-and-2 pitch 440 feet into the picnic area in center field off reliever Brad Clontz. It turned out to be the winning run.

Hershiser, who pitched against Braves teams for 12 years while he was a member of the Los Angeles Dodgers, and beat them 20 times in his NL career, including 12 in a row at one point, was masterful except for a pitch to Polonia in the fourth.

It landed in the right field seats for a solo home run.

The Braves tied the score, 2-2, in the fifth with an unearned run, the result of Hershiser's throwing error to second base on what should have been a double play.

The Indians were fortunate it didn't turn out worse. The Braves went on to load the bases with one out, and the run came home on a bounder back to the mound that Hershiser couldn't hold, and that went for a single.

Then, with the crowd hushed and fearing the worst, Polonia grounded to Vizquel who turned it into an inning ending double play.

When it ended and the Indians were alive to fight another night - but "still in a hole, a deep hole," as Hargrove said - their spirits were buoyed as they returned to Atlanta for the sixth game.

And, despite the Indians trailing, three-games-to-two, Hershiser said the pressure was on the Braves. "They definitely have something to lose. They have lost the last two World Series they'd participated in. The people in Atlanta are probably wondering what's going on."

He was alluding to the Braves history of losing big games - OK, *choking up* under pressure.

The Braves failed to hold a three-games-to-two lead and lost to Minnesota in seven games in 1991. In 1992, they lost in six games to Toronto. And they didn't make it back to the World Series in 1993, losing to Philadelphia in six games in the NLCS.

Sorrento agreed. "I think all the pressure is on them," he said. "They've been here before and haven't won. We weren't even supposed to get here. We're supposed to be at home because we were facing the best pitcher in baseball (Maddux) in Game 5."

But Cox, the feisty Atlanta manager scoffed. So did Justice.

"Orel should keep his mouth shut," snapped Cox. "He can play games with some babies somewhere. We're grown up around here."

Justice said, "For those guys to sit there and say that the pressure is on us, they're crazy."

Then, directing his remarks at Hershiser, Justice said, "(Expletive deleted) Orel! I don't know why he would say what he did. Sure, it makes me angry. I'm angry because each year this team fights its butt off. People don't know how hard we work.

"I don't think it's fair to say what he did because we haven't won a World Series."

**Cleveland fans, starved for a winning team, celebrate on Public Square after the Indians defeated Seattle to win the American League pennant.**

# GAME FIVE BOX SCORE

## Indians 5, Braves 4

| Atlanta | AB | R | H | RBI | BB | SO | AVG |
|---|---|---|---|---|---|---|---|
| Grissom, cf | 4 | 0 | 1 | 1 | 0 | 0 | .381 |
| Polonia, lf | 4 | 1 | 1 | 1 | 0 | 1 | .308 |
| Jones, 3b | 4 | 0 | 1 | 0 | 0 | 1 | .222 |
| McGriff, 1b | 4 | 1 | 1 | 0 | 0 | 2 | .316 |
| Justice, rf | 4 | 0 | 0 | 0 | 0 | 1 | .167 |
| Klesko, dh | 4 | 2 | 2 | 2 | 0 | 0 | .333 |
| Lemke, 2b | 4 | 0 | 0 | 0 | 0 | 1 | .250 |
| O'Brien, c | 1 | 0 | 0 | 0 | 0 | 0 | .000 |
| b-Lopez, ph-c | 1 | 0 | 0 | 0 | 0 | 0 | .214 |
| Belliard, ss | 1 | 0 | 0 | 0 | 0 | 1 | .000 |
| a-Smith, ph | 0 | 0 | 0 | 0 | 1 | 0 | .500 |
| Mordecai, ss | 1 | 0 | 1 | 0 | 0 | 0 | .333 |
| **Totals** | **32** | **4** | **7** | **4** | **1** | **7** | |

| Cleveland | AB | R | H | RBI | BB | SO | AVG |
|---|---|---|---|---|---|---|---|
| Lofton, cf | 4 | 0 | 0 | 0 | 0 | 0 | .238 |
| Vizquel, ss | 3 | 1 | 1 | 0 | 1 | 1 | .200 |
| Baerga, 2b | 4 | 1 | 1 | 0 | 0 | 0 | .227 |
| Belle, lf | 3 | 2 | 1 | 2 | 1 | 2 | .250 |
| Murray, dh | 3 | 0 | 0 | 0 | 1 | 0 | .118 |
| Thome, 3b | 4 | 1 | 2 | 2 | 0 | 0 | .250 |
| Ramirez, rf | 3 | 0 | 1 | 1 | 0 | 1 | .267 |
| Perry, 1b | 1 | 0 | 0 | 0 | 0 | 0 | .000 |
| Sorrento, 1b | 3 | 0 | 0 | 0 | 0 | 1 | .200 |
| Kirby, rf | 0 | 0 | 0 | 0 | 0 | 0 | .000 |
| Alomar, c | 3 | 0 | 2 | 0 | 0 | 0 | .200 |
| **Totals** | **31** | **5** | **8** | **5** | **3** | **5** | |

| | | | | |
|---|---|---|---|---|
| Atlanta | 000 | 110 | 002--4 | 7 0 |
| Cleveland | 200 | 002 | 01x--5 | 8 1 |

**a:** walked for Belliard in the 5th. **b:** grounded out for O'Brien in the 7th.
**E:** Hershiser. **LOB:** Atlanta 3, Cleveland 5 **2B:** Jones, McGriff, Baerga, Alomar. **HR:** Belle off Maddux, Thome off Clontz, Polonia off Hershiser, Klesko off Mesa. **S:** O'Brien. **GIDP:** Polonia. **DP:** Cleveland 2 (Vizquel, Baerga and Sorrento), (Hershiser and Perry)

| Atlanta | IP | H | R | ER | BB | SO | NP | ERA |
|---|---|---|---|---|---|---|---|---|
| Maddux L, 1-1 | 7 | 7 | 4 | 4 | 3 | 4 | 98 | 2.25 |
| Clontz | 1 | 1 | 1 | 1 | 0 | 1 | 20 | 2.70 |

| Cleveland | IP | H | R | ER | BB | SO | NP | ERA |
|---|---|---|---|---|---|---|---|---|
| Hershiser W, 1-1 | 8 | 5 | 2 | 1 | 1 | 6 | 100 | 2.57 |
| Mesa S, 1 | 1 | 2 | 2 | 2 | 0 | 1 | 18 | 4.50 |

**UMPIRES:** Pulli, Brinkman, Wendelstedt, McKean, Froemming, Hirschbeck
**T:** 2:33 **A:** 43,595

## GAME SIX: Atlanta 1, Indians 0

Two nights later, in the "Chop Shop," a.k.a. Atlanta-Fulton County Stadium, the Braves finally did win a World Series.

In a pressure-cooker environment, in front of 51,875 chanting, toma-hawk-chopping fans, they scored a run - *one lousy run!* - to defeat the Indians, 1-0, ending the most glorious year in Cleveland baseball history in 41 years, and to conclude the city's season of dreams.

It was the Braves' first world championship since the franchise moved to Atlanta in 1966, and their first in 38 years since 1957 when, as the Milwaukee Braves, they beat the New York Yankees in seven games.

It was a devastating, gut-wrenching loss for the Indians, but they had no reason to be ashamed. Not after all they'd done *almost* everything right to get to where they were on October 28.

They went down fighting valiantly, with pitching if not hitting.

"The only thing we didn't do was win this thing, the World Series," said Hargrove. "But we played like champions. I really feel we did."

Their legion of fans thought so, too, and more than 50,000 of them made those sentiments clear two days later with their exuberant outpouring of affection and respect - and anticipation of greater accomplishments to come.

Braves left-hander Tom Glavine made it all come undone for the Indians in that sixth game, pitching a near no-hitter for his second victory of the series, which won for him the Most Valuable Player award.

The Braves only run was a sixth inning homer by Justice. It was one of only six hits by Atlanta.

Dennis Martinez, the gutsy grandfather, pitched almost as well before he departed with two out in the fifth, his sore right elbow and aching left knee finally getting to be too much.

Poole replaced Martinez and got out of the inning, leaving two runners stranded, but couldn't escape the wrath of Justice in the sixth.

The outspoken right-fielder, who criticized Braves fans before the game for their lack of support for the team, smoked a 1-and-1 pitch from Poole over the right field fence for a home run.

It made Poole the loser of the last Indians game of the season - just as he was the pitcher of record in the first game they lost, 10-9, to Texas on April 28.

Poole faced the media afterwards and didn't make any excuses. "The score was 0-0 when I came in, and I was supposed to keep it 0-0. I didn't do my job," said Poole, admitting he missed badly on the pitch Justice creamed.

"It was supposed to be down and away, it was up an in," he said.

Glavine, whose record was 16-7 during the regular season, also got credit for the victory in Game 2, in which the Braves prevailed, 4-3.

The only hit the 29-year old southpaw allowed was a single off the broken bat of Pena that plopped down in center field leading the sixth inning. Glavine walked three and didn't permit a runner beyond first base through the eight innings he worked.

Wohlers pitched the ninth and was equally effective, retiring Lofton on a pop foul to Belliard, and Sorrento and Baerga on fly balls to Grissom in center field.

It was a remarkable performance by Glavine, the winningest pitcher in the major leagues over the last five years (with 95 victories), and was only the fifth one-hitter in World Series history.

"No one beats that kind of pitching, no one," said Hargrove. "We maybe had three good swings all night."

Pena also was quick to praise Glavine. "Give him credit. He kept the ball down the whole game. When I got the hit, I had to go down in the strike zone to get it."

Hart said, "We finally come back and beat Greg Maddux (in Game 5) and run right into Glavine. That pitching performance was as good as I've seen. We didn't have a chance against him.

"I never thought I'd see this lineup shut down like that for a full week," continued the Indians general manager. "We saw some pitchers do it sporadically during the season, but not like this. Not for a full week.

"We didn't swing the bats like we're capable of doing - but give the Braves pitching credit."

Everybody did.

"I've seen our hitters struggle for four or five games during the regular season, but never for more than 10 or 11 games like we've been doing, going all the way back to the Seattle (ALCS) series," said Alomar.

"If you had told me this would happen, I wouldn't have believed it."

Five of the six games were decided by one run. The Indians lost three of them, which was in direct contrast to the regular season when they were 28-14 in one-run games.

As a team they batted .179 (35-for-195), eighth-lowest average ever in the World Series, and the second lowest in a six game series. Only the New York Giants, who hit .175 against the Philadelphia Athletics in 1911, were more inept.

The heart of the Tribe's batting order, the 3-4-5 hitters - Baerga, Belle and Murray - hit a combined .177 (11-for-62) with three homers and 11 RBI.

Belle's .235 average (4-for-17) was the highest among the regulars, three of whom (Murray, Vizquel and Baerga) all hit less than .200.

Through the first three games of the series, Lofton was a leading candidate to win the MVP award. He was hitting .417 (5-for-12) with five runs and five stolen bases. In those three games Lofton reached base 10 times, including six in a row in Game 3.

After that game Braves manager Bobby Cox asserted, "We've got to find a way to keep (Lofton) off the bases."

They did. Thereafter, Lofton went 0-for-12 and wound up hitting .200 overall.

In the aftermath of the loss, Martinez perhaps said it best. "I think we should still feel good about ourselves," said the pitcher who battled injuries most of the second half of the season, but refused to give in to them.

"We don't feel good about losing, but we gave Cleveland a lot of joy, and I was happy to be part of that. I think the fans know, just as we know, that we accomplished something."

And so, though the Indians fell one game short of their goal - actually, only one inning, even one pitch short - 1995 was indeed a glorious year for baseball in Cleveland.

It was the season the Indians redeemed themselves after 41 long years of frustration and despair.

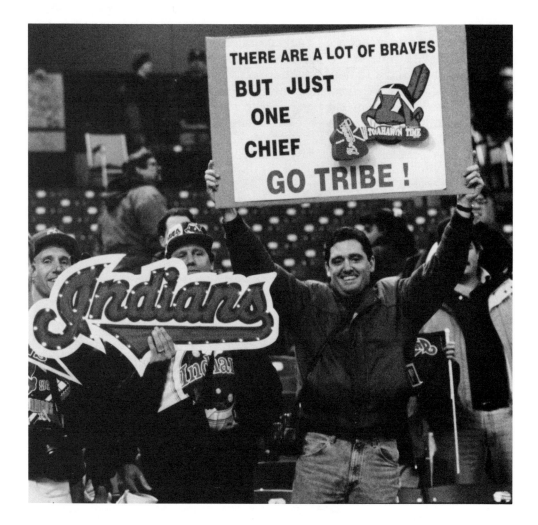

**Fans in the stands at Jacobs field cheer the Indians to a 5-4 victory over Atlanta in Game 5 of the World Series.**

# GAME SIX BOX SCORE

## Braves 1, Indians 0

| Cleveland | AB | R | H | RBI | BB | SO | AVG |
|---|---|---|---|---|---|---|---|
| Lofton, cf | 4 | 0 | 0 | 0 | 0 | 0 | .200 |
| Vizquel, ss | 3 | 0 | 0 | 0 | 0 | 2 | .174 |
| b-Sorrento, ph | 1 | 0 | 0 | 0 | 0 | 0 | .182 |
| Baerga, 2b | 4 | 0 | 0 | 0 | 0 | 0 | .192 |
| Belle, lf | 1 | 0 | 0 | 0 | 2 | 1 | .235 |
| Murray, 1b | 2 | 0 | 0 | 0 | 1 | 1 | .105 |
| Ramirez, rf | 3 | 0 | 0 | 0 | 0 | 1 | .222 |
| Embree, p | 0 | 0 | 0 | 0 | 0 | 0 | ----- |
| Tavarez, p | 0 | 0 | 0 | 0 | 0 | 0 | ----- |
| Assenmacher, p | 0 | 0 | 0 | 0 | 0 | 0 | ----- |
| Thome, 3b | 3 | 0 | 0 | 0 | 0 | 2 | .211 |
| Pena, c | 3 | 0 | 1 | 0 | 0 | 0 | .167 |
| Martinez, p | 1 | 0 | 0 | 0 | 0 | 1 | .000 |
| Poole, p | 1 | 0 | 0 | 0 | 0 | 0 | .000 |
| Hill, p | 0 | 0 | 0 | 0 | 0 | 0 | ----- |
| Amaro, rf | 1 | 0 | 0 | 0 | 0 | 0 | .000 |
| **Totals** | **27** | **0** | **1** | **0** | **3** | **8** | |

| Atlanta | AB | R | H | RBI | BB | SO | AVG |
|---|---|---|---|---|---|---|---|
| Grissom, cf | 4 | 0 | 1 | 0 | 0 | 0 | .360 |
| Lemke, 2b | 2 | 0 | 1 | 0 | 1 | 0 | .273 |
| Jones, 3b | 3 | 0 | 2 | 0 | 1 | 0 | .286 |
| McGriff, 1b | 4 | 0 | 0 | 0 | 0 | 2 | .261 |
| Justice, rf | 2 | 1 | 2 | 1 | 2 | 0 | .250 |
| Klesko, lf | 1 | 0 | 0 | 0 | 2 | 0 | .313 |
| Devereaux, lf | 1 | 0 | 0 | 0 | 0 | 0 | .250 |
| Lopez, c | 3 | 0 | 0 | 0 | 1 | 0 | .176 |
| Belliard, ss | 4 | 0 | 0 | 0 | 0 | 0 | .000 |
| Glavine, p | 3 | 0 | 0 | 0 | 0 | 1 | .000 |
| a-Polonia, ph | 1 | 0 | 0 | 0 | 0 | 1 | .286 |
| Wohlers, p | 0 | 0 | 0 | 0 | 0 | 0 | ----- |
| **Totals** | **28** | **1** | **6** | **1** | **7** | **4** | |

| | | | | | |
|---|---|---|---|---|---|
| **Cleveland** | **000** | **000** | **000--0** | **1** | **0** |
| **Atlanta** | **000** | **001** | **00x--1** | **6** | **0** |

**a:** struck out for Glavine in the 8th. **b:** flied out for Vizquel in the 9th
**E:** Thome. **LOB:** Atlanta 11, Cleveland 3. **2B:** Justice. **HR:** Justice off Poole.
**SB:** Lofton, Grissom. **CS:** Belle, Lemke. **S:** Lemke. **GIDP:** Belliard. **DP:**
Cleveland 1 (Vizquel, Baerga, Murray)

| Cleveland | IP | H | R | ER | BB | SO | NP | ERA |
|---|---|---|---|---|---|---|---|---|
| Martinez | 4-2/3 | 4 | 0 | 0 | 5 | 2 | 78 | 3.48 |
| Poole L, 0-1 | 1-1/3 | 1 | 1 | 1 | 0 | 1 | 25 | 3.86 |
| Hill | 0 | 1 | 0 | 0 | 0 | 0 | 5 | 4.26 |
| Embree | 1 | 0 | 0 | 0 | 2 | 0 | 9 | 2.70 |
| Tavarez | 2/3 | 0 | 0 | 0 | 0 | 0 | 15 | 0.00 |
| Assenmacher | 1/3 | 0 | 0 | 0 | 0 | 1 | 5 | 6.75 |

| Atlanta | IP | H | R | ER | BB | SO | NP | ERA |
|---|---|---|---|---|---|---|---|---|
| Glavine W, 2-0 | 8 | 1 | 0 | 0 | 3 | 8 | 109 | 1.29 |
| Wohlers S, 2 | 1 | 0 | 0 | 0 | 0 | 0 | 9 | 1.80 |

Hill faced 1 batter in the 7th.

# World Series Composite Box
**(Braves win, 4-2)**

## BATTING
## CLEVELAND INDIANS

| Cleveland | G | AB | R | H | 2B | 3B | HR | RBI | BB | SO | AVG | SB | CS | E |
|---|---|---|---|---|---|---|---|---|---|---|---|---|---|---|
| Espinoza, pr-3b | 2 | 2 | 1 | 1 | 0 | 0 | 0 | 0 | 0 | 0 | .500 | 0 | 1 | 0 |
| Belle, lf | 6 | 17 | 4 | 4 | 0 | 0 | 2 | 4 | 7 | 5 | .235 | 0 | 1 | 1 |
| Ramirez, rf | 6 | 18 | 2 | 4 | 0 | 0 | 1 | 2 | 4 | 5 | .222 | 1 | 0 | 0 |
| Thome, ph-3b | 6 | 19 | 1 | 4 | 1 | 0 | 1 | 2 | 2 | 5 | .211 | 0 | 0 | 1 |
| Lofton, cf | 6 | 25 | 6 | 5 | 1 | 0 | 0 | 0 | 3 | 1 | .200 | 6 | 1 | 0 |
| Alomar, c | 5 | 15 | 0 | 3 | 2 | 0 | 0 | 1 | 0 | 2 | .200 | 0 | 0 | 0 |
| Baerga, 2b | 6 | 26 | 1 | 5 | 2 | 0 | 0 | 4 | 1 | 1 | .192 | 0 | 0 | 1 |
| Sorrento, ph-1b | 6 | 11 | 0 | 2 | 1 | 0 | 0 | 0 | 0 | 4 | .182 | 0 | 0 | 1 |
| Vizquel, ss | 6 | 23 | 3 | 4 | 0 | 1 | 0 | 1 | 3 | 5 | .174 | 1 | 0 | 0 |
| Pena, c | 2 | 6 | 0 | 1 | 0 | 0 | 0 | 0 | 0 | 0 | .167 | 0 | 0 | 0 |
| Murray, 1b -dh | 6 | 19 | 1 | 2 | 0 | 0 | 1 | 3 | 5 | 4 | .105 | 0 | 0 | 0 |
| Perry, 1b | 3 | 5 | 0 | 0 | 0 | 0 | 0 | 0 | 0 | 2 | .000 | 0 | 0 | 0 |
| Martinez, p | 2 | 3 | 0 | 0 | 0 | 0 | 0 | 0 | 0 | 1 | .000 | 0 | 0 | 1 |
| Amaro, ph-rf | 2 | 2 | 0 | 0 | 0 | 0 | 0 | 0 | 0 | 1 | .000 | 0 | 0 | 0 |
| Hershiser, p | 2 | 2 | 0 | 0 | 0 | 0 | 0 | 0 | 0 | 0 | .000 | 0 | 0 | 1 |
| Kirby, ph-rf | 3 | 1 | 0 | 0 | 0 | 0 | 0 | 0 | 0 | 1 | .000 | 0 | 0 | 0 |
| Poole, p | 2 | 1 | 0 | 0 | 0 | 0 | 0 | 0 | 0 | 0 | .000 | 0 | 0 | 0 |
| Assenmacher, p | 4 | 0 | 0 | 0 | 0 | 0 | 0 | 0 | 0 | 0 | ----- | 0 | 0 | 0 |
| **Totals** | 6 | 195 | 19 | 35 | 7 | 1 | 5 | 17 | 25 | 37 | .179 | 8 | 3 | 6 |

## BATTING
## ATLANTA BRAVES

| ATLANTA | G | AB | R | H | 2B | 3B | HR | RBI | BB | SO | AVG | SB | CS | E |
|---|---|---|---|---|---|---|---|---|---|---|---|---|---|---|
| Smith,ph | 3 | 2 | 0 | 1 | 0 | 0 | 0 | 0 | 1 | 0 | .500 | 0 | 0 | 0 |
| Grissom, cf | 6 | 25 | 3 | 9 | 1 | 0 | 0 | 1 | 1 | 3 | .360 | 3 | 1 | 0 |
| Mordecai, ph-ss | 3 | 3 | 0 | 1 | 0 | 0 | 0 | 0 | 0 | 1 | .333 | 0 | 0 | 0 |
| Klesko, dh-lf | 6 | 16 | 4 | 5 | 0 | 0 | 3 | 4 | 3 | 4 | .313 | 0 | 0 | 0 |
| Jones, 3b | 6 | 21 | 3 | 6 | 3 | 0 | 0 | 1 | 4 | 5 | .286 | 0 | 0 | 1 |
| Polonia, ph-lf | 6 | 14 | 3 | 4 | 1 | 0 | 1 | 4 | 1 | 3 | .286 | 1 | 0 | 0 |
| Lemke, 2b | 6 | 22 | 1 | 6 | 0 | 0 | 0 | 0 | 3 | 2 | .273 | 0 | 1 | 1 |
| McGriff, 1b | 6 | 23 | 5 | 6 | 2 | 0 | 2 | 3 | 3 | 5 | .261 | 1 | 0 | 1 |
| Justice, rf | 6 | 20 | 3 | 5 | 1 | 0 | 1 | 5 | 5 | 1 | .250 | 0 | 0 | 0 |
| Devereaux, lf-rf | 5 | 4 | 0 | 1 | 0 | 0 | 0 | 1 | 2 | 1 | .250 | 0 | 0 | 1 |
| Lopez, ph-c | 6 | 17 | 1 | 3 | 2 | 0 | 1 | 3 | 1 | 1 | .176 | 0 | 0 | 0 |
| Belliard, ss | 6 | 16 | 0 | 0 | 0 | 0 | 0 | 1 | 0 | 4 | .000 | 0 | 0 | 2 |
| Glavine, p | 2 | 4 | 0 | 0 | 0 | 0 | 0 | 0 | 1 | 2 | .000 | 0 | 0 | 0 |
| O'Brien, c | 2 | 3 | 0 | 0 | 0 | 0 | 0 | 0 | 0 | 1 | .000 | 0 | 0 | 0 |
| Maddux, p | 2 | 3 | 0 | 0 | 0 | 0 | 0 | 0 | 0 | 1 | .000 | 0 | 0 | 0 |
| **Totals** | 6 | 193 | 23 | 47 | 10 | 0 | 8 | 23 | 25 | 34 | .244 | 5 | 2 | 6 |

# World Series Composite Box
### (Braves win, 4-2)

## PITCHING
## CLEVELAND INDIANS

| CLEVELAND | G | CG | IP | H | R | BB | SO | HB | WP | W | L | SV | ER | ERA |
|---|---|---|---|---|---|---|---|---|---|---|---|---|---|---|
| Tavarez | 5 | 0 | 4-1/3 | 3 | 0 | 2 | 1 | 1 | 0 | 0 | 0 | 0 | 0 | 0.00 |
| Hershiser | 2 | 0 | 14 | 8 | 5 | 4 | 13 | 0 | 0 | 1 | 1 | 0 | 4 | 2.57 |
| Embree | 4 | 0 | 3-1/3 | 2 | 1 | 2 | 2 | 0 | 0 | 0 | 0 | 0 | 1 | 2.70 |
| Martinez | 2 | 0 | 10-1/3 | 12 | 4 | 8 | 5 | 1 | 0 | 0 | 1 | 0 | 4 | 3.48 |
| Poole | 2 | 0 | 2-1/3 | 1 | 1 | 0 | 1 | 0 | 0 | 0 | 1 | 0 | 1 | 3.86 |
| Hill | 2 | 0 | 6-1/3 | 7 | 3 | 4 | 1 | 0 | 0 | 0 | 1 | 0 | 3 | 4.26 |
| Mesa | 2 | 0 | 4 | 5 | 2 | 1 | 4 | 0 | 0 | 1 | 0 | 1 | 2 | 4.50 |
| Nagy | 1 | 0 | 7 | 8 | 5 | 1 | 4 | 0 | 0 | 0 | 0 | 0 | 5 | 6.43 |
| Assenmacher | 4 | 0 | 1-1/3 | 1 | 2 | 3 | 3 | 0 | 0 | 0 | 0 | 0 | 1 | 6.75 |
| **TOTALS** | **6** | **0** | **53** | **47** | **23** | **25** | **34** | **2** | **0** | **2** | **4** | **1** | **21** | **3.57** |

## PITCHING
## ATLANTA BRAVES

| ATLANTA | G | CG | IP | H | R | BB | SO | HB | WP | W | L | SV | ER | ERA |
|---|---|---|---|---|---|---|---|---|---|---|---|---|---|---|
| Borbon | 1 | 0 | 1 | 0 | 0 | 0 | 2 | 0 | 0 | 0 | 0 | 1 | 0 | 0.00 |
| Glavine | 2 | 0 | 14 | 4 | 2 | 6 | 11 | 0 | 1 | 2 | 0 | 0 | 2 | 1.29 |
| Avery | 1 | 0 | 6 | 3 | 1 | 5 | 3 | 0 | 0 | 1 | 0 | 0 | 1 | 1.50 |
| Wohlers | 4 | 0 | 5 | 4 | 1 | 3 | 3 | 0 | 0 | 0 | 0 | 2 | 1 | 1.80 |
| Maddux | 2 | 1 | 16 | 9 | 6 | 3 | 8 | 0 | 0 | 1 | 1 | 0 | 4 | 2.25 |
| Clontz | 2 | 0 | 3-1/3 | 2 | 1 | 0 | 2 | 0 | 0 | 0 | 0 | 0 | 1 | 2.70 |
| McMichael | 3 | 0 | 3-1/3 | 3 | 2 | 2 | 2 | 0 | 1 | 0 | 0 | 0 | 1 | 2.70 |
| Mercker | 1 | 0 | 2 | 1 | 1 | 2 | 2 | 0 | 0 | 0 | 0 | 0 | 1 | 4.50 |
| Pena | 2 | 0 | 1 | 3 | 1 | 2 | 0 | 0 | 0 | 0 | 1 | 0 | 1 | 9.00 |
| Smoltz | 1 | 0 | 2-1/3 | 6 | 4 | 2 | 4 | 0 | 0 | 0 | 0 | 0 | 4 | 15.43 |
| **TOTALS** | **6** | **1** | **54** | **35** | **19** | **25** | **37** | **0** | **2** | **4** | **2** | **3** | **16** | **2.67** |

### SCORE BY INNINGS

| | | | | |
|---|---|---|---|---|
| **Cleveland** | **522** | **003** | **222** | **01--19** |
| **Atlanta** | **112** | **115** | **633** | **00--23** |

**DP:** Atlanta 2, Cleveland 8. **LOB:**Cleveland 39, Atlanta 44.**S:** Belliard 2, Mordecai, O'Brien, Lemke.**SF:** Jones

Hershiser faced 2 batters in the 7th (Game 1);Assenmacher faced 1 batter in the 7th (Game 1); Nagy faced 2 batters in the 8th (Game 3); Pena faced 3 batters in the 11th (Game 3); Wohlers faced 2 batters in the 9th (Game 4); Hill faced 1 batter in the 7th (Game 6).

**IBB:** Wohlers 2 (Lofton 2), off Pena (Belle), off Avery (Ramirez), off Assenmacher (Jones), off Maddux (Belle), off Hershiser (Smith), off Embree (Jones), off Martinez (Klesko). **HBP:** by Martinez (Grissom), by Tavarez (Lopez). **PB:** Alomar. **BALK:** Avery. **UMPIRES:** Wendelstedt, McKean, Froemming, Hirschbeck, Pulli, Brinkman. **T:** Game 1 at Atlanta. 2:37, Game 2 at Atlanta, 3:17. Game 3 at Cleveland, 4:09. Game 4 at Cleveland. 3:14, Game 5 at Cleveland, 2:33. Game 6 at Atlanta, 3:02. **A:** Game 1 at Atlanta. 51,876, Game 2 at Atlanta, 51,877. Game 3 at Cleveland, 43,584. Game 4 at Cleveland. 43,578, Game 5 at Cleveland, 43,595. Game 6 at Atlanta, 51,875.

# Epilogue

Before cleaning out their lockers at Jacobs Field for the last time in 1995, the Indians took one final curtain call. It was a beauty.

In a remarkable outpouring of affection, more than 50,000 fans rallied at Public Square on October 30. They came to salute the Indians, the American League champions who came within one game of beating the "team of the '90s," the heralded Atlanta Braves in the World Series.

Governor George V. Voinovich proclaimed, "Today, Cleveland is the greatest baseball town in the world!"

And Mayor Michael R. White said that 1995 was "a season we'll never forget," as he presented Indians owner Richard Jacobs with a ball and bat plaque in appreciation of the team's efforts.

Then Jacobs told the cheering crowd, and the players seated on the stage, "We are not selling hope and patience anymore. We have a proven winner."

Jacobs promised that the players would have a "single mission" when they return to Winter Haven, Florida for spring training. It will be, he said, "To prepare ourselves so the 1996 World Series will be won by the Cleveland Indians."

It was a joyous time, the likes of which had not been experienced by baseball fans in Cleveland since 1954, before the Indians were swept by the

New York Giants in the World Series that year.

When the rally ended a few hours later, the players, flushed with satisfaction despite having fallen one game - actually one inning, even one pitch - short of winning baseball's ultimate prize, departed, though many continue to make their home in Cleveland.

They left behind much to cherish: Eddie Murray's 3,000th hit, and then 71 more, placing him 15th on the all-time list, all but ensuring his eventual election to the Hall of Fame; Jose Mesa's remarkable record of 46 saves in 48 opportunities; Albert Belle's franchise record 50 home runs, and his becoming the first player in major league history to also hit 50 (actually 52) doubles in the same season; the emergence of Manny Ramirez as one of baseball's best hitters, for average (.308) and power (31 homers); and other memories which will not soon be forgotten.

Especially the wonderment in Dennis Eckersley's eyes, and the awe-struck, one word exclamation - "Wow!" - that he mouthed after Ramirez hammered one of his pitches for a two-run, 12th inning, game-winning homer at Jacobs Field on July 16.

But the way the 1995 season ended was not the only reason it was memorable.

Unforgettable, too, was the way it started, especially for those who reported for spring training as "replacement" players, a.k.a. "scabs," because the strike that shut down the game in 1994 was still in effect.

Before it was settled on April 1 and the regulars returned, Cleveland's hopes for winning a baseball championship for the first time in 41 years rested on the shoulders of men named Joe Biasucci, Darrin Campbell, Pete Kuld, Joe Slusarski, Mel Wearing and Eric Yelding, among others.

And when the regulars returned, the replacements were themselves replaced.

Some were retained in the Tribe's minor league system, but none was still in the organization when the season ended, with one exception - Joe Mikulik, though he wasn't kept as a player.

Mikulik, who would have been one of the Indians' outfielders if the replacement season had been played, was hired as a coach for Canton-Akron of the Class AA Eastern League. When that league finished its season, Mikulik was appointed manager of the Tribe's Florida Instructional League team in Winter Haven.

Yelding, the best of the replacement players, started the season at Class AAA Buffalo, but didn't stay there long, despite a .346 average in 29 games. He was demoted in May to Canton-Akron where he also did well, hitting .351 in 10 games, but soon was let go.

Dickie Brown, who was penciled in as the Indians' opening day pitcher before the strike ended, was 8-5 with a 4.67 ERA in 37 games, nine as a starter for Canton-Akron, but he didn't finish the season either.

So, for those who would have been Indians, the replacement era ended, abruptly and, appropriately, without fanfare.

And that which, seven months earlier, began as the best of times - but also the worst of times - became a glorious Indian summer, when a season of dreams became reality in Cleveland.

# *1995 Cleveland Indians Batting Statistics*

| | G | AB | R | H | 2B | 3B | HR | RBI | SB | AVG |
|---|---|---|---|---|---|---|---|---|---|---|
| Sandy Alomar | 66 | 203 | 32 | 61 | 6 | 0 | 10 | 35 | 3 | .300 |
| Ruben Amaro | 28 | 60 | 5 | 12 | 3 | 0 | 1 | 7 | 1 | .200 |
| Carlos Baerga | 135 | 557 | 87 | 175 | 28 | 2 | 15 | 90 | 11 | .314 |
| David Bell | 2 | 2 | 0 | 0 | 0 | 0 | 0 | 0 | 0 | .000 |
| Albert Belle | 143 | 546 | 121 | 173 | 52 | 1 | 50 | 126 | 5 | .317 |
| Jeromy Burnitz | 9 | 7 | 4 | 4 | 1 | 0 | 0 | 0 | 0 | .571 |
| Alvaro Espinoza | 66 | 143 | 15 | 36 | 4 | 0 | 2 | 17 | 0 | .252 |
| Brian Giles | 6 | 9 | 6 | 5 | 0 | 0 | 1 | 3 | 0 | .556 |
| Wayne Kirby | 101 | 188 | 29 | 39 | 10 | 2 | 1 | 14 | 10 | .207 |
| Jesse Levis | 12 | 18 | 1 | 6 | 2 | 0 | 0 | 3 | 0 | .333 |
| Kenny Lofton | 118 | 481 | 93 | 149 | 22 | 13 | 7 | 53 | 54 | .310 |
| Eddie Murray | 113 | 436 | 68 | 141 | 21 | 0 | 21 | 82 | 5 | .323 |
| Tony Pena | 91 | 263 | 25 | 69 | 15 | 0 | 5 | 28 | 1 | .262 |
| Herb Perry | 52 | 162 | 23 | 51 | 13 | 1 | 3 | 23 | 1 | .315 |
| Manny Ramirez | 137 | 484 | 85 | 149 | 26 | 1 | 31 | 107 | 6 | .308 |
| Billy Ripken | 8 | 17 | 4 | 7 | 0 | 0 | 2 | 3 | 0 | .412 |
| Paul Sorrento | 104 | 323 | 50 | 76 | 14 | 0 | 25 | 79 | 1 | .235 |
| Jim Thome | 137 | 452 | 92 | 142 | 29 | 3 | 25 | 73 | 4 | .314 |
| Scooter Tucker | 17 | 20 | 2 | 0 | 0 | 0 | 0 | 0 | 0 | .000 |
| Omar Vizquel | 136 | 542 | 87 | 144 | 28 | 0 | 6 | 56 | 29 | .266 |
| Dave Winfield | 46 | 115 | 11 | 22 | 5 | 0 | 2 | 4 | 1 | .191 |
| | | 5028 | 840 | 1461 | 279 | 23 | 207 | 803 | 132 | .291 |

# *1995 Cleveland Indians Pitching Statistics*

| | W | L | G | GS | CG | IP | H | BB | SO | ERA |
|---|---|---|---|---|---|---|---|---|---|---|
| Paul Assenmacher | 6 | 2 | 47 | 0 | 0 | 38.1 | 32 | 12 | 40 | 2.82 |
| Bud Black | 4 | 2 | 11 | 10 | 0 | 47.1 | 63 | 16 | 34 | 6.85 |
| Mark Clark | 9 | 7 | 22 | 21 | 2 | 124.2 | 143 | 42 | 68 | 5.27 |
| Dennis Cook | 0 | 0 | 11 | 0 | 0 | 12.2 | 16 | 10 | 13 | 6.39 |
| Alan Embree | 3 | 2 | 23 | 0 | 0 | 24.2 | 23 | 16 | 23 | 5.11 |
| John Farrell | 0 | 0 | 1 | 0 | 0 | 4.2 | 7 | 0 | 4 | 3.86 |
| Jason Grimsley | 0 | 0 | 15 | 2 | 0 | 34 | 37 | 32 | 25 | 6.09 |
| Orel Hershiser | 16 | 6 | 26 | 26 | 1 | 167.1 | 151 | 51 | 111 | 3.87 |
| Ken Hill | 4 | 1 | 12 | 11 | 1 | 74.2 | 77 | 32 | 48 | 3.98 |
| Albie Lopez | 0 | 0 | 6 | 2 | 0 | 23 | 17 | 7 | 22 | 3.13 |
| Dennis Martinez | 12 | 5 | 28 | 28 | 3 | 187 | 174 | 46 | 99 | 3.08 |
| Jose Mesa | 3 | 0 | 62 | 0 | 0 | 64 | 49 | 17 | 58 | 1.13 |
| Charles Nagy | 16 | 6 | 29 | 29 | 2 | 178 | 194 | 61 | 139 | 4.55 |
| Chad Ogea | 8 | 3 | 20 | 14 | 1 | 106.1 | 95 | 29 | 57 | 3.05 |
| Greg Olson | 0 | 0 | 3 | 0 | 0 | 2.2 | 6 | 3 | 0 | 13.60 |
| Eric Plunk | 6 | 2 | 56 | 0 | 0 | 64 | 48 | 27 | 71 | 2.67 |
| Jim Poole | 3 | 3 | 42 | 0 | 0 | 50.1 | 40 | 17 | 41 | 3.75 |
| Joe Roa | 0 | 1 | 1 | 1 | 0 | 6 | 9 | 2 | 0 | 6.00 |
| Paul Shuey | 0 | 2 | 7 | 0 | 0 | 6.1 | 5 | 5 | 5 | 4.26 |
| Julian Tavarez | 10 | 2 | 57 | 0 | 0 | 85 | 76 | 21 | 68 | 2.44 |
| | 100 | 44 | | 144 | 10 | 1301 | 1262 | 445 | 926 | 3.83 |

**Shutouts:** Martinez (2), Hershiser, Nagy
**Saves:** Mesa (46), Plunk (2), Embree, Grimsley

# *Standings*

## AMERICAN LEAGUE

## NATIONAL LEAGUE

| CENTRAL | W | L | Pct | GB | CENTRAL | W | L | Pct | GB |
|---|---|---|---|---|---|---|---|---|---|
| **INDIANS** | 100 | 44 | .694 | — | Cincinnati | 85 | 59 | .590 | — |
| Kansas City | 70 | 74 | .486 | 30.0 | Houston | 76 | 68 | .528 | 9.0 |
| Chicago | 68 | 76 | .472 | 32.0 | Chicago | 73 | 71 | .507 | 12.0 |
| Milwaukee | 65 | 79 | .451 | 35.0 | St. Louis | 62 | 81 | .434 | 22.5 |
| Minnesota | 56 | 88 | .389 | 44.0 | Pittsburgh | 58 | 86 | .403 | 27.0 |

| EAST | W | L | Pct. | GB | EAST | W | L | Pct. | GB |
|---|---|---|---|---|---|---|---|---|---|
| Boston | 86 | 58 | .597 | — | Atlanta | 90 | 54 | .625 | — |
| New York | 79 | 65 | .549 | 7.0 | New York | 69 | 75 | .479 | 21.0 |
| Baltimore | 71 | 73 | .493 | 15.0 | Philadelphia | 69 | 75 | .479 | 21.0 |
| Detroit | 60 | 84 | .417 | 26.0 | Florida | 67 | 76 | .469 | 22.5 |
| Toronto | 56 | 88 | .389 | 30.0 | Montreal | 66 | 78 | .458 | 24.0 |

| WEST | W | L | Pct. | GB | WEST | W | L | Pct. | GB |
|---|---|---|---|---|---|---|---|---|---|
| Seattle | 79 | 66 | .545 | — | Los Angeles | 78 | 66 | .542 | — |
| California | 78 | 67 | .538 | 1.0 | Colorado | 77 | 67 | .535 | 1.0 |
| Texas | 74 | 70 | .514 | 4.5 | San Diego | 70 | 74 | .486 | 8.0 |
| Oakland | 67 | 77 | .465 | 11.5 | San Francisco | 67 | 77 | .465 | 11.0 |

# Day-by-Day

| GAME | DATE | OPP. | SCORE | WINNING PITCHER | LOSING PITCHER | RECORD | POS. | GB | ATTEND. | HOME TOTAL |
|---|---|---|---|---|---|---|---|---|---|---|
| 1 | 4/27 | at Tex | 11-6 | Martinez (1-0) | Gross (0-1) | 1-0 | T2 | .5 | 32,161 | |
| 2 | 4/28 | at Tex | 9-10 | r Whiteside (1-0) | r Poole (0-1) | 1-1 | T3 | 1.5 | 23179. | |
| 3 | 4/29 | at Tex | 5-6 | r Burrows (1-0) | r Shuey (0-1) | 1-2 | T3 | 2.5 | 28,048 | |
| 4 | 4/30 | at Tex | #7-6 | r Mesa (1-0) | r Whiteside (1-1) | 2-2 | T2 | 1.5 | 26,026 | |
| 5 | 5/2 | at Det | 11-1 | Martinez (2-0) | Bergman (0-2) | 3-2 | T2 | 1.5 | 39,398 | |
| 6 | 5/3 | at Det | 14-7 | Clark (1-0) | Doherty (0-2) | 4-2 | 2 | 1.5 | 29,996 | |
| 7 | 5/4 | at Det | 3-4 | Wells (1-1) | Hershiser (0-1) | 4-3 | T2 | 1.5 | 28,446 | |
| 8 | 5/5 | MIN | 5-1 | Nagy (1-0) | Erickson (0-3) | 5-3 | T2 | .5 | 41,434 | 41,434 |
| 9 | 5/6 | MIN | 2-5 | Radke (1-0) | Black (0-1) | 5-4 | T2 | 1.5 | 37,325 | 78,759 |
| 10 | 5/7 | MIN | #10-9 | r Poole (1-1) | r Guthrie (1-1) | 6-4 | T2 | 1.5 | 39,431 | 118,190 |
| 11 | 5/8 | K C | 6-2 | Clark (2-0) | Appier (3-1) | 7-4 | 2 | 1.0 | 26,704 | 144,894 |
| 12 | 5/9 | K C | 10-0 | Hershiser (1-1) | Linton (0-1) | 8-4 | 2 | .5 | 27,225 | 172,119 |
| 13 | 5/10 | K C | #3-2 | r Plunk (1-0) | r Meacham (1-2) | 9-4 | T1 | | 27,749 | 199,868 |
| 14 | 5/12 | at Bal | 3-2 | Martinez (3-0) | Brown (2-1) | 10-4 | 1 | +.5 | 40,516 | |
| 15 | 5/13 | at Bal | 1-6 | MUSSINA (2-1) | Clark (2-1) | 10-5 | 1 | +.5 | 40,185 | |
| 16 | 5/14 | at Bal | 3-1 | Hershiser (2-1) | Rhodes (1-2) | 11-5 | 1 | +1.5 | 39,167 | |
| 17 | 5/16 | at NY | 10-5 | Nagy (2-0) | Key (1-2) | 12-5 | 1 | +2.5 | 18,246 | |
| 18 | 5/18 | at Bos | 3-4 | r Belinda (2-0) | r Poole (1-2) | 12-6 | 1 | +3.0 | 24,285 | |
| 19 | 5/19 | at Bos | 9-5 | r Tavarez (1-0) | r Ryan (0-1) | 13-6 | 1 | +3.0 | 23,507 | |
| 20 | 5/20 | at Bos | 7-5 | r Plunk (2-0) | r Pena (1-1) | 14-6 | 1 | +3.0 | 29,412 | |
| 21 | 5/21 | at Bos | 12-10 | r Assenmacher (1-0) | r Pierce (0-2) | 15-6 | 1 | +4.0 | 32339. | |
| 22 | 5/22 | MIL | 5-7 | Bones (3-1) | Nagy (2-1) | 15-7 | 1 | +5.0 | 34,464 | 234,332 |
| 23 | 5/23 | MIL | 5-3 | Martinez (4-0) | Sparks (1-1) | 16-7 | 1 | +4.0 | 35,373 | 269,705 |
| 24 | 5/24 | MIL | 5-7 | r Rightnowar (1-0) | Clark (2-2) | 16-8 | 1 | +5.0 | 29,638 | 299,343 |
| 25 | 5/26 | at Tor | 7-4 | Hershiser (3-1) | Hentgen (3-2) | 17-8 | 1 | +4.0 | 47,113 | |
| 26 | 5/27 | at Tor | 0-3 | Leiter (2-2) | r Plunk (2-1) | 17-9 | 1 | +4.5 | 47,143 | |
| 27 | 5/28 | at Tor | 5-4 | Nagy (3-1) | Darling (1-4) | 18-9 | 1 | +4.5 | 42,362 | |
| 28 | 5/29 | CHI | 7-6 | r Tavarez (2-0) | r Deleon (2-1) | 19-9 | 1 | +4.5 | 41,736 | 341079.00 |
| 29 | 5/30 | CHI | 2-1 | r Assenmacher (2-0) | FERNANDEZ (2-4) | 20-9 | 1 | +4.5 | 33,038 | 374,117 |

# *Day-by-Day*

| GAME | DATE | OPP. | SCORE | WINNING PITCHER | LOSING PITCHER | RECORD | POS. | GB | ATTEND. | HOME TOTAL |
|---|---|---|---|---|---|---|---|---|---|---|
| 30 | 5/31 | CHI | 6-3 | Hershiser (4-1) | Abbott (2-2) | 21-9 | 1 | +5.5 | 36,771 | 410,888 |
| 31 | 6/1 | CHI | 7-4 | Black (1-1) | Bere (1-4) | 22-9 | 1 | +6.0 | 33,260 | 444,148 |
| 32 | 6/2 | TOR | 0-5 | Leiter (3-2) | Nagy (3-2) | 22-10 | 1 | +5.0 | 41,545 | 485,693 |
| 33 | 6/3 | TOR | 3-0 | MARTINEZ (5-0) | Darwin (1-5) | 23-10 | 1 | +5.0 | 41,566 | 527,259 |
| 34 | 6/4 | TOR | 9-8 | r Tavarez (3-0) | r Hall (0-1) | 24-10 | 1 | +5.0 | 41,688 | 568,947 |
| 35 | 6/5 | DET | 8-0 | HERSHISER (5-1) | Bergman (1-4) | 25-10 | 1 | +5.0 | 34,615 | 603,562 |
| 36 | 6/6 | DET | 4-3 | r Tavarez (4-0) | r Boever (3-3) | 26-10 | 1 | +6.0 | 36,115 | 639,677 |
| 37 | 6/7 | DET | #3-2 | r Plunk (3-1) | r Maxey (2-1) | 27-10 | 1 | +7.0 | 36,363 | 676,040 |
| 38 | 6/8 | at Mil | 8-7 | r Tavarez (5-0) | r Lloyd (0-5) | 28-10 | 1 | +8.0 | 17,641 | |
| 39 | 6/9 | at Mil | 7-4 | Ogea (1-0) | Roberson (1-0) | 29-10 | 1 | +8.5 | 13,136 | |
| 40 | 6/10 | at Mil | 1-6 | Miranda (3-2) | Hershiser (5-2) | 29-11 | 1 | +7.5 | 18,869 | |
| 41 | 6/11 | at Mil | 11-5 | Black (2-1) | Scanlon (3-4) | 30-11 | 1 | +7.5 | 18,706 | |
| 42 | 6/12 | BAL | 4-3 | Nagy (4-2) | Brown (5-4) | 31-11 | 1 | +7.5 | 41,845 | 717,885 |
| 43 | 6/13 | BAL | 11-0 | MARTINEZ (6-0) | Mussina (5-4) | 32-11 | 1 | +7.5 | 41,927 | 759,812 |
| 44 | 6/14 | BAL | 5-2 | Ogea (2-0) | Klingenbeck (1-1) | 33-11 | 1 | +7.5 | 41,839 | 801,651 |
| 45 | 6/16 | NY | 2-4 | r Wickman (2-1) | r Poole (1-3) | 33-12 | 1 | +6.0 | 41,643 | 843,294 |
| 46 | 6/17 | NY | 7-4 | Black (3-1) | Pettitte (1-4) | 34-12 | 1 | +7.0 | 41,662 | 884,956 |
| 47 | 6/18 | NY | 5-9 | McDowell (3-4) | Nagy (4-3) | 34-13 | 1 | +7.0 | 41,667 | 926,623 |
| 48 | 6/19 | BOS | #4-3 | r Plunk (4-1) | r Ryan (0-3) | 35-13 | 1 | +7.0 | 41,645 | 968,268 |
| 49 | 6/20 | BOS | 9-2 | Ogea (3-0) | Eshelman (3-1) | 36-13 | 1 | +8.0 | 40,190 | 1,008,458 |
| 50 | 6/21 | BOS | 1-3 | Hanson (7-1) | Hershiser (5-3) | 36-14 | 1 | +7.0 | 41,948 | 1,050,406 |
| 51 | 6/23 | at Chi | 5-12 | Bere (3-6) | Nagy (4-4) | 36-15 | 1 | +6.0 | 31,962 | |
| 52 | 6/24 | at Chi | 3-8 | FERNANDEZ (3-4) | Black (3-2) | 36-16 | 1 | +6.0 | 35,028 | |
| 53 | 6/25 | at Chi | 2-3 | r Deleon (3-3) | Assenmacher (2-1) | 36-17 | 1 | +5.5 | 27,514 | |
| 54 | 6/26 | at KC | 2-0 | Ogea (4-0) | GORDON (5-3) | 37-17 | 1 | +6.5 | 24,296 | |
| 55 | 6/27 | at KC | 7-1 | Clark (3-2) | Haney (3-2) | 38-17 | 1 | +7.5 | 19,510 | |
| 56 | 6/28 | at KC | 5-2 | Nagy (5-2) | Appier (11-3) | 39-17 | 1 | +8.5 | 18,596 | |
| 57 | 6/29 | at Min | 10-5 | Black (4-2) | Erickson (3-5) | 40-17 | 1 | +9.0 | 17,116 | |
| 58 | 6/30 | at Min | 4-1 | Martinez (7-0) | Trombley (0-3) | 41-17 | 1 | +9.0 | 27,416 | |

# Day-by-Day

| GAME | DATE | OPP. | SCORE | WINNING PITCHER | LOSING PITCHER | RECORD | POS. | GB | ATTEND. | HOME TOTAL |
|---|---|---|---|---|---|---|---|---|---|---|
| 59 | 7/1 | at Min | 5-6 | Redke (4-7) | Ogea (4-1) | 41-18 | 1 | +9.0 | 18,820 | |
| 60 | 7/2 | at Min | 7-0 | Clark (4-2) | Harris (0-2) | 42-18 | 1 | +10.0 | 16,790 | |
| 61 | 7/3 | TEX | 9-1 | Nagy (6-4) | Rogers (8-4) | 43-18 | 1 | +11.0 | 41,713 | 1,092,119 |
| 62 | 7/4 | TEX | 6-7 | r McDowell (4-0) | Assenmacher (2-2) | 43-19 | 1 | +11.0 | 41,769 | 1,133,888 |
| 63 | 7/5 | TEX | 2-0 | Martinez (8-0) | Gross (3-8) | 44-19 | 1 | +11.0 | 71,881 | 1,175,769 |
| 64 | 7/6 | SEA | 8-1 | OGEA (5-1) | Belcher (4-4) | 45-19 | 1 | +12.0 | 41,661 | 1,217,430 |
| 65 | 7/7 | SEA | 3-5 | JOHNSON (9-1) | Clark (4-3) | 45-20 | 1 | +12.0 | 41,741 | 1,259,171 |
| 66 | 7/8 | SEA | 7-3 | NAGY (7-4) | Bosio (6-3) | 46-20 | 1 | +12.0 | 41,893 | 1,301,064 |
| 67 | 7/9 | SEA | 3-9 | Torres (3-4) | Hershiser (5-4) | 46-21 | 1 | +12.0 | 41,897 | 1,342,961 |
| 68 | 7/14 | O A K | 1-0 | r Embree (1-0) | PRIETO (0-2) | 47-21 | 1 | – | – | – |
| 69 | 7/14 | O A K | 7-6 | Nagy (8-4) | Darling (2-5) | 48-21 | 1 | +12.5 | 41,862 | 1,384,823 |
| 70 | 7/15 | O A K | 7-2 | Hershiser (6-4) | Ontiveros (8-4) | 49-21 | 1 | +13.5 | 41,726 | 1,426,549 |
| 71 | 7/16 | O A K | #5-4 | r Embree (2-0) | r Eckersley (2-3) | 50-21 | 1 | +14.5 | 41,767 | 1,468,316 |
| 72 | 7/17 | C A L | 3-8 | Anderson (3-2) | Ogea (5-2) | 50-22 | 1 | +13.5 | 41,583 | 1,509,899 |
| 73 | 7/18 | C A L | 7-5 | r Assenmacher (3-2) | r Smith (0-3) | 51-22 | 1 | +13.5 | 41,763 | 1,551,662 |
| 74 | 7/19 | at Tex | 14-5 | NAGY (9-4) | Cross (4-9) | 52-22 | 1 | +13.5 | 42,929 | |
| 75 | 7/20 | at Tex | 6-3 | Hershiser (7-4) | Brandenburg (0-1) | 53-22 | 1 | +14.5 | 28,160 | |
| 76 | 7/21 | at Oak | 6-1 | MARTINEZ (9-0) | Stottlemyre (8-3) | 54-22 | 1 | +14.5 | 21,158 | |
| 77 | 7/22 | at Oak | 6-4 | r Tavarez (6-0) | r Eckersley (2-4) | 55-22 | 1 | +15.5 | 33,019 | |
| 78 | 7/23 | at Oak | 2-0 | Clark (5-3) | Prieto (1-3) | 56-22 | 1 | +16.5 | 26,763 | |
| 79 | 7/24 | at Cal | #9-7 | r Assenmacher (4-2) | r Smith (0-4) | 57-22 | 1 | +16.5 | 30,367 | |
| 80 | 7/25 | at Cal | 5-6 | Finley (9-7) | Hershiser (7-5) | 57-23 | 1 | +16.5 | 42,468 | |
| 81 | 7/26 | at Cal | 3-6 | Hervey (5-6) | Martinez (9-1) | 57-24 | 1 | +15.5 | 35,650 | |
| 82 | 7/27 | at Sea | 5-11 | BELCHER (7-5) | Ogea (5-3) | 57-25 | 1 | +15.5 | 20,121 | |
| 83 | 7/28 | at Sea | 6-5 | r Plunk (5-1) | r Frey (0-3) | 58-25 | 1 | +16.5 | 17,608 | |
| 84 | 7/29 | at Sea | 3-5 | Bosio (7-5) | r Embree (2-1) | 58-26 | 1 | +16.5 | 43,874 | |
| 85 | 7/30 | at Sea | 5-2 | HERSHISER (7-5) | Torres (3-7) | 59-26 | 1 | +17.5 | 24,089 | |
| 86 | 8/1 | MIN | 5-6 | r Mahomes (1-4) | r Tavarez (6-1) | 59-27 | 1 | +17.5 | 42,023 | 1,593,685 |
| 87 | 8/2 | MIN | 12-6 | Clark (6-30) | Harris (0-5) | 60-27 | 1 | +17.5 | 41,947 | 1,635,632 |

# *Day-by-Day*

| GAME | DATE | OPP. | SCORE | WINNING PITCHER | LOSING PITCHER | RECORD | POS. | GB | ATTEND. | HOME TOTAL |
|------|------|------|-------|-----------------|----------------|--------|------|----|---------|-----------|
| 88 | 8/3 | MIN | 6-4 | Hill (1-0) | Radke (7-10) | 61-27 | 1 | +18.5 | 41,907 | 1,677,539 |
| 89 | 8/4 | CHI | 13-3 | Nagy (10-4) | Bere (5-10) | 62-27 | 1 | +18.5 | 41,895 | 1,719,434 |
| 90 | 8/5 | CHI | 11-7 | Hershiser (9-5) | Fernandez (5-8) | 63-27 | 1 | +19.5 | 41,657 | 1,761,091 |
| 91 | 8/6 | CHI | 1-5 | Righetti (3-0) | Martinez (9-2) | 63-28 | 1 | +18.5 | 41,975 | 1,803,066 |
| 92 | 8/8 | at Bos | 1-5 | WAKEFIELD (13-1) | Clark (6-4) | 63-29 | 1 | +17.5 | 34,574 | |
| 93 | 8/9 | ar Bos | 5-9 | Hanson (10-4) | r Plunk (5-2) | 63-30 | 1 | +16.5 | 34,240 | |
| 94 | 8/10 | at NY | 10-9 | r Poole (2-3) | r Wetteland (1-2) | 64-30 | 1 | | | |
| 95 | 8/10 | at NY | 5-2 | Ogea (6-3) | Hitchcock (5-7) | 65-30 | 1 | +18.0 | 48,155 | |
| 96 | 8/11 | at NY | #5-4 | r Tavarez (7-1) | r Wetteland (1-3) | 66-30 | 1 | +18.0 | 33,739 | |
| 97 | 8/12 | at NY | 2-3 | McDOWELL (10-8) | Martinez (9-3) | 66-31 | 1 | +18.0 | 35,795 | |
| 98 | 8/13 | at NY | 1-4 | CONE (13-6) | Clark (6-5) | 66-32 | 1 | +17.0 | 45,866 | |
| 99 | 8/14 | at Bal | 9-6 | r Assenmacher (5-2) | r Benitez (1-4) | 67-32 | 1 | +17.0 | 47,198 | |
| 100 | 8/15 | at Bal | 3-8 | ERICKSON (8-9) | Nagy (10-5) | 67-33 | 1 | +17.0 | 46,346 | |
| 101 | 8/16 | at Bal | 8-5 | Hershiser (10-5) | Brown (5-8) | 68-33 | 1 | +17.0 | 47,140 | |
| 102 | 8/17 | MIL | 3-7 | McAndrew (1-2) | Martinez (9-4) | 68-34 | 1 | +16.0 | 40,505 | 1,843,571 |
| 103 | 8/18 | MIL | 7-5 | Clark (7-5) | Bones (7-9) | 69-34 | 1 | +17.0 | 41,755 | 1,885,326 |
| 104 | 8/19 | MIL | 4-3 | r Plunk (6-2) | r Wegman (5-5) | 70-34 | 1 | +18.0 | 41,939 | 1,927,265 |
| 105 | 8/20 | MIL | 8-5 | r Tavarez (8-1) | Sparks (7-7) | 71-34 | 1 | +19.0 | 41,799 | 1,969,064 |
| 106 | 8/21 | at Tor | 7-3 | Hershiser (11-5) | Hurtado (5-2) | 72-34 | 1 | +19.5 | 39,187 | |
| 107 | 8/22 | at Tor | 4-5 | r Castillo (1-2) | r Tavarez (8-2) | 72-35 | 1 | +18.5 | 39,293 | |
| 108 | 8/23 | at Tor | 6-5 | r Poole (3-3) | Carrara (1-3) | 73-35 | 1 | +19.0 | 41,169 | |
| 109 | 8/24 | DET | #6-5 | r Tavarez (9-2) | r Lira (8-9) | 74-35 | 1 | +18.5 | 41,676 | 2,010,740 |
| 110 | 8/25 | DET | 6-2 | Nagy (11-5) | Moore (5-14) | 75-35 | 1 | +18.5 | 41,744 | 2,052,484 |
| 111 | 8/26 | DET | 9-2 | Hershiser (12-5) | Lima (1-6) | 76-35 | 1 | +18.5 | 41,646 | 2,094,100 |
| 112 | 8/27 | TOR | 9-1 | Ogea (7-3) | Carrara (1-4) | 77-35 | 1 | +19.5 | 40,283 | 2,134,383 |
| 113 | 8/28 | TOR | 4-1 | CLARK (8-5) | Guzman (3-10) | 78-35 | 1 | +20.5 | 41,257 | 2,175,640 |
| 114 | 8/29 | TOR | #4-3 | r Assenmacher (6-2) | r Castillo (1-3) | 79-35 | 1 | +21.5 | 41,807 | 2,217,447 |
| 115 | 8/30 | TOR | #6-4 | r Mesa (2-0) | r Rogers (2-3) | 80-35 | 1 | +21.5 | 41,746 | 2,259,193 |
| 116 | 9/1 | at Det | 14-4 | Nagy (12-5) | Lima (1-7) | 81-35 | 1 | +21.5 | 16,155 | |

# Day-by-Day

| GAME | DATE | OPP. | SCORE | WINNING PITCHER | LOSING PITCHER | RECORD | POS. | GB | ATTEND. | HOME TOTAL |
|------|------|------|-------|-----------------|----------------|--------|------|----|---------|-----------|
| 117 | 9/2 | at Det | 2-3 | Lira (9-9) | Hershiser (12-6) | 81-36 | 1 | +21.5 | 22,426 | |
| 118 | 9/3 | at Det | #9-8 | r Mesa (3-0) | r Boever (5-7) | 82-36 | 1 | +21.5 | 25,393 | |
| 119 | 9/4 | at Det | 2-3 | Sodowsky (1-0) | CLARK (8-6) | 82-37 | 1 | +21.0 | 24,987 | |
| 120 | 9/5 | at Mil | 7-3 | Martinez (10-4) | Sparks (7-8) | 83-37 | 1 | +21.0 | 12,129 | |
| 121 | 9/6 | at Mil | 12-2 | Hill (2-0) | Givens (5-3) | 84-37 | 1 | +22.0 | 10,042 | |
| 122 | 9/7 | SEA | 4-1 | Nagy (13-5) | Bosio (9-8) | 85-37 | 1 | +22.5 | 41,450 | 2,300,643 |
| 123 | 9/8 | BAL | 3-2 | Hershiser (13-6) | Brown (7-9) | 86-37 | 1 | +23.5 | 41,656 | 2,342,299 |
| 124 | 9/9 | BAL | 2-1 | Ogea (2-1) | KRIVDA (2-4) | 87-37 | 1 | +24.5 | 41,729 | 2,384,028 |
| 125 | 9/10 | BAL | 5-3 | r Tavarez (10-2) | r Orosco (2-4) | 88-37 | 1 | +25.5 | 41,647 | 2,425,675 |
| 126 | 9/11 | N Y | 0-4 | McDOWELL (14-10) | Martinez (10-5) | 88-38 | 1 | +25.0 | 41,835 | 2,467,510 |
| 127 | 9/12 | N Y | 2-9 | Kamieniecki (5-5) | Hill (2-1) | 88-39 | 1 | +24.0 | 41,276 | 2,508,786 |
| 128 | 9/13 | N Y | 5-0 | Nagy (14-5) | Cone (15-8) | 89-39 | 1 | +25.0 | 41,708 | 2,550,494 |
| 129 | 9/14 | BOS | 5-3 | Hershiser (14-6) | Eshelman (5-3) | 90-39 | 1 | +25.0 | 41,812 | 2,592,306 |
| 130 | 9/15 | BOS | 3-6 | Hanson (14-5) | r Embree (2-2) | 90-40 | 1 | +24.0 | 41,833 | 2,634,139 |
| 131 | 9/16 | BOS | 6-5 | Clark (9-6) | Clemens (8-5) | 91-40 | 1 | +24.0 | 41,765 | 2,675,904 |
| 132 | 9/17 | BOS | 6-9 | r Suppan (1-2) | r Shuey (0-2) | 91-41 | 1 | +23.0 | 41,723 | 2,717,627 |
| 133 | 9/18 | at Chi | 11-1 | HILL (3-1) | Alvarez (7-10) | 92-41 | 1 | +23.5 | 20,439 | |
| 134 | 9/19 | at Chi | 8-2 | Nagy (15-5) | Andujar (2-1) | 93-41 | 1 | +24.5 | 18,468 | |
| 135 | 9/20 | at Chi | 3-4 | Bere (8-13) | Roa (0-1) | 93-42 | 1 | +24.5 | 17,171 | |
| 136 | 9/22 | at KC | 5-3 | Hershiser (15-6) | r Olson (3-3) | 94-42 | 1 | +26.0 | 16,562 | |
| 137 | 9/23 | at KC | 7-3 | Martinez (11-5) | Gubicza (11-14) | 95-42 | 1 | +27.0 | 23,816 | |
| 138 | 9/24 | at KC | 2-4 | Appier (15-9) | Clark (9-7) | 95-43 | 1 | +26.0 | 17,277 | |
| 139 | 9/26 | at Min | 4-13 | Trombley (4-8) | Nagy (15-6) | 95-44 | 1 | +26.0 | 9,825 | |
| 140 | 9/27 | at Min | 9-6 | Hill (4-1) | Radke (11-14) | 96-44 | 1 | +27.0 | 9,614 | |
| 141 | 9/28 | at Min | 12-4 | Martinez (12-5) | Rodriguez (5-8) | 97-44 | 1 | +27.0 | 9,442 | |
| 142 | 9/29 | K C | 9-2 | Hershiser (16-6) | Appier (15-10) | 98-44 | 1 | +28.0 | 41,701 | 2,759,328 |
| 143 | 9/30 | K C | #3-2 | r Embree (3-2) | Montgomery (2-3) | 99-44 | 1 | +29.0 | 41,578 | 2,800,906 |
| 144 | 10/1 | K C | 17-7 | Nagy (16-6) | Gordon (12-12) | 100-44 | 1 | +30.0 | 41,819 | 2,842,725 |

# *Awards and Honors*

As expected, individual awards for the Indians were plentiful following the season that, it says here, was "glorious," and which Mike Hargrove called "magical."

And though there can be no argument with either adjective to describe the 1995 baseball season in Cleveland, there is much room for disagreement about two awards that weren't won by the Indians.

One was Boston's Mo Vaughn being named the American League's Most Valuable Player over Albert Belle.

The other was that voters failed to select Hargrove as AL Manager of the Year, an honor he richly deserved for the second straight season.

In the case of Belle, it is significant that AL players - Belle's peers - elected him Player of the Year, an award that includes both leagues.

But members of the Baseball Writers Association of America, specifically two scribes in each of the 28 AL franchise cities, decided that Vaughn should receive the coveted MVP award.

It was *The Sporting News* that conducted the vote by the players who placed Vaughn second to Belle, and Greg Maddux of Atlanta third.

In the balloting by the BBWAA, Vaughn won by 308 total points over Belle, who polled 300.

Obviously, Belle's often uncooperative attitude with the media hurt his candidacy as Vaughn, more popular among the writers, received 12 first place votes, 12 seconds and four thirds. Belle was named first on 11 ballots, second on 10, and third on seven.

Seattle's Edgar Martinez, the AL batting champion, was third with 244 points, including 56 as a result of receiving four first place votes.

Indians ace reliever Jose Mesa got the other first place vote, and finished with 130 points.

*The Sporting News,* in its balloting among major league players, managers and coaches, also named Hargrove the AL Manager of the Year, though the BBWAA again saw it differently.

Hargrove didn't even finish second in the poll by the writers, He was beaten out for the prize by Lou Piniella of the Seattle Mariners. Boston's Kevin Kennedy dame in second.

Don Baylor of Colorado was the National League Manager of the Year, according to *The Sporting News.*

It was the second season in a row that Hargrove failed to be picked by the writers, though he probably deserved it both times. Buck Showalter of the New York Yankees was awarded the honor over the Tribe manager in 1994.

Belle also was second in the voting for the Indians Man of the Year award as selected by the Cleveland Chapter of the BBWAA.

Mesa was the winner on the basis of his outstanding performance - 46 saves in 48 opportunities and a 1.13 earned run average in 61 appearances - though there also probably was ample reason for having co-winners.

In five of the previous 49 seasons, scribes named co-winners. The award wasn't presented in 1994 because of the players' strike. The first winner was Bill Veeck, then owner of the Indinas, in 1946.

Mesa edged Belle by three votes, 8-5, in the balloting among the local writers, who also unanimously elected Jim Thome winner of their Good Guy award.

The latter is co-named in honor of former Cleveland Press sportswriter Frank Gibbons and Steve Olin, the Tribe pitcher who was killed in a boating accident in Winter Haven, Florida in 1993.

It goes to the person in the Indians organization judged to be the best and most cooperative to deal with by the media.

*The Sporting News* poll also recognized the Indians 1995 achievements with awards for General Manager John Hart, as well as Mesa and rookie reliever Julian Tavarez.

Hart, who is primarily responsible for putting together the team that won 100 games and the AL Central Division championship by 30 lengths, was voted Executive of the Year for the second consecutive season.

Mesa, who also was named the Rolaids Relief Man of the Year, was elected Fireman of the Year by the players in *The Sporting News* poll, and Tavarez won the Rookie Pitcher of the Year award from the publication.

"This reflects well on the success we've had," Hart said on behalf of all the Indians' winners. "The players played well, Mike and his staff did a good job, and that makes the front office look good."

Mesa also finished second in the balloting for the AL Cy Young award. It went to Seattle's Randy Johnson, whose record was 18-2 with an AL best 2.48 earned run average. Johnson also led the major leagues for the fourth straight year in strikeouts with 294 in 214 innings.

Johnson, with his 100 miles-per-hour fast ball and improved control, led the Mariners to the AL West championship, and was 0-1 in two starts against the Indians in the ALCS. He garnered 26 of the 28 first place votes in the balloting by the BBWAA, and was the only pitcher listed on every ballot, finishing with 136 points.

Mesa received the other two first place votes, and had 54 points. Boston knuckleballer Tim Wakefield was third with 29, followed by the 1994 winner, David Cone of New York, and Mike Mussina of Baltimore.

Many, including Hargrove (as well as the author of this book), believe Belle should have won the MVP award based on the outstanding season he had: .317 batting average (eighth-best in the AL) and a league-leading 50 homers. Belle also tied Vaughn for the most runs batted in, 126; and Martinez for the most runs, 121; and most doubles, 52.

Vaughn batted .300 with 39 homers, 98 runs, and 165 hits (to Belle's 173).

Belle's homers and doubles established him as the first player in major league history to hit 50 of each in one season, a feat that even such great players as Babe Ruth, Lou Gehrig, Rogers Hornsby, Stan Musial, Roberto Clemente, Willie Mays, Mickey Mantle and other Hall of Famers never accomplished.

Making it even more remarkable is the fact that Belle did it in 144 games (he actually played in only 143) because of the players' strike that delayed the start of the 1995 season, and shortened it by 18 games.

As Hargrove said, "To me, Albert Belle is the MVP - hands down."

And Mesa remarked before the MVP results were announced, "If Albert Belle doesn't win this year, I don't think anyone else would win it."

The voting was conducted prior to post season play, during which Vaughn went 0-for-14 in the Division Series against the Indians, while Belle was 3-for-14 with one homer and three RBI. Belle batted .222 (4-for-18, one home run) in the ALCS against Seattle, and .235 (4-for-17, two homers) against Atlanta in the World Series.

Both Cleveland writers who voted for the MVP award - Paul Hoynes of *The Plain Dealer* and Sheldon Ocker of the *Akron Beacon-Journal,* named Belle No. 1 and Vaughn second.

Ironically, it was Mesa who, through no fault of his, prevented Belle from beating out Vaughn. That's because one writer gave Mesa his first place vote for MVP. Had that not been done, had it been cast for Belle instead, the Indians left fielder would have finished ahead of Vaughn in one of the closest races since the BBWAA took over the voting in 1931.

If it is any consolation, at least Belle is getting closer. He finished third in the voting in 1994 when Chicago's Frank Thomas won the award.

Only two Indians previously were MVP winners: Al Rosen in 1953, and Lou Boudreau in 1948.

Two Indians also won Gold Glove awards, as voted by opposing managers. They were center fielder Kenny Lofton and shortstop Omar Vizquel.

# Mike Hargrove: Manager

Few have paid their managerial dues more faithfully or completely than Mike Hargrove, who should have won - in 1995 as well as 1994 - the American League Manager of the Year award, though he has too much class to complain.

"I did the best I could ... we all did, myself, my staff and my players. We won the pennant and very nearly won the World Series, and I'm happy about that," Hargrove said after the Indians were beaten by Atlanta in six games in the World Series.

And well Hargrove should have been happy, and proud. Very proud.

But still, it says here as emphatically as possible, Hargrove deserved to be named Manager of the Year, because that's what he was.

Hargrove took over the Indians in mid-1991, when they were a team in disarray and destined to lose a franchise record 105 games.

It wasn't easy for Hargrove then, and it wasn't easy in the years that followed, especially 1992 and 1993, as the Indians embarked upon a plan designed to keep their best young players in Cleveland, without the addition of any high-priced free agents.

It required the nurturing and developing of the promising but inexperienced talent, a job for which Hargrove was well suited. He came to be recognized as a "player/s manager," and the results of his hard work, combined with the planning and efforts of John Hart and Dan O'Dowd in the front office, began paying dividends in 1994.

But for the players' strike that cut short the 1994 season, the Indians - and Hargrove - might have reached the World Series a year before they did.

But it all came together in 1995 and Hargrove earned a lion's share of the credit. He took a team of diverse personalities, including several players whose combative attitudes toward the media often created problems for everybody, especially Hargrove.

There were distractions, many of which went unreported, but Hargrove held the Indians together through those difficult periods, and kept his players focused on one goal - winning the franchise's first pennant in 41 years.

It has been a long journey for Hargrove to reach this level of success and respect in his managerial career; in fact, a lesser man would have given up even before it began, back in 1986.

He concluded - unwillingly, to be sure - a 12 year playing career that began with Texas (when he won the AL Rookie of the Year award in 1975), continued in San Diego 1979, and with the Indians for 6 1/2 seasons through

1985.

His acquisition by the Tribe on June 14, 1979 was one of the best trades made by the club: Hargrove came in an even-up deal for third baseman-outfielder Paul Dade.

Hargrove was named the Indians' Man of the Year in 1980, when he batted .304, and again in 1981, when his average climbed to .317, and also won the Good Guy award in 1985, his final season as a player.

Then, at age 35, though Hargrove thought he could still play, he was released by the Indians. He was given a trial with Oakland in 1986, but was let go the final week of spring training, and it appeared that Hargrove's baseball career was finished.

But he refused to give up, finally convincing the Indians to give him a job in their farm system that summer.

Hargrove started at the lowest rung in professional baseball - he was the hitting instructor at Batavia (New York) of the short season Class A New York-Penn League.

It was all Hargrove needed to prove his worth, though his climb back to the major leagues would still be long and difficult.

Hargrove took over the Kinston (North Carolina) Indians of the Class A Carolina League in 1987, moved up to Williamsport (Pennsylvania) of the Class AA Eastern League in 1988, and to Colorado Springs (Colorado) of the Class AAA Pacific Coast League in 1988.

When John McNamara was named manager of the Indians in 1990, Hargrove was appointed first base coach. And when McNamara was dismissed on July 6, 1991, Hargrove's comeback was complete.

Again, if ever a man paid his managerial dues, it was Hargrove.

Nobody worked harder, more faithfully, and with greater dedication than Hargrove.

And nobody deserves the plaudits he's now receiving more than Mike Hargrove.

# Richard E. Jacobs: Indians Owner

The year was 1986 and, while the Indians were doing relatively well on the field - they were en route to a fifth place finish with their first .500-plus record in five years - the front office was in a state of disorder and near turmoil.

F.J. "Steve" O'Neill, owner of the club since 1978, had died in 1983 and the Indians were being operated by his estate, under the direction of nephew Patrick J. O'Neill, who placed Peter Bavasi in charge as president.

O'Neill solicited potential buyers of the franchise, but little progress was being made and the American League was anxious for stability to be restored.

Bavasi had ties with a Tampa Bay group that wanted to obtain a franchise for that area, and rumors were rampant that the Indians would be moved out of Cleveland if local ownership was not found.

It was then, in early July, that two prominent Cleveland developers, brothers Richard E. and David H. Jacobs, stepped forward to buy the franchise, and by December their purchase was approved by AL owners.

The reported price was $35 million, plus the assumption of debts accumulated by the financially-strapped Indians dating back to the early 1970s.

"We did it (purchased the club) out of a sense of civic responsibility and to have a little fun," Richard Jacobs stated then. "We want to bring a contender to Cleveland, and we don't think this team is far away."

Soon after the Jacobs brothers took over, Bavasi was replaced by Hank Peters, the franchise was steadied and progress began. Soon, too, plans for a new ball park were developed, construction started in 1992, and the facility was opened in April 1994.

Named "Jacobs Field," it became an immediate hit - and so did the Indians, under the direction of Richard Jacobs, whose brother David died September 17, 1992 at age 71.

While there is no question but that Jacobs is in total control, that he has the final word on all decisions regarding every aspect of the operation of the club, he's not one to seek the spotlight, and has delegated authority to his lieutenants.

A self-made millioniare, Jacobs is quoted in a May 3, 1992 newspaper article as saying, "I want a contender, positive cash flow and fair return on our investment."

There's no doubt the Indians under Jacobs' direction have achieved those three goals since he and his brother bought the franchise - and saved it for Cleveland - nine years ago.

A graduate of Indiana University in 1949, Jacobs is chairman and chief executive officer of The Richard E. Jacobs Group, whose primary business includes the development, ownership and management of office towers, hotels and regional enclosed malls.

# John Hart: Executive Vice President/ General Manager

John Hart, the primary architect of the Indians' return to glory, is a former high school coach, minor league catcher and manager, and third base coach of the Baltimore Orioles who learned under a master, Hank Peters.

It was Peters who saw great potential in Hart, and brought him to Cleveland in 1989.

"I'd known John for a long time and respected his values, work ethic and ability to evaluate players," said Peters. "When I was hired by (Indians owner) Dick Jacobs, John Hart was one of the men I wanted to join me, to help me do what needed to be done."

Obviously, Hart learned well. *The Sporting News* named him "Major League Executive of the Year" for 1995, the second year in a row that Hart was so honored.

A baseball, football and basketball star at Winter Park (Florida) High School, Hart went on to Seminole (Florida) Junior College on a baseball scholarship and earned Junior College All-America honors in 1969 as a catcher, and was drafted by Montreal.

Hart played minor league baseball for seven seasons in the Montreal and Baltimore organizations, then served as a minor league manager for the Orioles under Peters for six years at the Class A, AA and AAA levels. He compiled an impressive won-lost record of 436-334, and twice won Manager of the Year honors

Hart was third base coach of the Orioles in 1988, prior to joining Peters in Cleveland as a special assignment scout. He managed the team on an interim basis the final 19 games of that season during which the Tribe's record was 8-11.

Hart, 47, was promoted to director of baseball operations in 1990 and, upon Peters' retirement, was named general manager of the Indians on September 18, 1991. In 1993, Hart became executive vice president and general manager.

Three years after Hart took over as general manager, in the 1994 season that was cut short by the players strike, the Indians became a contender for the first time since 1959.

And the following season they won their first pennant in 41 years.

All of which proves that Peters was right when he recognized something special in John Hart, and brought him to Cleveland six years ago.

# Dan O'Dowd: Director of Baseball Operations/Assistant General Manager

It was under Dan O'Dowd's tutelage, as overseer of player development and scouting, that the Indians were honored as "Organization of the Year" in 1992 by the publication that covers minor league baseball, *Baseball America.*

O'Dowd was another of the bright young men brought to Cleveland in 1989 by Hank Peters when he became president and general manager of the Indians.

As did John Hart, O'Dowd had worked for the Baltimore Orioles under Peters in a variety of positions.

Since coming to Cleveland, O'Dowd, 35, has worked closely with Hart as they rebuilt the Tribe farm system into one of the most progressive and productive in professional baseball.

Winnigest, too, as attested to by three of their minor league teams in 1995:

Buffalo finished second with an 82-62 record in the Class AAA International League, and went to the finals of the playoffs before losing to Louisville, three games to two; Kinston of the Class A Carolina League won the first and second half races in the Southern Division, then swept Wilmington for the championship; and Watertown won the (short season) Class A New York-Penn League title.

O'Dowd was closely involved with Hart in the implementation of the plan devoloped by the Indians in 1992 to sign their best young players to multi-year contracts, ensuring their presence for seasons to come.

It was a plan that other major league organizations have copied because it obviously has worked so well for the Indians.

Prior to joining the Indians, O'Dowd, who was with the Orioles for five years, served in a variety of roles, including assistant director of player development and scouting. He also worked as director of corporate marketing, director of broadcasting, and sales manager.

A graduate of Rollins College in Winter Park, Florida where he played four years of varsity baseball, O'Dowd joined the Orioles in 1984 after a stint as an executive trainee in the office of the Baseball Commissioner.

Attesting to the reputation O'Dowd has developed as an administrator and judge of baseball talent, when the 1995 season ended, the Baltimore Orioles requested permission to interview him for the vacant job of general manager.

# How the Indians Were Built

|      | NON-DRAFTED FREE AGENTS | FREE AGENT DRAFT (Beginning 1965) | PURCHASES AND TRADES |
|------|-------------------------|-----------------------------------|----------------------|
| 1987 |                         | Albert Belle, of (2)              |                      |
| 1988 |                         | Charles Nagy, rhp (1)             |                      |
| 1989 |                         | Alan Embree, lhp (5)<br>Jim Thome, inf (13) | Sandy Alomar, c<br>  from San Diego<br>Carols Baerga, inf<br>  from San Diego |
| 1990 | Julian Tavarez, rhp     |                                   |                      |
| 1991 | Wayne Kirby, of         | Manny Ramirez, of (1)<br>Herbert Perry, inf (2)<br>Chad Ogea, rhp (3) | Kenny Lofton, of<br>  from Houston |
| 1992 | Alvaro Espinoza, inf<br>Eric Plunk rhp |                    | Paul Sorrento, inf<br>  from Minnesota<br>Jose Mesa, rhp<br>  from Baltimore |
| 1993 | Dennis Martinez, rhp<br>Eddie Murray, inf |                 | Mark Clark, rhp<br>  from St. Louis<br>Ruben Amaro<br>  from Philadelphia<br>Omar Vizquel<br>  from Seattle |
| 1994 | Tony Pena, c            |                                   |                      |
| 1995 | Jim Poole, lhp<br>Dave Winfield, of<br>Orel Hershiser, rhp<br>Paul Assenmacher, lhp | | Ken Hill, rhp<br>  from St. Louis |

# *Transactions*

April 25        Purchased the contracts of left handed pitcher Bud Black, left handed pitcher Jim Poole, and catcher Tony Pena; placed catcher Sandy Alomar on the 15 day disabled list with a strained left knee, retroactive to April 19; recalled infielder David Bell from Class AAA Buffalo; designated outfielder Tony Mitchell and right handed pitcher James Lewis for assignment

May 5        Placed right handed pitcher Paul Shuey on the 15 day disabled list with a pulled right hamstring, retroactive to May 4; recalled right handed pitcher Chad Ogea from Class AAA Buffalo

May 14        Optioned infielder David Bell and right handed pitcher Chad Ogea to Class AAA Buffalo

May 15        Acquired catcher Scooter Tucker from the Houston Astros in exchange for left handed pitcher Matt Williams; designated catcher Jesse Levis for assignment; outrighted outfielder Ruben Amaro to Class AAA Buffalo

May 22        Placed right handed pitcher Paul Shuey on the active roster and optioned him to Class AAA Buffalo

May 25        Optioned right handed pitcher Mark Clark to Class AAA Buffalo; recalled right handed pitcher Chad Ogea from Buffalo

June 12        Placed outfielder Dave Winfield on the 15 day disabled list with a partial tear of his left rotator cuff, retroactive to June 11; recalled first baseman Herbert Perry from Class AAA Buffalo

June 18        Purchased the contract of right handed pitcher Gregg Olson from Class AAA Buffalo; designated left handed pitcher Dennis Cook for assignment

June 23        Placed right handed pitcher Orel Hershisher on the 15 day disabled list with a lower back sprain, retroactive to June 22; recalled right handed pitcher Albie Lopez from Class AAA Buffalo

June 27        Recalled right handed pitcher Mark Clark from Class AAA Buffalo; optioned right handed pitcher Albie Lopez to Buffalo

June 29        Placed catcher Sandy Alomar on the active roster; catcher Scooter Tucker was claimed on waivers by the Atlanta Braves

July 3        Placed first baseman Eddie Murray on the 15 day disabled list with two broken ribs; purchased the contract of outfielder Ruben Amaro from Class AAA Buffalo

July 7          Placed right handed pitcher Orel Hershiser on the active roster; optioned right handed pitcher Chad Ogea to Class AAA Buffalo

July 13          Outrighted right handed pitcher Jason Grimsley to Class AAA Buffalo; recalled left handed pitcher Alan Embree from Buffalo

July 14          Placed left handed pitcher Bud Black on waivers for the purpose of giving him his unconditional release; recalled right handed pitcher Albie Lopez from Class AAA Buffalo

July 17          Designated right handed pitcher Gregg Olson for assignment; placed outfielder Dave Winfield on the active roster; optioned left handed pitcher Alan Embree to Class AAA Buffalo; recalled right handed pitcher Chad Ogea from Buffalo

July 21          Placed outfielder Kenny Lofton on the 15 day disabled list retroactive to July 17, with a strained right rib cage; recalled left handed pitcher Alan Embree from Class AAA Buffalo

July 27          Acquired right handed pitcher Ken Hill from the St. Louis Cardinals in exchange for minor leaguers infielder David Bell, right handed pitcher Rick Heiserman, and catcher Pepe McNeal

July 28          Optioned right handed pitcher Albie Lopez to Class AAA Buffalo

August 1          Placed outfielder Kenny Lofton on the active roster; optioned left handed pitcher Alan Embree to Class AAA Buffalo

August 12          Placed outfielder Dave Winfield on the 15 day disabled list with an aggravated left rotator cuff; recalled left handed pitcher Alan Embree from Class AAA Buffalo

September 1   Placed outfielder Dave Winfield and outfielder Ruben Amaro on the active roster; recalled right handed pitcher Albie Lopez from Class AAA Buffalo

September 16  Recalled right handed pitcher Joe Roa, outfielder Brian Giles, and outfielder Jeromy Burnitz from Class AAA Buffalo; purchased the contracts of infielder Billy Ripken, catcher Jesse Levis, and right handed pitcher John Farrell from Class AAA Buffalo

September 17  Recalled right handed pitcher Paul Shuey from Class AAA Buffalo

# *Injuries by the Indians in 1995*

April 26          Catcher Sandy Alomar suffered an injury to the lateral miniscus cartilage in his left knee and underwent surgery performed by Dr. Richard Steadman in Vail, Colorado

May 3            Right handed pitcher Paul Shuey left the game in Detroit with a strained right hamstring

May 12           Right handed pitcher Dennis Martinez left the game in Baltimore after being hit in his right hand by a line drive off the bat of Brady Anderson

May 14           Outfielder Kenny Lofton visited Dr. Keppler in Cleveland for an examination of his sore right leg ... he received a shot of cortisone on May 15 and returned to the lineup on May 18

May 19           Right handed pitcher Jason Grimsley left the game in the fourth inning at Boston with a strained left hamstring

June 3            Right handed pitcher Paul Shuey visited Dr. Keppler for treatment of an impingement in his right shoulder

June 10           Outfielder Dave Winfield left the game in the sixth inning at Milwaukee with tightness in his right shoulder and a strained muscle in his left shoulder ... placed on the disabled list June 12

June 12           Outfielder Dave Winfield underwent an MRl and was diagnosed as having a slight tear in his left rotator cuff

June 12           Right handed pitcher Dennis Martinez underwent an MRI and was diagnosed as having a floating cartilage in his left knee

June 21           Right handed pitcher Orel Hershiser left the game after three plus innings against Boston with tightness in his lower back ... placed on the disabled list June 23

June 26           Outfielder Kenny Lofton left the game in the second inning at Kansas City with a strained left hamstring ... his status was described as day-to-day

June 28          Right handed pitcher Chad Ogea left the game in the seventh inning at Kansas City after being hit in the right rib cage area, but did not miss a start

July 2          Infielder Eddie Murray broke two ribs in a play at the plate in the third inning at Minnesota upon crashing into catcher Matt Walbeck

July 13          Outfielder Kenny Lofton strained his right rib cage muscle in a game against Oakland

July 13          Infielder Jim Thome suffered a suspected attack of food poisoning

July 14          Outfielder Kenny Lofton came out of the starting lineup after one at-bat against Oakland because of pain in his right rib cage

July 21          Outfielder Kenny Lofton was in the starting lineup, but scratched after suffering more pain in his right rib cage prior to a game in Oakland

July 22          Outfielder Kenny Lofton was placed on the disabled list with a strained right rib cage, retroactive to July 17

July 28          Catcher Sandy Alomar left the game at Seattle with a slightly strained right quadriceps muscle

July 30          Infielder Carlos Baerga left the game at Seattle with a twisted ankle

August 1          Outfielder Ruben Amaro was placed on the disabled list with a strained left hamstring

August 1          Left handed pitcher Paul Assenmacher broke the small toe on his left foot in a game against Minnesota

August 10          Infielder Jim Thome was hit in the right hand by a pitch from Sterling Hitchcock in a game against New York ... precautionary x-rays disclosed no fracture

August 12          Outfielder Dave Winfield re-aggravated an injury to his left shoulder in a game at New York

August 29              First baseman Paul Sorrento strained his right hamstring in a game against Toronto

September 4            Catcher Sandy Alomar left the game against Detroit in the fifth inning with a sore left knee

September 6            Right handed pitcher Eric Plunk was diagnosed as having tendinitis in his right shoulder

September 10           First baseman Paul Sorrento suffered a slight aggravation of a previous injury to his right hamstring

September 12           Infielder Carlos Baerga sprained his left wrist in a collision with Bernie Williams in a game against New York

September 16           First baseman Paul Sorrento re-aggravated a previous injury to his left rib cage

# *Ejections*

April 27               Left handed pitcher Dennis Cook ejected by Darrell Mason for arguing a home run call in the eighth inning of a game against Texas

August 11              Shortstop Omar Vizquel and manager Mike Hargrove ejected by Darryl Cousins for arguing balls and strikes in the fifth inning of a game against New York

August 22              Manager Mike Hargrove ejected by Chuck Meriwether for arguing balls and strikes in the eighth inning of a game against Toronto

September 28           Pitching coach Mark Wiley ejected by Tim Tschida for arguing after Albert Belle was hit by a pitch in the second inning of a game against Minnesota

# Cleveland Indians 1995

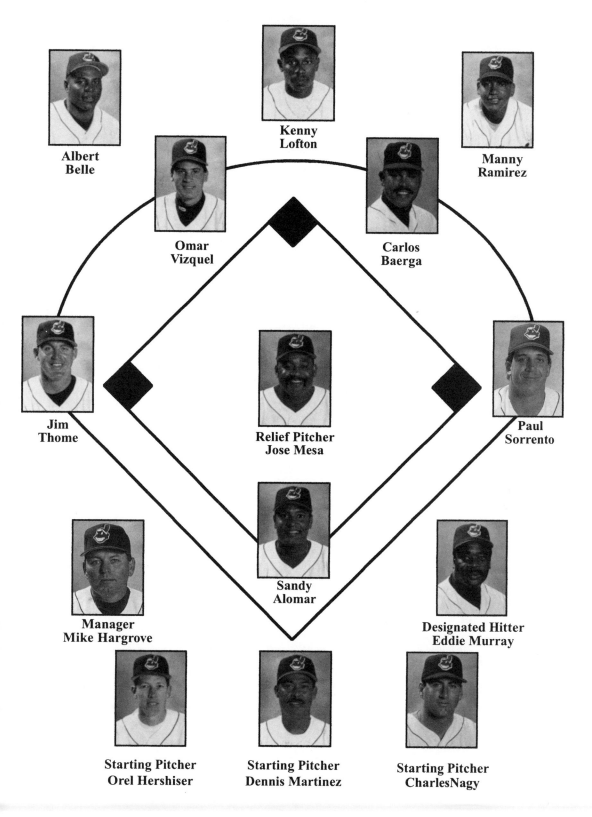

Albert
Belle

Kenny
Lofton

Manny
Ramirez

Omar
Vizquel

Carlos
Baerga

Jim
Thome

Relief Pitcher
Jose Mesa

Paul
Sorrento

Sandy
Alomar

Manager
Mike Hargrove

Designated Hitter
Eddie Murray

Starting Pitcher
Orel Hershiser

Starting Pitcher
Dennis Martinez

Starting Pitcher
CharlesNagy

# *Other Tribe Memory Books*

Collections of Memories ... By Russell Schneider

| | |
|---|---|
| Tribe Memories I | Bob Feller ... Andre Thornton ... Herb Score<br>Len Barker ...Jack Graney ... Rocky Colavito<br>Mel Harder ... Bill Veeck ... Larry Doby<br>Early Wynn ... Ken Keltner... Ray Chapman<br>Shoeless Joe Jackson ...Al Rosen<br>Oscar Vitt ... Gene Bearden ... Bill Wambsganss<br>Al Lopez ... Lou Boudreau ... Joe Sewell<br>Earl Averill ... Sam McDowell ... Johnny Allen<br>and many more from the 1990-91<br>Schedule/Engagement Book |
| Tribe Memories II | Tris Speaker ... Luke Easter ... Al Milnar<br>George Uhle ... Pat Seerey ... Satchel Paige<br>Ray Fosse... Dale Mitchell ... Jeff Heath<br>Johnny Burnett ... Ken Harrelson ... Joe Adcock<br>Stan Coveleski ... Tony Horton ... Emil Levsen<br>Hal Trosky ... Joe Azcue ... Joe Gordon<br>Ray Narleski ... Denny Galehouse ... Jim Piersall<br>Ray Caldwell ... Tito Francona ... Wes Ferrell<br>and many more from the 1991-92<br>Schedule/Engagement Book |
| Tribe Memories III | George Burns ... Vic Wertz ... Mike Garcia<br>Al Benton ... Rich Rollins ... Ken Aspromonte<br>Al Luplow ... C.C. Slapnicka ... Sonny Siebert<br>Odell Hale ... Mudcat Grant ... Ralph Kiner<br>Don Rudolph ... Dick Radatz ...Jim Bagby Sr.<br>Napoleon Lajoie...Gomer Hodge ...Charlie Spikes<br>Jim Bagby Jr. ... Hal Newhouser ...Ed Farmer<br>Hank Ruszkowski ...Gene Woodling<br>and many more from the 1992-93<br>Schedule/Engagement Book |

Now offered at close-out prices of $3 each (Ohio Sales Tax included),
or three for $8, plus $3 for postage and handling per order.
To order: complete the following (or facsimile) and mail to
Tribe Memories, P.O. Box 347156, Cleveland, Ohio 44134.

Name _____ Please specify: Tribe I

(CIRCLE CHOICE) Tribe II

Address _____ Tribe III

All three

City/State/Zip _____

Len Barker, the once-perfect man after he pitched a perfect game on May 15, 1981, to beat the Toronto Blue Jays, 3-0, at the Cleveland Stadium.

(Photo courtesy of the Cleveland Indians)

Herb Score is signed by Indians scout C.C. Slapnicka for a reported $40,000 on June 15, 1952.
(Photo courtesy of Herb Score)

Indians second baseman Bill Wambsganss with the three Brooklyn players who were his "victims" in the only unassisted triple play in World Series history, on October 10, 1920, in the fifth game, won by Cleveland, 8-1. The Brooklyn base runners who were wiped out by Wambsganss: (left to right) Pete Kilduff, Otto Miller and Clarence Mitchell.

(Photo courtesy of Wambsganss' grand daughter Effie Lydon)

The great Napoleon Lajoie (right), whom many consider to have been the greatest player ever to wear a Cleveland uniform, poses with Ty Cobb (center) and Shoeless Joe Jackson (left), who played left field for the Indians from 1910-15. Lajoie was a second baseman who was the Indians' player-manager from 1905-09.

(Photo courtesy of Bill Wambsganss' grand daughter Effie Lydon)

Center fielder Tris Speaker (second from left), the Indians player-manager from 1919-26, with Lou Gehrig (left), Ty Cobb (second from right), and Babe Ruth.

(Photo courtesy of Bill Wambsganss' grand daughter Effie Lydon)

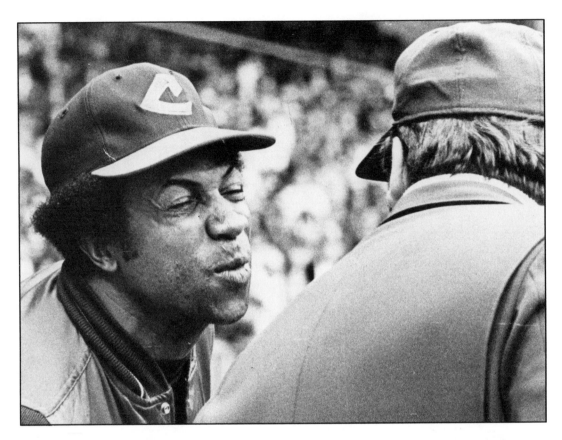

Frank Robinson, major league baseball's first black manager in 1975, argues with umpire Russ Goetz.

(Photo courtesy of the Cleveland Indians)

Indians broadcaster Mike Hegan (left), then a five-year old toddler, tries on the equipment worn by his father, Indians catcher Jim Hegan, prior to a 1947 spring training practice session at Hi Corbett Field in Tucson, Arizona.

(Photo courtesy of the Cleveland Indians)

Everybody expected Sam McDowell (right) to be as good as Sandy Koufax, shown here comparing pitching grips in spring training at Hi Corbett Field in Tucson, Arizona in 1966.

(Photo courtesy of the Cleveland Indians)

# American League Champion Cleveland Indians

First row, left to right: Stan Hunter, clubhouse manager; Fernando Montes, strength and conditioning coach; Mike Seghi, director of team travel; coach Luis Isaac, coach Dave Nelson, coach Jeff Newman, coach Buddy bell, coach Charlie Manuel, coach Mark Wiley, coach Dan Williams, Paul Spicuzza, assistant trainer; Jim Warfield, trainer; Jeff Sipos, equipment manager.
Second row: Jose Mesa, Julian Tavarez, Omar Vizquel, Orel Hershiser, Alan Embree, Mark Clark, Charles Nagy, Manager Mike Hargrove, Jim Poole, Chad Ogea, Gregg Olson, Albie Lopez, Eric Plunk, Paul Assenmacher, Eddie Murray.
Third row: Dave Winfield, Sandy Alomar Jr., Dennis Martinez, Paul Sorrento, Herbert Perry, Albert Belle, Manny Ramirez, Alvaro Espinoza, Kenny Lofton, Wayne Kirby, Carlos Baerga, Ruben Amaro, Jim Thome, Tony Pena.

Photo courtesy of the Cleveland Indians

Two of Cleveland's all-time greatest athletes trade equipment (but only temporarily) in this 1956 gag shot. That's football Hall of Fame quarterback Otto Graham (left), wearing an Indians cap, pitcher's glove and holding a baseball, and baseball Hall of Fame pitcher Bob Feller wearing a Browns helmet and holding a football.

(Photo courtesy of the Cleveland Indians)